Pius VII

by Jacques Louis David
Louvre, Paris

THE LEASING OUT OF ENGLAND

This book is for C. W. B.

Contents

Acknowledgements

I wish to thank Bowdoin College, particularly President A. Leroy Greason and Dean of the Faculty Alfred Fuchs for most generous support in writing this book. My thanks to colleagues David Bradshaw and William Watterson for incisive critiques and for pointing me towards materials I had missed in my own research. Peter Saccio clarified some vexing historical questions for me. I was fortunate to read a brilliant manuscript by Raymond Reno while I was working on this book, and have incorporated some of Professor Reno's valuable insights herein. I hope that by now his own book has seen the light of day. The original version of my Henry V chapters appeared as "Henry the Fifth and the Nature of Kingship," in Discourse XIII (1970). An outline of the II Henry IV material appeared as an introduction to the play in The Blackfriars Series (1971). The original version of the Richard II chapters was written at the Folger Library in the Spring of 1971. To Amherst College, Folger, and O. B. Hardison — again — my thanks. I am grateful as well for encouragement given me by the late C. L. Barber, and by Roy Battenhouse, Peter Erickson, James Fisher, Alvin Kernan, and Norman Rabkin.

1

2

Preface

E.M.W. Tillyard is only partially correct to assert that "when Shakespeare deals with the concrete facts of English history he never forgets the principle of order behind all the terrible manifestations of disorder."1/ The problem for those inhabiting the world of the Second Henriad is that "the principle of order" enunciated by the dying John of Gaunt (Richard II: II.i) already lies deep in the past. The principle recedes further and further into the Fourteenth Century, becoming a forgotten mythology, as a very different "ethic" ramifies outward from the devastating actions of King Richard II, and from the reactions of men like Bolingbroke, Northumberland, and even Fitzwater, who "intend to thrive in this new world" (Richard II : IV.i.78).

Alvin Kernan, talking of the world the Lancastrians encourage into being, says that "Having confidently relied on themselves to make of life whatever they will it to be, they now begin to discover what it means to live without some of the ultimate comforts provided by the older system: without the grace and mercy of God, without an unchanging nature which continues to circle in its great patterns and manifest an order and meaning in the universe quite independent of the actions of men, without a stable society in which the individual man can achieve permanence and meaning by living the same life his father did and passing that life on to his children."2/ Tillyard's "principle of order" is present, then, only as an ironic reminder of "the way it was," but will never be again. Like the perfect harmony of Eden, the principle of order in England as Richard II begins is already an element of paradise lost.

A recent article by J. Scott Colley argues that "a sophisticated and thorough Marxist approach [to Richard II] will allow us to see Shakespeare's ideas from a perspective that in both 'critical' and 'historical'."3/ While Marx is implicit in much that follows, as perhaps he must be in any detailed study of the Second Henriad, I am not convinced that the materials of these plays can be neatly incorporated into a Marxist formula, where, as Engels says of the development of law in England: "It is possible. . .to retain in the main the forms of the old feudal laws while giving them a bourgeois content."4/ The "revolution" Shakespeare explores in the Second Henriad does involve a movement towards "economic determinism," and towards the exploitation of a population by a central capitalistic authority. I do not believe, however, that Lenin's interpretation of Plekhanov's "dialectical materialism" pertains to the Second Henriad: that is, that the nature of the cosmos Shakespeare describes coincides with positive revolutionary aspirations. In a sense, cosmic or universal law is rendered null and void by the revolution depicted in The Second Henriad; the historical process Shakespeare depicts is, I believe, profoundly negative and devoid of any teleology other than the pressure of "the event" itself. I believe that to impose an overtly Marxist perspective upon the Second Henriad might be to obscure the profound ironies that Shakespeare discovers in his materials. I do not, however, believe that the plays can be approached only through "the ideas of Shakespeare's time." Certainly Elizabethan England was a time of debate on all issues, social and religious, a debate emerging from and encouraging the radical transitions that the Sixteenth Century was experiencing. It is out of that "dialectic" that Shakespeare shapes his plays, although obviously he deepens and dramatizes the debate into a context that, so far, is "not of an age, but for all time."

A detailed exploration — a kind of "new criticism" integrated by a thesis — seems demanded if I am to demonstrate how relentlessly the plays show that once the England of Gaunt's great speech has been eroded by King Richard's actions, the country becomes increasingly dominated by a version of social Darwinism. The characters inhabiting the world of these plays are no longer "placed" in an inherited social hierarchy, but must complete with each other ruthlessly in a world drained of intrinsic value. The "Lancastrian norm," stripped of any rationalizations, is that of John of Lancaster at Gaultree Forest. The "ethic" is "what works." The most successful of them, Henry V, can reinvoke a semblance of "traditional order," but that "imitation of the sun" is based solely on the qualities of Henry's leadership that can summon forth an English spirit only temporarily reminiscent of the deeper community of "souls" celebrated by John of Gaunt. Henry V's leadership is as transitory as the life that shapes it.

Shakespeare is not "taking sides" on the issue of the "medieval" (i.e. static, traditional, hereditary, God-ordained-and-oriented) vs. the "modern" world, however negatively that latter area of history is depicted. Shakespeare demonstrates what must happen granted certain premises and their radical alteration. If the sacramental basis of kingship and kingdom is erased, another ethic must emerge to replace it. In a world where God does not intervene in the lives of men — seems indeed blocked from contact with mankind — the emerging ethic must be empirical, tangible, and quantitative. The actions of men who recognize the world they inhabit must be pragmatic, based on the economy of self-interest. Let an abstract concept, like "honor," lead a man on and that man is doomed. But a king can employ "honor," rolling it out when necessary from his arsenal of rhetoric and role-playing, and can succeed. In a world devoid of essential religious premises, lesser men may persist in a belief in God. Henry V may realize that contact with God is a possibility lost in the past, literally deep in his grandfather's memory, but he can continue to employ words and gestures that confirm for his followers what he himself recognizes as absolute anachronism. Henry V knows how to administer "the opiate of the masses." But his skills must die with him. The Wars of the Roses, so full of opportunism, treachery, and atrocity, can only continue to pursue the prophecy Carlisle makes at the eleventh hour, when it is too late to save King Richard, and when King Richard has made it too late for anyone to save England from its movement into a world very much like our own in its economy and politics, regardless of its robes and rhetoric. Kernan's isolation of the basic cause of the transition is accurate: "Richard's internal disorders and conflicting values grow into the increasingly bitter political and social disorders of a world racked by rebellion, strife, ambition, self-seeking, squabbling, and desperate attempts to hold things together."5/ One of the most successful efforts to keep things from falling apart, Henry V's war on France, is also one of the most desperate — and perhaps one of the most ultimately destructive for England.

I attempt here to give these four great plays a close reading that will validate the artistic integrity and thematic unity of The Second Henriad. If such a reading succeeds, it becomes its own validation. That a book-length treatment is justified seems obvious to me on the basis of the plays themselves, the brilliant outline provided by Alvin Kernan's article, an explosion of excellent recent articles on the plays by Anne Barton, James Black, Sherman Hawkins, Frank Manley, Norman Rabkin, Gordon Ross Smith, Karl P. Wentersdorf, and others, Peter Saccio's superb Shakespeare's English Kings, and on the basis of recent major productions, particularly John Barton's controversial Richard II, and Terry Hand's monumental Henry V, with Alan Howard in the title role.

Quotations from the plays accord with The Complete Signet Classic Shakespeare, ed. Sylvan Barnet (Harcourt Brace Jovanovich, New York, 1972).

Bowdoin College
January, 1980

1.   E.M.W. Tillyard, Shakespeare's History Plays (Macmillan, New York, 1946), p. 18.

2.   Alvin Kernan, "The Henriad: Shakespeare's Major History Plays," Modern Shakespearean Criticism, ed. Alvin Kernan (Harcourt, Brace & World, New York, 1970), p. 262.

3.   J. Scott Colley, "The Economics of Richard II?" Shakespeare Jahrbuch (Band 113/ 1977), 158-163.

4.   Quoted in A.A. Smirnov, "Shakespeare:" A Marxist Interpretation," Approaches to Shakespeare, ed. Norman Rabkin (McGraw-Hill, New York, 1964), p. 161.   See also Paul N. Siegel, "Marxism and Shakespearean Criticism," Shakespeare Newsletter XXIV: 4-5 (September-November, 1974), 37.

5.   Kernan, p. 253.

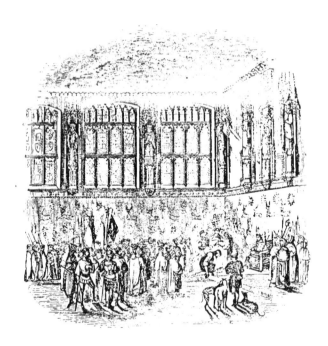

THE LEASING OUT OF ENGLAND: THE SECOND HENRIAD

Introduction

> The Persies with this answer and fradulent
> excuse were not a little fumed, insomuch that
> Henrie Hotspur said openlie: "Behold, the heire of
> the realme is robbed of his right, and yet the robber
> with his owne will not redeeme him!" So in this
> furie the Persies departed, minding nothing more
> than to depose King Henry from the high type of
> roialtie, and to place in his seat their cousin
> Edmund earle of March...
>
> Holinshed's Chronicles

By the time Shakespeare depicts this episode, the confrontation between Henry IV and the Northumberland faction in I Henry IV, England is hopelessly sundered. Edmund Mortimer, the man Richard II has inadvertently cursed by naming him heir, will be the theme of civil wars and conspiracies reaching even into the reign of Henry V (the Cambridge Plot: II.i.). Bolingbroke, the "robber," will be haunted by the purely political specters rising from his usurpation and regicide. Even his son will be troubled by his father's ascension, on the eve of Agincourt (Henry V: IV.i.292 ff.). That "bright exception" to the so-called Tudor Mythology, which explains the dark years between 1399 and 1485, will die young. The England Henry V so skillfully unites will lose France and will itself "bleed," as the final Chorus of Henry V tells us, and as Shakespeare has already "oft...shown" on his "stage" (Henry V: Epilogue: 13).

By the time Shakespeare dramatizes the Percy - Henry IV argument, England has suffered a profound separation from the intangible spiritual values that John of Gaunt claimed for "this dear, dear land" (Richard II: II.i.57). The realm that remains after the sundering effects of Richard's murder of his uncle, Gloucester, his seizure of the Lancastrian estates, Bolingbroke's premature return, the deposition and murder of Richard — the England that survives this sequence is an empirical place, a land of specific quantity, not of inestimable quality, of precisely defined weights and measures, wages and prices. It is the artistotelian world that survives the destruction of the platonic. From a timeless and sacramental premise of government, England shifts to a predatory and exploitative economics similar to that which Marx describes in Das Kapital and to a population largely composed of "social darwinists," with an occasional exception like Hotspur around to enforce the point.

I propose to examine the transition in detail and to suggest that, granted the premises of the world he inherits, Henry V has no choice but to exercise brilliant personal leadership and to simulate sacrament through effective ceremonial. But such leadership, based on "the cult of personality," must be temporary. Shakespeare does not try to escape the shadow already cast by the history between Henry V's reign and the latter days of Elizabeth's monarchy. Henry V makes us wonder whether England is really better off for this magnificent leader. His skill may delay but does not avert the civil wars that wait in the wings. One might ask whether his virtuosity doesn't make those wars worse when they do burst onto centerstage. The opening sequences of the Henry VI plays are full of reminiscences of Henry V, memories of a lost leader that echo ironically against the lowering skies of the fifteenth century England Shakespeare presents.]/ One wonders whether the transition into the "modern" world might not have been more orderly had Henry V not delayed that movement with the tour de force reign Shakespeare depicts. I do not believe that Shakespeare shows Henry V as designing a starring vehicle merely for the display of Henry's talents. That Henry does so seems an inevitable corollary to his concern for the welfare of England. But Henry V seems incapable of going behind his politics to ask, will it work when I am not here to stage-manage it? And to answer, probably not. Since Henry has an alternative to his war on France -- the establishment of yet another feudal system in England, a possibility outlined by Canterbury (Henry V: I.i. 12-14), an analysis of how Henry employs his brilliance is not the irrelevant imposition of the critic.

Whether Shakespeare had a personal "theory of history" or not is probably irrelevant and undiscoverable. We do know that he would subordinate historical fact to dramatic purpose, in, for example, changing the middle-aged Hotspur into the impetuous young rebel who becomes Prince Hal's rival, foil, and "factor" (I Henry IV: III.ii.147). We do know that Shakespeare viewed the single historical moment as "continuum"; the instant we witness on stage emerges from a matrix of prior events and contains within it the vectors of the future. Young Mowbray will look back upon the moment when Richard II "did throw his warder down" (II Henry IV: IV.i.123) and define it as the instant that dictated the future. Mowbray's perspective is limited, however, conditioned as it must be by his father's banishment, which followed hard upon Richard's interruption of the combat at Coventry. But Mowbray is no less "right" in his interpretation than is the Westmoreland who predictably defends Bolingbroke (II Henry IV: IV.i.128 ff.). Young Mowbray might well carry his mind ahead to include his intuition (IV.i.79-80) that "something is wrong" here at Gaultree Forest also, but he does not, and goes with the "shallow" Hastings (IV.i.50) and the over-credulous Archbishop of York to the block.

The "non-battle" of Gaultree Forest consolidates the kingdom Henry V will inherit and predicts the conduct of Henry V's politics. The "looking back" and "looking ahead" characteristic of the histories, the prophecies, portents, ironic self-cursings — Lady Anne's curse of whoever may become Gloucester's wife, for example (<u>Richard III</u>: I.ii.25-27), suggest that history is inevitability once certain forces have been released within certain contexts. Once Richard of Gloucester begins his pursuit of the throne, it must inevitably be his. He is superior to his rivals, and intrinsic "rightness" has long ceased to have any bearing on who is king. But once he is on the throne, the activist will be unhappy. As in courtship, the enjoyment has been in the game itself, not in the victory. What Richard says of Anne is true of his crown as well: "I'll have her, but I will not keep her long" (I.ii.229). Neither character nor environment can be said to dominate in <u>Richard III</u>. Indeed, Richard talks in his opening soliloquy of personal deformities that emerge only when the kingdom is at peace, only when time exists to examine one's own shadow.

"History" in Shakespeare seems often to be the product of the decisions made by great men. But such a Carlylian thesis is complicated, if not refuted, by the mastery that the decisions of the great men achieve over <u>them</u>. The Hegelian might argue that a pattern of thesis - antithesis - synthesis works out in Richard II - Bolingbroke - Henry V and in Henry VI - Richard III - Henry VII, and that Cranmer's blessing of Elizabeth at the end of <u>Henry VIII</u> represents Shakespeare's version of the ultimate synthesis of English history. Certainly many of Shakespeare's characters are "historians" — and that is really the point. The aspirations, short-sightedness, and insufficient theorizing of political men ramify into a series of conflicts between different premises and the men who represent them — "honor" vs. <u>Realpolitik</u> at Gaultree Forest, for example. Shakespeare promotes no "theory" in that episode. He shows what works and what does not in a world in many ways similar to our own, where Munich Agreements of 1938 or Geneva Accords of 1954 become "scraps of paper" to national leaders, where in Budapest in 1956 a resistance leader is summarily executed after approaching the Russians under a flag of truce. Shakespeare's characters, as James Black suggests of many of the characters of <u>Henry V</u>, are trapped within their concepts of the past: "What they would have the king be is limited to their dreams, and their dreams are of history, of chivalry, and of epic."2/ The French are similarly trapped, remembering history as motive for revenge but forgetting the specifics of Crecy to which their own king would recall them. For Shakespeare to have held a theory of history might have been an inhibition. But Shakespeare knew that <u>people</u> hold such theories; that knowledge is the material from which drama emerges, particularly if Shakespeare's characters are once, future, present, or would-be kings.

What G. R. Elton says generally of English History can be applied to the Second Tetralolgy: "In England at least, more often than not, political events precede mental reorientation; events are commonly the result of physical forces and personalities, and many a thinker has limped along after the party to offer his quota of ideas in explanation

9

and justification."3/ We observe in the Second Tetralogy rationalization and recognition, as the great men struggle with the forces that even their own decisions have released. Some history can be "rewritten." But some emerges to an increasingly clear focus, with a stubbornness that vexes the powers-that-be. It would seem that, for Shakespeare, "history" is a complex of competing dynamics not reducible to a statement or formula. One has only to recognize, for example, that both Calpurnia's and Decius Brutus's interpretations of her dream are valid, although in very different contexts, to recognize that history is and is not what any individual says it is. Among other things, Shakespeare is intent upon exploring the subjectivity of his characters, and, in doing so, exciting the subjectivity of his spectator into response.

The Second Henriad focuses on the actions of men. We are told of a few strange, unnatural events — bay trees wither in Wales (in Holinshed, a withering attributed to the bay trees of England, trees that become green again, as they do not in Shakespeare), an event to be read at least partly back to the character of the speaker, presumably Glendower (Richard II: II.iv.7 ff.). The warping of nature prior to the death of Henry IV, described by Gloucester and Clarence (II Henry IV: IV.iv. 121-128), suggests that the death of any king, de jure or de facto, reverberates into the cosmos. The prodigies might also suggest some final embodiment of the crimes of the dying king, or that unnaturalness dies with him. We must remember that Bolingbroke leaves his country at peace, and Westmoreland's metaphor seems to reflect back to those shriveled bay trees: "Peace puts forth her olive everywhere" (II Henry IV: IV, iv. 87). But Westmoreland employs metaphor; he does not claim to describe an actual event in nature. Glendower, of course, claims that the heavens greeted his birth ambiguously, if not ominously (I Henry IV: III.i.12. ff.), but Glendower was too young at the time to have been an eye-witness. These exceptions noted, we find the Second Henriad focussing on the actions of political men and on the results of those actions in a purely political world.4/   Shakespeare seems consciously to eliminate the reality of the cosmos in the Second Henriad, the super-nature or "outer mystery" so much a part of Richard III and, later, so intimately woven into the poetic and thematic fabric of plays like Julius Caesar, Hamlet, Macbeth, and The Tempest.5/

One question raised by the Second Henriad, as it is more profoundly in King Lear, is why is God (or "the gods") absent in this sequence? While characters in Richard II and King Lear constantly talk about "God" or "the gods," "He" or "they" are emphatically inactive in each play. Even Carlisle's prediction, couched in Christian terms, that England will become another "Golgotha" (Richard II: IV.i.144) is more attributable to Carlisle's political acumen than to divinely-inspired foreknowledge. Richard, not the shrewdest of politicians, can "create a perfect guess" (II Henry IV: III.i.88) about the future defection of Northumberland from the Lancastrians (Richard II: V.i.55-68). While Gaunt can tell Gloucester's widow that "God's is the quarrel" (I.ii.37),

Richard's nemesis becomes some combination of his own unexamined psyche and Gaunt's opportunistic son. York can warn Bolingbroke that "the heavens are over our heads" (III.iii.17), but Bolingbroke's blithe reply is interrupted by his eagerness for intelligence:

> I know it uncle, and oppose not myself
> Against their will. But who comes here?
>
> (III.ii.18-19)

The nature of Bolingbroke's alignment with "the will of God," even if such a link is presumed to exist, is hardly an issue as he confronts Richard. Bolingbroke is backed by the glitter of his armor, while Richard is left to rant desperately that "God for his Richard hath in heavenly pay/ A glorious angel" (III.ii.60-61). Were there such an angel, we would anticipate that Bolingbroke, like Richard III, Brutus, Macbeth, and Lady Macbeth would experience fearsome visitations, rather than mere insomnia. While Henry IV's "soul" is "full of woe" by the end of the play (Richard II: V.vi.45), that pain is the personal product of a political dilemma that allowed of no valid solution, as Bolingbroke knew even before Exton took things into his own fierce hands. One could argue that Bolingbroke must be allowed to "grow," however nourished by anti-sacramental "blood" (V.vi.46), because Shakespeare cannot manipulate Holinshed as freely as he will when he turns to the dimmer Scottish materials from which he shapes Macbeth. But the more basic argument, I believe, is that the worlds of the Second Henriad and Macbeth are different, and that the difference is Shakespeare's conscious choice. While the exploration of tyranny in Macbeth is profound, full of Hitlerian overtones,6/ the equally penetrating exploration of politics and of the changes dictated by redefinition of political premises in the Richard II - Henry V sequence occurs in a world seldom, if ever, visited by cosmic foreboding or reaction. While the world of the Second Henriad is charted out by its creator, Shakespeare, the dramatic effect of that world is that it is being created by the characters themselves. And, to a large extent, this is true. Once the world is devoid of divine sanction, it becomes what men, particularly powerful men, make of it. But great men — even a Henry V — must, like chimney sweepers, come to dust. The Second Henriad charts the movement from a God-ordained body politic to a more sequential, though not necessarily more orderly, pragmatic, modern politics.

The movement is analogous to that of Paradise Lost, from the timeless relationship of Adam, Eve, Eden, and God to the linear history detailed by Michael in Book XII. But beyond Shakespeare's Second Henriad waits no ultimate reconciliation, no proof of a "fortunate fall." The final chorus of Henry V predicts what Shakespeare has already dramatized at length — the Wars of the Roses.7/

1.   A character from the past can haunt a historical present with possibilities opposite to those that events seem to be demonstrating. The Black Prince, Richard's father, is such a figure during his son's reign.   Richard himself becomes that figure during Bolingbroke's kingship.   Henry V is consistently remembered during the early stages of his son's unsuccessful career.   Richard I is such a figure during the reign of his brother, John.   America has had a recent similar experience with John F. Kennedy, who might have been a scapegoat had he survived rather than a savior killed before he could save us.

2.   James Black, "Shakespeare's Henry V and the Dreams of History," English Studies in Canada I #1 (Spring, 1975), 13.

3.   G. R. Elton, "The Henrician Revolution," The English Tradition, ed. Norman F. Cantor and Michael S. Werthman (Macmillan, New York, 1967), I, p. 186.

4.   I would argue that Julius Caesar is, generically, a "history play," containing obvious "tragic elements," but elevating no single character as "tragic hero."   At various moments in the play, the action is dominated by Cassius, Julius Caesar, Brutus, Marc Antony, and Octavius Caesar. The primary issue is not "character," but, as in the history play, the disposition of political power. Admittedly, First Folio does not make this distinction regarding Richard II or Julius Caesar.   The storm in Julius Caesar portends drastic change in the political sphere (a thesis reiterated by Horatio in the first scene of Hamlet: 113-125). One of the storm's dramatic functions is to draw a variety of responses from those who witness it.   The storm in King Lear can be traced to no cause. Perhaps it reflects the overturning of political hierarchy, but "the Elizabethan World Picture" in its cosmic dimension pertains far less clearly to the world of King Lear than it does to the world of Macbeth. The storm may suggest the terrible energy Lear has released, but, if so, it is "metaphor," not "result."   And the storm may suggest a Jacobean "end of the world" motif.   It does, of course, absorb what people say about it, but what is said must be read back to character rather than accepted as "the meaning of the storm."   The storm in King Lear, like the play in which it rages, is a mystery.   The storm in Macbeth seems clearly a manifestation of cosmic outrage, and Prospero's storm, like Keats's in "The Eve of St. Agnes," is a benevolent tempest. In Macbeth and The Tempest, we have a good grasp of what the cosmic facts are.   In King Lear, we do not. In the Second Tetralogy, Shakespeare renders the cosmos largely irrelevant.

5.   For the wild meteorology Shakespeare could have imported into the Second Henriad, see Daniel's Civil Wars (Book I: 108-121, for example).

6.   Macbeth's claim that he must "wail [Banquo's] fall/ Who I myself struck down" (III.i.122-123), for example, resembles Hitler's forcing Rommel to commit suicide, then holding a giant state funeral for The Desert Fox. Hitler, like Macbeth, was also afraid of being captured and displayed in a cage, according to John Tolland, Adolph Hitler (New York, 1976), p. 1204. Before his suicide Hitler ordered his corpse to be burned to avoid some ironic version of Lenin's fate: "After my death, I don't want to be put on exhibition in a Russian wax museum," Tolland, p. 1217.

7.   One could argue the "Tudor myth," of course, and suggest that the earthly analogue to ultimate reconciliation with God is the reign of Elizabeth. The argument could be buttressed by citing the allusion to the Queen at the end of II Henry IV (Epilogue: 30), and the reference to Essex in the Chorus to Act V of Henry V. The latter reference, of course, is soon to develop negatively against the fin de siecle.

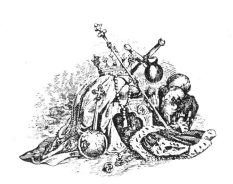

CHAPTER I

John of Gaunt's England

The Second Tetralogy represents a long denouement beginning with Richard's defection from duty, but comprehensible for us only through Gaunt's evocation of a paradise lost, a sacrament drained of its intangible efficacy. The Tower to which Bolingbroke will order Richard overlooks a Thames already "chartered" by the time the play begins. Indeed, Blake's lament in "London" is similar to Gaunt's complaint.

Shakespeare manipulates his sources so that the forces threatening Richard's kingship dominate the opening scenes of <u>Richard II</u>. Holinshed leaves no doubt that Gloucester's murder is Richard's responsibility, although the matter is complicated by Mowbray's disavowal of direct responsibility, a disclaimer delivered to Bagot, who was riding "behind the duke of Norfolke in the Savoy street towards Westminster." According to Peter Saccio, "Almost certainly [Gloucester] was murdered. Whether he was murdered at Richard's orders, and if so whether Norfolk was the agent, and if so whether Norfolk obeyed the command willingly or complied with it only after conscience-stricken delay, are questions that have never been satisfactorily settled."1/ Shakespeare allows the suspicion about Richard's complicity to run through the opening scene, emphasizing the other anti-Richard aspect — Bolingbroke's apparent ambition and obvious usurpation of royal prerogative (I.i.70-71, for example). We learn in I.ii from Gaunt that Richard is indeed the guilty party. Gaunt, however, invokes what Shakespeare makes the "medieval" argument in this play:

> God's is the quarrel: for God's substitute,
> His deputy anointed in His sight,
> Hath caused his death, the which if wrongfully,
> Let heaven revenge, for I may never lift
> An angry arm against His minister.
>   (I.ii.37-41)2/

As Henry Kelly says, "In these words of Gaunt, Shakespeare would seem to be setting up a code of morality by which subsequent events of the play are to be judged, if we can infer such a meaning from Gaunt's character, which is unalloyed with any unworthy motives,"3/ and, I might add, not undermined by authorial irony.

A brief examination of the sources will suggest that Shakespeare's placement of patriotic sentiments in Gaunt's mouth is the dramatist's invention, therefore <u>intention</u>. Gaunt's speech serves as chorus for the entire tetralogy. His vision of England will be a dimension against which all subsequent visions and versions of England will be measured.

15

England, of course, will never return to the explicitly immeasurable England Gaunt describes, even as he mourns England's descent into tangibility.

In writing The Second Henriad, Shakespare shapes his sources to emphasize first an anti-sacramental crime — the shedding of "sacred blood" (I.ii.12 and 17), as the Duchess of Gloucester says of her husband's murder, a sentiment with which Gaunt concurs. Bolingbroke's bold thrust at Richard results from this initial crime. Although the murder of Gloucester undermines Richard's kingship in a basic way, destroying the God-ordained and sacramental nature of his "body politic," neither Gaunt nor Bolingbroke can assert an effective countervailing force, as Gaunt admits in his confrontation with the Duchess and in acquiescing in his son's banishment. Richard retains that de facto control of which Macbeth boasts to his Murderers: "I could/ With barefaced power sweep him from my sight/ And bid my will avouch it" (III.i.118-120). But once Richard descends to the plane of mere power politics, he commits a sequence of errors that alienate both nobility and commons. Act II, scene one brings forward the copious fiscal material from Holinshed, in the wake of Richard's seizure of Hereford's inheritance. Shakespeare suppresses Richard's financial motive in Mowbray's banishment, reserving Richard's economic mismanagement as a "second stage" in Richard's downfall, a crucial blow to Richard's de facto kingship. In "deny[ing Bolingbroke's] off'red homage" (II.i.293), Richard discards a basic premise of the contractual feudal system, refusing to accept even the stewardship required of the "landlord of England." Richard has cracked spiritual bonds with God in conspiring to murder Gloucester. In his confiscation of the Lancastrian estates, he breaks both a legal and a sequential link with the premises of "order." Shakespeare manipulates his sources to suggest a sequence in which, first, the God-ordained and then the legally predicated premises of kingship are abandoned. Between Richard's two great errors, Shakespeare places Gaunt's majestic vision of an England-that-was, to emphasize that Richard, not Shakespeare, is denying a "providential pattern" to these plays. Richard insists upon a world drained of spiritual essence, stripped of heritage, devoid of orderly historical rhythm. Against the rich backdrop of Gaunt's evocation, we view a king who willfully destroys sacramental value, both in English blood and English soil. That the characterization of Richard is meant to be willful is suggested by Shakespeare's providing no trace of a motive for Richard's complicity in Gloucester's murder, though such a motive resides amply in the sources. The events which open out from the first two acts of Richard II must be reflected constantly against the ideal qualities projected by Gaunt's speech, and against Richard's heedless translation of "quality" into a world that can only be known in the context of "quantity."

Gaunt's appeal to God's justice in Shakespeare differs markedly from Gaunt's response to the Duchess of Gloucester in Woodstock:

> Go to our tents, dear sister, cease your sorrows,
> We will revenge our noble brother's wrongs
> And force that wanton tyrant to reveal
> The death of his dear uncle, harmless Woodstock,
> So traitorously betrayed.
>
> (V.ii.44-49)

It is intriguing to speculate that Bolingbroke acts as Gaunt's agent in Shakespeare's version; father and son have discussed the matter (I.i.8-14), Gaunt knows who is really guilty, and Gaunt encourages Bolingbroke's return to England on the basis of an unspecified "cause" (I.iii.304),4/ a cause that cannot yet be Richard's seizure of the Lancastrian estates. Such speculation about Gaunt's role goes beyond textual evidence — although complicity between Gaunt and Bolingbroke could be suggested in performance.

Certainly Shakespeare's Gaunt does attempt to persuade Richard to return to kingly duties, but not because of a specific objection to Richard's involvement in Gloucester's murder. That is not to suggest that Shakespeare accepts Holinshed's characterization of Gloucester as "presumptuous," as kindling "such displeasure...that it never ceased to increase into flames, till the duke was brought to his end." In Holinshed, Gaunt and York attempt to intercede between Richard and a Gloucester described as "fierce of nature, hastie, willful, and given more to war than to peace: and in this greatlie to be discommended, that he was ever repining against the king in all things, whatsoever he wished to have forward." In Holinshed, Gloucester is a threat recognized even by Gaunt and York, a characterization accepted by Daniel (Civil Wars: I.31). Shakespeare suggests the far milder Gloucester rendered by the York of Woodstock:

> Alack, good man,
> It was an easy task to work on him.
> His plainness was too open to their view.
> He feared no wrong, because his heart was true
> (V.ii.50-53)

Shakespeare's Gaunt reiterates this version of Gloucester, though it must be remembered that Gloucester is invoked only after Richard and Gaunt have become furious with each other at Ely House:

> O, spare me not, my brother Edward's son,
> For that I was his father Edward's son,
> That blood already, like the pelican,
> Hast thou tapped out and drunkenly caroused:
> My brother Gloucester, plain, well-meaning soul —
> Whom fair befall in heaven 'mongst happy souls! —

> May be a precedent and witness good
> That thou respect'st not spilling Edward's blood.
> (II.i.124-131)

While Richard's hand in Gloucester's murder is left motiveless in Shakespeare, seemingly a reflex of Richard's capricious malevolence, it is hardly a prime motive for Gaunt's attempted "correction" of Richard. Gaunt dismisses the subject when pressed by the Duchess of Gloucester, and utters the lines quoted above under obvious provocation. Gloucester's murder is a pretext for Bolingbroke's accusation of Mowbray, although Bolingbroke does not mention Gloucester in his condemnation of Bushy and Green (III.i.1-30). York lists Gloucester among many other indices of York's patience (II.i.163-185).

Shakespeare's Gaunt leaves the death of Gloucester to "the will of heaven" (I.ii.6). Gaunt will not attempt personal redress for "the fault that we cannot correct" (I.ii.5). Gaunt tries to recall Richard to that area of royal responsibility that can still be addressed. And here the sources agree. Froissart has Gaunt say:

> Our nephew, the King of England, will shame all ere
> he cease. He believeth too lightly evil counsel who
> shall destroy him: and simply, if he live long, he
> will lose his realm, and that hath been gotten with
> much cost and travail by our predecessors and by us.

In Froissart, Gaunt says, "He hath caused my brother to die, which is one thing to be noted," but Gaunt's primary emphasis is on England as political entity, not on any single crime, on the alienation of Richard from wise counsel, and on the expense and effort of past and present generations to secure and to expand English hegemony over its neighbors.

Gaunt's basic complaint in <u>Richard II</u>, however, will be about the reduction of something sacred to a merely economic meaning. Gaunt's precise description of that degradation becomes the best way of understanding the world that gradually opens out from the first two acts of <u>Richard II</u>, a beginning increasingly shadowed by the negative potentiality of kingly failure. Gaunt describes a basic and — as he seems to sense — inalterable transition, not merely in "world picture," but in the invisible elements that project such a picture, in the shapes that cast the shadows on the walls of Plato's cave. While Shakepeare is hardly a "Marxist," he understands that fundamental changes in the premises of government, a basic alienation between king and kingdom, between the king and his function as "body politic," are bound to have deep economic ramifications. Economic change in <u>Richard II</u> would seem to be a result of a change in theory of government rather than a cause of governmental change. Richard's violation of sacramental premises in killing Gloucester precedes his violation of legal sanction in seizing the Lancastrian estates, although in the latter instance, feudal "economics" and the basis of rule are synonymous, as York urges. Suffice it that Richard undercuts the premises of his rule partly for economic reasons and gets the economics he demands. In doing so, however, he changes the basis of everything, including rule itself, to quantitative terms. It would seem that Richard must erase the sacramental aspects of his kingship before he can destroy the more strictly legal basis of his rule. His leasing out of sacred land, of course, represents in one action a blow to both sacramental <u>and</u> legalistic premises.

Shakespeare's Gaunt, in his debate with the Duchess of Gloucester, seems not to grasp the full implications of his argument, which suggests, as Gaunt will see, the alienation of God and England. The <u>intrinsic</u> losses suffered by England under Richard's reign are stressed in both <u>Woodstock</u> and Daniel's <u>Civil Wars</u>. <u>Woodstock's</u> Gaunt mourns Richard's birth at Bordeaux:

> And England now laments that heavy time;
> Her royalties are lost, her state made base,
> And thou no king but landlord now become
> To this great state that terrored Christendom.
> (V.ii.151-154)

Gaunt has earlier said that Richard has "Rent out our kingdom like a pelting farm" (<u>Woodstock</u>: II.i.113), a line emerging almost directly into Shakespeare's version (II.i.59-60). For Daniel, the confrontation between Bolingbroke and Richard has fearful consequences, translated by Shakespeare into Gaunt's memory of the England-that-was. Daniel's England is

> A place...where proudly raised there stands
> A huge aspiring rock neighboring the skies,
> Whose surly brow imperiously commands
> The sea his bounds that at his proud feet lies:
> And spurns the waves that in rebellious bands
> Assault his Empire and against him rise...
> (II.49)

Daniel also emphasizes the debasement of England, and Richard's elevation of self to the detriment of crown and kingdom:

> And who as let in lease do farm the crown
> And joy the use of Majesty and might,
> While we hold but the shadow of our own...
> Bereave the rest of joy and us of love,
> And keep down all to keep themselves above.
> (II.19)

Daniel, however, does not ascribe such sentiments directly to Gaunt. For Daniel, Gaunt and York are hardly the staunch patriots we observe in the early sequences of Richard II.

While Holinshed deals in detail — however conflicting the evidence on Mowbray — with the murder of Gloucester, Holinshed's primary emphasis is on Richard's financial mismanagement. Bolingbroke's accusation of Mowbray, in Holinshed, as in Shakespeare, consists partly in Mowbray's having "received eight thousand nobles" (I.i.88), which Mowbray admits (I.i.126). In Shakespeare, as in Holinshed, Mowbray implies that Richard owes him the money (I.i.129-130), but in Holinshed, Richard not only banishes Mowbray for life, but stays "the profits of his lands, till he had levied thereof such summes of money as the duke had given up of the king's treasuror for the wages of the garrison of Calis, which were still unpaid." Shakespeare, it seems, wishes to suggest Richard's reluctance to banish a faithful subject. Richard, as Daniel has it, "thought best to loose a friend to rid a foe" (I.65.7). While Shakespeare's Richard has no financial motive in banishing Mowbray, Shakespeare later follows Holinshed closely in detailing Richard's other fiscal irresponsibilities:

> The common brute ran, that the king had set to farm the realm of England unto Sir William Scroop, earle of Wiltshire, and then treasuror of England, to Sir John Bushie, sir William Bagot, and sir Henrie Green, Knights.

> But yet to content the kings mind, manie blanke charters were devised, and brought into the citie, which manie of the substantiall and wealthie citizens were faine to seale, to their great charge, as in the end appeared. And the like charters were sent abroad into all shires within the realme, whereby great grudge and murmuring arose among the people: for, when they were so sealed, the kings officers wrote in the same what liked them, as well for charging the parties with paiment of monie, as otherwise.

> The spiritualitie alledged against him, that he, at his going into Ireland, exacted manie notable summes of monie, beside plate and jewels, without law or custome, contrarie to his oth taken at his coronation... The nobles, gentlemen, and commons of those shires were inforced also to receive a new oth to assure the king of their fidelitie in time to come; and withall certein prelats and other honorable personages were sent into the same shires

to persuade men to this paiment, and to see things ordered at the pleasure of the prince: and suerlie the fines which the nobles, and other the meaner estates of those shires were constreined to paie, were not small, but exceeding great, to the offense of manie.

While Shakespeare's Bolingbroke moves with politic indirection, accusing Mowbray, then Bushy and Green, of what Bolingbroke knows are Richard's crimes, and while Northumberland, Bolingbroke's "hatchet man," is less cautious (II.i.224-300 and III.iii.5-14, for example), the thrust against Richard is clearly motivated in Holinshed:

diverse of the nobilitie, as well prelats as others, the likewise manie of the magistrats and rulers of the cities, townes, and communalitie, here in England, perceiving dailie how the realme drewe to utter ruine, not like to be recovered to the former state of wealth whilst king Richard lived and reigned...devised...to send and signifie by letters unto duke Henrie...requiring him with all convenient speed to conveie himselfe into England, promising him all their aid, power, and assistance, if he, expelling K. Richard, as a man not meet for the office he bare, would take upon him the scepter, rule, and diademe of his native land and region.5/

By this time, of course, Gaunt is dead, both in Shakespeare and in Holinshed. While Shakespeare ignores the specific pleas cited above, he renders Gaunt's death in detail, if offstage. Holinshed merely notes that "In this meane time the duke of Lancaster departed out of this life at the bishop of Elies place in Holborne." Holinshed describes the subsequent confiscation, and York's reaction to it:

The death of this duke gave occasion of increasing more hatred in the people of this realme toward the king, for he seized into his hands all the goods that belonged to him, and also received all the rents and revenues of his lands which ought to have descended unto the duke of Hereford by lawful inheritance; in revoking his letters patents, which he had granted to him before, by vertue wherof he might make his attorneis generall to sue liverie for him, of any maner of inheritances or possessions that might from thenceforth fall unto him; and that his homage might be respited, with making resonable fine: whereby it was evident, that the king meant his utter undooing...

This hard dealing was much misliked of all
the nobilitie, and cried out against of the meaner
sort; but namelie the duke of Yorke was therewith
sore mooved; who, before this time, has borne
things with so patient a mind as he could, though
the same touched him verie neere, as the death of
his brother the duke of Glocester, the banishment of
his nephue the said duke of Hereford, and other mo
injuries in great number...

Shakespeare's treatment of the events following Gaunt's death is
similar, of course, although its rendition in dramatic terms is obviously
worth consideration.   First, however, one must notice Shakespeare's
crucial inclusion of the "patriotic" material he inherits from Daniel,
incorporated into Gaunt's celebration of England's past.   While York,
more a political realist than his brother, cannot convince Gaunt that
good advice will be wasted on Richard, York does not stem the tide of
Gaunt's oration, words which, we should note, do not reach Richard's
ear:6/

> This royal throne of kings, this scept'red isle,
> This earth of majesty, this seat of Mars,
> This other Eden, demi-paradise,
> This fortress built by Nature for herself
> Against infection and the hand of war,
> This happy breed of men, this little world...
>   (II.i.40-45)

England, it would seem, has been granted a scepter by God. The
earth itself is "majestic," and represents a creative principle; it is both
"nurse, and teeming womb of royal kings" (II.i.51).   The land is so
profoundly fecund that it is, for Gaunt, an "other Eden, demi-paradise."
Gaunt feels his words, we infer, as more than metaphor.7/   England,
"built by Nature for herself," is a model of platonic perfection that
Nature creates for her own enjoyment.8/   Gaunt's England is a
"fortress... Against infection [both physical and moral corruption] and
the hand of war." While Gaunt's metaphors are historically "medieval" —
"a moat defensive to a house" (II.i.48) — the inestimable value of
England removes it, or should remove it, from post-lapsarian history. It
is a "precious stone set in the silver sea" (II.i.46) — a jewel of
incalculable price — a "dear dear land...of such dear souls" (II.i.57). The
repetition suggests that Gaunt's own diction cannot capture the
valuation of England and the souls (i.e. "people," but with obvious
Christian connotations) inhabiting it. While the "blessed plot" (II.i.50) is
free of the incursions of "less happier lands" (II.i.49), England itself is a
progenitor of Christian value.

English soldiery are

> Renowned for their deeds as far from home,
> For Christian service and true chivalry,
> As is the sepulcher in stubborn Jewry
> Of the world's ransom, blessed Mary's son.
>   (II.i.53-56)

Thus England is not merely a prototype of perfection, but generates its virtue through Christian service in holy wars, the goal of which is to redeem the "stubborn" rest of the world, or, at least, to bring within England's pale a land equally precious, being held in ransom by unbelievers, as man's soul is "ransomed" to Christ. Gaunt's view is not merely "sacramental," seeing invisible power and grace in tangible form; for him, England _is_ sacrament, a visible manifestation of God's power and grace, and a transmitter of that energy. England, in Gaunt's equation, _is_ a "holy land."

While Gaunt's metaphors express value in material terms — a "precious stone," a "silver sea," the "world's ransom" — the terms are inadequate to the supreme qualities that quantitative language cannot encompass. Gaunt strains against the limits of finite language invented by man. As God's creation, England cannot be captured in man's words.

But Gaunt's England, "this seat of Mars," capable of withstanding "the envious seige/ Of wat'ry Neptune" (II.i.62-63), an England equal to one and superior to another of the greatest pagan deities, "is now bound in with shame,/ With inky blots, and rotten parchment bonds" (II.i.63-64). Sacramental value, the reflection of great Nature's purpose through England, has been subverted. The reduction of sacred soil to a "tenement" (tenant) and "pelting [paltry] farm" (II.i.60) has robbed the land of intrinsic value, reducing inexpressible quality to commercial quantity, bankrupting England of its sacred energy, divorcing it from essential value by translating the soil into a set of "rotten" (corrupt) commercial "bonds." Gaunt's metaphor implies that "bonds" bind, that is, render potential power useless by tying it up. England is in bondage, no better than a holy land held by infidels. England is "bond-slave to the law" (II.i.114); its "holy-supernatural"9/ aspect of the soil, that which gave it its profound procreative power, has evaporated, and Richard is "landlord of England...not king" (II.i.113). England's link with God and Nature, a fusion based on more than similitude, is gone. Richard's "waste is no whit lesser than [his] land" (II.i.103) because, as King, he is keeper of the "holy metaphor." In his descent to landlord, he has broken the metaphoric bridge between England's soil and God, a linkage that, for Gaunt, is more than metaphor.

Gaunt's world is "timeless," in that its value-system is fixed, its relationship to God constant. Kingship as office, as "body politic," embodies the basic principle Gaunt enunciates to the Duchess of

Gloucester. The King is "God's deputy," though "human by nature" is "divine by grace."10/ Under the dispensation Gaunt accepts, time exists in the Old Testament, "Hebraic," sense, as an index of moral purpose. If a king violates his relationship with God, "God's is the quarrel," as it is with the erring soul of individual man.11/ Ritual, as opposed to ceremony, is part of the patterned movement of history, reflecting the intersection of kingship and divinity. Ritual, as Rossiter puts it mildly, is "a gesture of regard or respect for something which goes beyond the state-of-affairs or the event."12/ While Gaunt puts no emphasis on time — there being no "modern" time in Eden — York must, as Richard prepares to seize the Lancastrian estates, for heritage, at least, remains a value:

> Take Hereford's rights away, and take from Time
> His charters and his customary rights,
> Let not tomorrow then ensue today;
> Be not thyself. For how art thou a king
> But by fair sequence and succession?
> (II.i.195-199)

Gaunt emphasizes Richard's basic betrayal of trust and responsibility towards his realm. The kingdom may survive the murder of a kinsman by a king — if God takes up the quarrel — but Gaunt would try to prevent Richard from sundering England permanently from any possibility of God's positive or negative intervention. York's emphasis is, as it must be, on Richard's specific betrayal of the legal principle that makes him king. Though kings change, kingship as office is a continuum on which the state is predicated. Richard interrupts the continuity, not merely altering theories of time, but, as York sees it, defying time per se as emanation of the supernature, the rhythm within man shapes his destiny, the pattern a king must recognize as a premise of his royal plurality. Time is not destroyed in Richard II; England does not descend to primal chaos, as Britain seems to during King Lear's inexplicable storm. Instead, the world of the play swings from "Biblical" to "aristotelian" time, the latter a measurement of motion and movement. Time is what passes as motion occurs, or, in this play, time measures the sequences of Bolingbroke's movement towards a throne to which he has no right, but to which Richard has denied Time's de jure rhythm. In killing Gloucester and in reducing English soil to real estate, Richard ushers in a strictly de facto ordering of politics. In seizing Bolingbroke's inheritance, Richard compromises even the de facto premises of his office. In "this new world" (IV.i.78), time becomes strict measurement, quantitative, not qualitative, and all things within time are capable of measurement, of the assignment of a numerical equivalency profoundly base compared to Gaunt's inestimable England.

Richard's "commerical exploitation of a sacred trust," as Dorius suggests,13/ erodes principle. York's speech follows Richard's decision to

> seize to us
> The plate, coin, revenues, and movables
> Whereof our uncle Gaunt did stand possessed.
> (II.i.160-162)

Richard's use of his plurality in this command suggests again his misunderstanding of his role as king, specifically his failure to heed Gaunt's warning that Richard is "possessed now to depose [himself]" (II.i.108). Richard's "waste is no whit lesser than [his] land" (II.i.103), and, as he squandered the concept of time under which he might have functioned even as king de facto, he will discover that "now doth Time waste [him]" (V.v.49). At the beginning of the play, time has already become for Richard at best a medium of compromise. "Our doctors," he says lamely, "say this is no month to bleed" (I.i.157). But Richard lacks the healing power of his predecessor, Edward the Confessor (cf. Macbeth: IV.iii.141-159). He cannot persuade Mowbray and Bolingbroke to a peace. Nor can Richard mediate between man and the "outer mystery." He is trapped in the ironies of his own faulty leadership. As so often happens in the history plays, Richard's words palter with him in a double sense: "time [or the violation of 'time'] shall call [Bolingbroke] home from banishment" (I.iv.21), but prematurely, as Richard creates a "time" within which Bolingbroke can function. In leaving for Ireland, Richard creates "the absent time" (III.iii.79), but he has done as much already by vacating the basic premises of kingship. Bolingbroke is pulled inevitably into the vacuum, regardless of the legalistic premises Richard himself has given Bolingbroke for repealing his own banishment. While the summons of Bolingbroke to leadership is made explicit in Holinshed, Shakespeare makes it implicit, thereby rendering it more complex and ambiguous. As Ornstein suggests, Bolingbroke, posing as the exponent of conservative values both in his indictment of Mowbray and in his return to England, becomes an instrumentality which destroys those values.14/ The basic and prior destructive agent, however, is Richard, who gives Bolingbroke the pretext for each of his crucial actions.

The banishment scene suggests what will happen to "time" in England. Gaunt warns Richard about the limits of a king's control of time:

Gaunt.   My inch of taper will be burnt and done,
               And blindfold death not let me see my son.

Richard.   Why, uncle, thou has many years to live.

Gaunt.   But not a minute, king, that thou canst give;
            Shorten my days thou canst with sullen sorrow
            And pluck nights from me, but not lend a morrow;
            Thou canst help time to furrow me with age,
            But stop no wrinkle in his pilgrimage:
            Thy word is current with him for my death,
            But dead, thy kingdom cannot buy my breath.
                            (I.iii.222-231)

Gaunt contrasts superhuman power with mere worldly "currency." He
attempts to cheer his banished son with an obviously metaphoric jewel, a
contrast to the different medium he will employ in his speech on
England:

            The sullen passage of thy weary steps
            Esteem as foil wherein thou art to set.
            The precious jewel of thy home return.
                            (I.iii.264-266)
Bolingbroke turns the metaphor around:

            Nay, rather, every tedious stride I make
            Will but remember me what a deal of world
            I wander from the jewels that I love.
                            (I.iii.267-269)

Gaunt, almost desperately one infers, exhorts Bolingbroke to fantasy:

            Suppose the singing birds musicians,
            The grass whereon thou tread'st the presence strewed,
            The flowers fair ladies, and thy steps no more
            Than a delightful measure or a dance.
                            (I.iii.287-290)

While Gaunt's reference to "the presence strewed," i.e. the royal
chamber strewn with rushes, might be interpreted along with the
ambiguous "cause" (I.iii.304) as encouraging Bolingbroke towards
kingship, the literal Bolingbroke responds scornfully and specifically to
"fantasy":

            O, who can hold a fire in his hand
            By thinking on the frosty Caucasus?
            Or cloy the hungry edge of appetite
            By bare imagination of a feast?
            Or wallow naked in December snow
            By thinking on fantastic summer's heat?
                            (I.iii.293-298)

Bolingbroke values things as they are, not as they should be or as they might be. Time itself is translated into empirical measure, unlike the time of Gaunt's vision. Bolingbroke, whose response is demanded by Richard's seizure of the Lancastrian estates and by Richard's denial of any legal redress, is a predictable entity. An empiricist moving into an increasingly empirical world can hardly be expected to reverse the process. Ironically, however, Bolingbroke will show that he would like very much to "bid time return" (III.ii.69) once he takes the measure of the crown he has seized. By then, England will be reduced to the commercial getting and spending Gaunt evokes in his warning to Richard about time and that Gaunt deplores at the end of his paean of English glories.

The Elizabethan would have been familiar with Gaunt's sentiments regarding kingship and England, having heard them of a Sunday, as the Homilies rolled forth the official doctrine with considerable splendor. But the Elizabethan walking towards the Thames from old St. Paul's or from St. Martin's, or crossing towards the City of London from Bankside, would have been what De Maisse, the French Ambassador to England, saw in 1597: "From Greenwich to London, it is a magnificent sight to see the numbers of ships and boats which lie in anchor, insomuch that for two leagues you see nothing but ships..."15/ Whether an historian agrees with Tawney, that landowners, having achieved a literally solid economic base, sought to achieve political power, only to clash with a conservative Stuart stewardship backed by the older aristocracy,16/ and/or with Trevor-Roper, that the achieving or the failure to achieve high office within the government was the dividing line between worldly success or failure,17/ sacramental sanctions, as dictated from the pulpit, were essentially irrelevant to that part of Elizabethan man that lived in this world. The question of his soul's destiny was still vital, and he may have believed that England was linked to the will of God and that her sovereign was mediator between God and man, but his operative principle was the exercise of political - commercial power for the sake of its own maintenance and growth in an England, where, as Hurstfield says, "Drake strove for the destruction of Spanish supremacy, Hawkins for a trading imperialism based on sea power, Raleigh for a colonial civilization in the new world."18/

The court, as M. St. Clare Byrne notes "was overrun with place-seekers, all scrambling for perquisites, offices, money, favour. [The Court] was undeniably the focus of the national life."19/ Some members of Parliament may well have accepted Elizabeth's claim, in 1601, that her power "acknowledged no superior on earth and did not share its authority in the making of war or the settling of peace, in governing the church or managing the state,"20/ but still they insisted on an Act of Parliament on monopolies. Elizabeth's successor would say of Parliament: "I am surprised that my ancestors should ever have permitted such an institution to come into existence... I am obliged to put up with what I cannot get rid of."21/ But underlying a monarch's struggle with Parliament was a monarch's need for money, a need that explains Elizabeth's "compromise" with Parliament in 1601. As B. R. Outhwaite says:

> The crown was deep in debt: Elizabeth owed the Corporation [of London] 80,000 pounds, and had failed to pay the interest charges on the last loan, and a further 120,000 pounds was outstanding in privy seal loans. Crown lands were being sold on an unprecedented scale and the proceeds were being used, not to repay these debts, but to keep the crown's head above the continuously high level of expenditure. Moreover, the queen was old, there were doubts about the succession, and there was never any guarantee that her successor would honour her debts. These factors combined to produce a situation in which Elizabeth's credit reached its nadir.[22]

As Hurstfield says, "No wonder Elizabeth yielded on monopolies. An immediate grant of taxation was urgent, and she bowed to necessity."[23]

It is tempting to see Richard II as a topical satire on the financial realities of divine-right monarchy.[24] It is also tempting to view Richard II as an allegory demonstrating the transition from Elizabeth's divinely sanctioned power to the "popular" government Bolingbroke promotes in Richard II. Richard's version of kingship became as obsolete as Elizabeth's, though for very different reasons, if Byrne is correct: "the Stuart dynasty never had a chance from the beginning; Elizabeth had served her country's needs so effectively, given it peace in which to develop and grow, and by the time her long reign was over she had enabled her people to outgrow the need of her and her kind."[25] Shakespeare's prescience, then, looks ahead to the civil wars of the mid-Seventeenth Century, as inevitable in their way as were the Wars of the Roses after the deposition of Richard II.[26] It is equally tempting, and perhaps more plausible, to view Gaunt's great speech, his doctrinal response to the Duchess of Gloucester, and York's argument for "degree," as Elizabethan rhetoric conflicting with fiscal realities. The latter thesis, at least, has some bearing on the way a play is written, and on a spectator who had witnessed the contrast between theory and action so apparent at the end of Elizabeth's reign. Better yet, however, to assume that, while the spectator had some inkling of all that was happening in London at the century's close, he came to see plays in which Gaunt's speech stands as a vivid contrast to all that happens in the Richard II – Henry V epoch. It is in the plays and not in their possible reference to the end of Elizabeth's reign that the continuing topicality of these plays resides.

We can only know the "England-that-was" if it is brought to our ears by a character with the authority and the experience to recall it for us. Gaunt's vision is not challenged by anyone in the play. York, though more realistic than Gaunt, extends the thesis by recalling the specific exploits of the two Edwards (II.i.171-183). Against the England qua sacrament Gaunt projects, we must place what England becomes, a realm of mere tangibility, in which things are in the saddle and ride mankind, in which the element of fire is quite put out. The translation, or debasement, of England is the central issue explored by the Second Henriad, but the issue cannot be explored unless the other side of the equation — Gaunt's England — is provided in detail. The Second Henriad demonstrates the inexorable process ramifying outward from Richard's complicity in shedding Gloucester's sacred blood, and, equally, from Richard's economic exploitation, his denial of the laws of inheritance and his viewing of the land as land, his violation of the land as sacrament.

Appropriately, the only Englishman who fulfills Gaunt's vision is the banished Mowbray, whose career reflects England's crusading chivalry only though the irony of his alienation:

> Many a time has banished Norfolk fought
> For Jesu Christ in glorious Christian field,
> Streaming the ensign of the Christian cross
> Against black pagans, Turks, and Saracens;
> And, toiled with works of war, retired himself
> To Italy, and there at Venice gave
> His body to that pleasant country's earth,
> And his pure soul unto his captain, Christ,
> Under whose colors he had fought so long.
> (IV.i.91-100)

Carlisle, who talks of the "pleasant...earth" of Venice, will soon predict that England will "be called/ The field of Golgotha and dead men's skulls" (IV.i.143-144). The dying Gaunt has called England "a grave/ Whose hollow womb inherits naught but bones" (I.ii.82-83). His "other Eden, demi-paradise" becomes, in Henry V, not England, but France: "this best garden of the world" (as reflected by the varietal prejudice of Burgundy: V.ii.36), and, according to the Final Chorus of Henry V, "the world's best garden" (7). 27/

1.   Peter Saccio, Shakespeare's English Kings (Oxford Galaxy, New York, 1977), p. 24.

2.   Gaunt's utterances in the play, and many of York's, represent standard Elizabethan doctrine. The Homily of Obedience suggests that "David might have killed his enemie King Saul," but prayed instead: "keepe me that I lay not my hand upon him, seeing he is the anointed of the Lord."   Nothing justifies "any insurrection, sedition, or tumults, either by force of armes (or otherwise) against the anointed of the Lord, or any of his officers: But wee must in such case patiently suffer all wrongs, and injuries, referring the judgement onely to God."   One must wonder how Essex's followers could have considered Richard II a justification for rebellion, particularly since the Homily against Rebellion which, with the Homily of Obedience, converges so prominently with the doctrinal context of the play, was written in 1571, specifically to prevent rebellions like those led by the seventh Earl of Northumberland and by the sixth Earl of Westmoreland.   Elizabeth herself declared, more than a decade after these homiletic warnings, that princes were "not bound to yield account or render the reasons of their actions to any others but to God."   She herself was "therefore accountable only to his Divine Majesty." A declaration of the causes moving the Queene of England to give aid to the defence of the people afflicted and oppressed in the Low Countries (October, 1585: printed in Holinshed's Third Edition, 1587). The same doctrine is reiterated in the Prayer Book's Prayers for the Queen of England, which the Elizabethan would have repeated every Sunday from 1559 to 1603. The Sixteenth Century was divided on the question, of course, as it was divided on all questions, with Erasmus, for example, advocating resistence to an evil King, Bodin, insisting with Gaunt that even the tyrant is accountable only to God.

3.   Henry A. Kelley, Divine Providence in the England of Shakepeare's Histories (Cambridge, Mass., 1970), p. 204.

4.   The word encourages directly opposite interpretations. See the Variorum note on it: Richard II, ed. Matthew Black (Philadelphia, 1955), p. 85, n. 278.

5.   Cf. Hall, where similar sentiments are echoed by the English ruling class, "preceavyng daily more and more the realme to fall into ruyne and desolacion (in maner irrecuperable as long as Kyng Richard either lived or reigned)." In Hall, Bolingbroke is crowned by acclamation, "with one voyce of the nobles and the commons." The Union of the Two Noble and Illustrious Families of York and Lancaster (1548: reprinted, London, 1809), pp. 6 and 13.

6. Michael Manheim talks of Richard as if he were present during II.i.1-68. Few, Manheim argues, could be "more icily impenetrable than the Richard who can listen with such insufferable indifference to Gaunt's famed and ringing patriotism..." — as if Gaunt were already, like Pistol, reciting lines from old plays! The Weak King Dilemma in the Shakespearean History Plays (Syracuse University Press, 1973), p. 57.

7. Critics like Dover Wilson, Richard II (Cambridge, England, 1939), pp. lviii and 156, who find Gaunt's speech originating in Froissart, should note that the relevant passage in Froissart, quoted previously, is only "negatively patriotic," as is much of Richmond's speech to his army: cf. "A base foul stone, made precious by the foil/ Of England's chair" (Richard III: V.iii.251-252) vs. Gaunt's "This precious stone set in the silver sea" (II.i.46). One should further note that Shakespeare has already written a precis of Gaunt's speech in Hasting's "Let us be backed by God, and with the seas,/ Which He has given for fence impregnable" (III Henry VI: IV.i.43-44).

8. Gaunt's speech consistently reminds me of Hopkins' "sacramental vision" in his "celebratory poems," particularly the sestet of "Spring":

> What is all this juice and all this joy?
> A strain of the earth's sweet being in the beginning,
> In Eden garden — Have, get, before it cloy,
> Before it cloud, Christ, Lord, and sour with sinning...

Like Gaunt, Hopkins senses an Eden being "sold out," particularly in "God's Grandeur" and "Binsey Poplars." Cf. also Blake's "Milton" and "London," and Wordsworth's "Westminster Bridge."

9. The phrase is L. C. Knights': Explorations (New York, 1964), p. 37.

10. The distinction is that of Ernst Kantorowicz, The King's Two Bodies (Princeton, 1957).

11. The Mirror for Magistrates emphasizes Richard's wild deviation from leadership, as Gaunt does when he faces Richard. Richard rules "all by lust/ That forced not of vertue, ryght, or lawe." "This lawles life, to lawles deth ey draws,/ Wherefore byd Kynges be rulde and rule by right,/ Who worketh his will, and shunneth wisedomes sawes,/ In flateries clawes, and shames foule pawes shal light." ed. Lily B. Campbell (Cambridge, England, 1938), p.120. Gaunt's emphasis to York had been on the premises of "right," not merely on Richard's abandonment of law. As Kelly says of Gaunt's "England" speech, it "should no doubt be classified as belonging to the anti-Lancastrian tradition. [my ital.] This is an aspect of providential speculation that receives far more emphasis in Shakespeare, and especially in this play, than in any of the chronicle sources before him." Divine Providence in the England of Shakespeare's Histories (Harvard University Press, 1970),

p. 205. The "pro-Lancastrian" case is put forward by Irving Ribner, The English History Play in the Age of Shakespeare (Princeton, 1957). J. W. Lever makes a strong case for John Eliot's translation of the Ortho-epia Gallica as the source of Gaunt's speech: "Shakespeare's French Fruits," Shakespeare Survey 6 (Cambridge, England, 1953), 79-90. For a convincing case that Shakespeare is indebted to Daniel, and not vice versa, see George M. Logan, "Lucan - Daniel - Shakespeare: New Light on the Relation Between The Civil Wars and Richard II," Shakespeare Studies IX (1976), 121-140.

12. A. P. Rossister, "Angel With Horns" and Other Shakespeare Lectures, ed. Graham Storey (London, 1961), p. 35.

13. R. J. Dorius, "A Little More Than a Little," Shakespeare Quarterly, XI (1960), 19.

14. Robert Ornstein, A Kingdom for a Stage (Cambridge, Mass., 1972), p. 104.

15. Quoted in Joel Hurstfield, The Elizabethan Nation (New York, 1964), p. 100.

16. R. H. Tawney, The Agrarian Problem in the Sixteenth Century (New York, 1967).

17. Hugh Trevor-Roper, "The Political Failure of the Gentry," The English Political Tradition, I, pp. 339-341.

18. Hurstfield, The Elizabethan Nation, p. 85.

19. M. St. Clare Byrne, Elizabethan Life in Town and Country (New York, 1961), p. 28.

20. Quoted in Hurstfield, The Elizabethan Nation, p. 80.

21. Quoted in Hurstfield, The Elizabethan Nation, p. 81.

22. Quoted in Hurstfield, The Elizabethan Nation, pp. 81-82.

23. Hurstfield, The Elizabethan Nation, p. 82.

24. For one of the more telling attacks on "occasional" and topical interpretations of Shakespearean (and Elizabethan and Jacobean) drama, see Richard Levin's, the "The King James Version of Measure for Measure," Clio (III, 2, February, 1974), 129-163. For a sane and balanced attack on the specificity of topical allusions in Tudor - Stuart drama, see David Bevington, Tudor Drama and Politics (Harvard University Press, 1968).

25. Bryne, Elizabethan Life in Town and Country, p. 26.

26. Cf. Colley: "If Richard II is not an image of Queen Elizabeth, he is Shakespeare's uncanny (yet unconscious) prophetic vision of the Stuarts." "The Economics of Richard II?" 162.

27. I believe that this chapter is in general accord with the conclusions of H. A. Kelly, whose exploration of the sources is far more complete than mine: "After viewing the providential themes in Richard II, we may ask if there is any indication that Shakespeare intended us to feel that God was active in bringing about any of the actions of the play, or in aiding any of the characters. It would seem that we must answer in the negative, for not even the characters themselves are dramatized as considering any of the play's vicissitudes to have been brought about by God" (Dramatic Providence in the England of Shakespeare's Histories, p. 214). The latter generalization is too sweeping, ignoring as it does Bolingbroke's suggestion that he does not oppose the will of heaven (III.ii.18-19), lines that could be read as Bolingbroke's oblique and self-serving suggestion that he is God's instrumentality ("In God's name, I'll ascend the regal throne": IV.i.113), York's suggestion that "God for some strong purpose steeled/ The hearts of men" against pity for Richard (V.ii.34-35), York's "But heaven hath a hand in these events" (V.ii.37), and Carlisle's indictment of Bolingbroke, a speech "Stirred up by God," as Carlisle feels it (IV.i.133). But certainly the tetralogy dramatizes, if not the alienation of England from God, the absence of the "supernature," an absence we feel strongly in King Lear, as we feel its presence within and surrounding the two tragic characters of Macbeth, and, positively, within King Duncan and King Edward.

II

Richard's England

Into a world where ceremony reflects intrinsic reality, and is therefore Ritual, where blood and soil are sacramental, where the king incorporates a priestly function, where his "body politic" includes the concept of Christus,1/ Shakespeare projects an unroyal crime, an uncle's murder perpetrated by a king. Richard's opening lines suggest the sanctions of a medieval world:

> Old John of Gaunt, time-honored Lancaster,
> Hast thou according to thy oath and band
> Brought hither Henry Hereford, thy bold son,
> Here to make good the boist'rous late appeal,
> Which then our leisure would not let us hear,
> Against the Duke of Norfolk, Thomas Mowbray?
> (I.i.1-6)

Beyond the stately opening cadences, Richard talks of conflict. And we quickly learn (in I.ii) that the source of the conflict is the very king who speaks of time's honors, oaths and bonds, the very king who seems so aware of heritage. Even before the play has begun, sacramental potency has evaporated from the forms and formalities of Richard's world. This loss of essence will not be immediately apparent, however. The world of this doomed king will witness the demonstration of the loss, but will seldom express it directly — Carlisle being an exception to this statement, as he tends to be an exception to the world into which he survives. Regardless of the "high sparks of honor" even Bolingbroke discerns in Carlisle (Richard II: V.vi.29), Richard's example in destroying the spiritual premises of his kingship becomes the destiny his kingdom must gradually recognize.

The historical Richard II — more than had monarchs before him — insisted on anointment as the sacramental action that confirmed his absolute right to rule. He was, according to Figgis, "king by virtue of unction."2/ Gaunt respects the status of God's "deputy anointed in His sight" (I.ii.38), and Richard will insist that "Not all the water in the rough rude sea/ Can wash the balm off from an anointed king" (III.ii.54-55). The significance of Richard's "With mine own tears I wash away my balm" (IV.i.206) cannot be over-emphasized, because, with that balm, one of the basic means by which a king is king is rinsed away.3/ A central sacramental action has been erased (appropriately by Richard), not to be reinstated, except perhaps as mere ceremony, since its sacred premises have been evaporated.4/ As Fritz Kern says, "above all it was the anointing that embodied the theocratic monarchical element in constitutional law."5/ When what Figgis calls a "ceremony conferring a sacramental grace"6/ is rendered violable, monarchy must base its claim on other premises, no matter what ceremonies it indulges. The difference between Richard's coronation and any that might follow it after his deposition is described by Percy Schramm:

> [Coronation] is far more than drama: for God is looking down upon it, asking whether the crown has been passed on from head to head as it should be. Only if the forms have been truly observed, and nothing has been omitted, does the coronation have its due effect. That is why it is quite different from a pageant, a term...reducing it to the level of fetes and state ceremonies...manifestations of royal power that could be abandoned, changed, or devised anew.7/

Gaunt, of course, sees "God looking down," and predicts divine vengeance for Richard's violation of sacramental premises. But nemesis would seem to be profane rather than divine, for Bolingbroke's intervention merely confirms an already unsacramental concept of kingship, denying the mystical incorporation described by Lucas de Penna:

> And just as men are joined together spiritually in the spiritual body the head of which is Christ...so are men joined together morally and politically in the respublica...a body the head of which is the Prince.8/

The prince begins to destroy that body if, like Richard, he fails to recognize his central place in the structure.

According to the Duchess of Gloucester, Richard has ravaged a "Jesse Tree," and has perpetrated an obvious anti-sacrament. She tells Gaunt that

> Edward's seven sons, whereof thyself art one,
> Were as seven vials of his sacred blood,
> Or seven fair branches springing from one root.
> Some of those seven are dried by nature's course,
> Some of those branches by the destinies cut:
> But Thomas, my dear lord, my life, my Gloucester,
> One vial full of Edward's sacred blood,
> One flourishing branch of his most royal root,
> Is cracked, and all the precious liquor spilt,
> Is hacked down, and his summer leaves all faded
> By envy's hand and murder's bloody ax.
> (I.ii.11-21)

Gaunt grants as much, but refuses to take "the part [he] had in Woodstock's blood" (I.ii.1), that is, to accept the argument based on the quasi-sacramental ties of family that will be employed increasingly in Richard II. Instead, Gaunt commits the argument to the sacred premises of Richard's coronation. If Richard has violated those premises, as Gaunt agrees he has, then the God who approved the coronation must also respond to its violation:

> Put we our quarrel to the will of heaven,
> Who, when they see the hours ripe on earth,
> Will rain hot vengeance on offenders' heads.
> (I.ii.6-8)

In one sense, Richard's tears will be that "rain," but, by then, Bolingbroke's "rain" (III.iii.58) of steel will have dictated deposition. 9/ In neither case can an act of God be discerned.

Richard's coronation, as Reno points out, 10/ reversed the usual ordo, a startling historical fact when we consider the "reversal" that the Deposition Scene represents. According to Holinshed, the people vowed after the coronation to submit "unto such a prince and governor, and obeie his commandments." Thus, as Schramm suggests, the Archbishop's question to the people was "not a collaudatio [that is an election, or acclamation: cf. Richard III: III.vii and Macbeth: V.viii.54-59]...but primarily a recognition of the legal position bestowed by inheritance, and secondarily, an act of homage complementary to the king's oath made by the people in fulfillment of an historical covenant." 11/ Thus the people acceded not to a man about to be anointed and crowned, but to God's will in anointing and crowning the king. The people, here, ratify God's will, after their participation in its conferral, granting an already established cosmic truth, rather than giving their voices as an element of that truth. The reversal of the ordo is more than "significant"; it lends far greater historical weight to Gaunt's "God's deputy anointed in His sight" than we might suspect, for Richard, it would seem, insisted on being anointed in God's sight alone, the "voice of God" being the only collaudatio necessary to seal Richard's kingship. In responding to the Archbishop's question, then, the people must perforce assent to the conception of "divine coronation." Shakespeare does not make use of this material directly, although it is available from what we assume to be his prime source, Holinshed, but reserves it, as I will argue, for the Deposition Scene, where Richard's coronation will be reversed. The Deposition Scene will reflect negatively the context in which the coronation was set.

Richard's defection from sovereignty, as both Holinshed and Gaunt depict it, is profound. He has descended before the play begins to an unroyal culpability that reverberates into the opening scenes. Such defection releases dangerous energies into the kingdom, energies that manifest themselves before we learn of Richard's guilt in I.ii. Richard calls Bolingbroke "bold" and "boist'rous," and tries to gather as much intelligence from Gaunt as he can before Bolingbroke launches his indictment at Richard's alter ego, Mowbray.

While Richard uses the royal plurality in excusing himself for not attending to Bolingbroke's "late [recent] appeal...which then our leisure would not let us hear," he requests that Gaunt "tell me" (I.i.9) what Bolingbroke's accusations are. Should Richard not say "tell us"?12/ Should he not still be acting as king concerned for his state and his subjects? He is "acting," as we will learn, and the shift to "body natural" in "tell me" betrays his personal uneasiness in the face of Bolingbroke's charge.13/ Richard's ambiguous references point as much at Bolingbroke as at Mowbray:

> hast thou sounded him,
> If he appeal the duke on ancient malice,
> Or worthily, as a good subject should,
> On some known ground of treachery in him?
> (I.i.9-11)

The final "him" obviously applies to "the duke" (Mowbray), but the nearest antecedent is "a good subject" (Bolingbroke). Thus, the sentence defines Richard's position, standing on the ground of treachery that, again, as we will learn, is of his own creating. Richard's cautionary lecture on what good subjects should do — a speech delivered to Gaunt! — is undermined by what the king has done. While we do not yet know that Bolingbroke's appeal is a response to Richard's crime, we infer that, beneath his commanding facade, Richard is vulnerable, faced as he is with two great noblemen, running beyond control, like nature, whether in conflagration or in tempest:

> High-stomached are they both, and full of ire,
> In rage, deaf as the sea, hasty as fire.
> (I.i.18-19)

Richard himself introduces the elements of fire and moisture that will form so important a part of the imagistic/thematic patterning of the play.

Richard, poised between two nobles, each accusing the other of treason, knows that "one but flatters us" (I.i.25). Whatever has happened, the lines of loyalty, of "oath and band," the premises that insure "a good subject," have been disturbed. Two great men come angrily before the King, an action reflecting an equivocal status within the kingdom. We do not yet know the basis of the conflict.

Richard's position between the two accusers might seem that of an independent judge, justicer of the kingdom, the king's proper role. We quickly learn, however, that Bolingbroke has assumed that role, accusing Mowbray of "all the treasons for these eighteen years/Complotted and contrived in this land" (I.i.95-96), in other words of virtually every crime committed during Richard's reign, which began in 1377 (Richard assigns the date for the Bolingbroke - Mowbray trail by combat in April, 1398). We find, further, that Bolingbroke arrogates to himself "Disclaiming... the kindred of the king"14/ (I.i.70), a disclaimer that Richard can only second, while emphasizing that Bolingbroke is not heir apparent and that the king's blood is sacramental:

> Were he my brother, nay, my kingdom's heir,
> As he is but my father's brother's son,
> Now by my scepter's awe I make a vow,
> Such neighbor nearness to our sacred blood
> Should nothing privilege him nor partialize
> The unstooping firmness of my upright soul.
> (I.i.116-121)15/

While Richard may score a point or two here, we remember that he merely ratifies the disclaimer Bolingbroke has already made, and while the lines can be read as a threat to Bolingbroke, alluding, as they do, to Mortimer, the heir Richard has named, one feels that Richard protests too much. He must admit that Bolingbroke's blood is a "neighbor" to his own. We do not yet know, of course, how far Richard has stooped in shedding the blood of a closer neighbor, that of his father's brother, Gloucester.

Bolingbroke ascribes "the primal eldest curse" to his uncle's murder. Gloucester's blood, he claims,

> like sacrificing Abel's, cries
> Even from the tongueless caverns of the earth
> To me for justice and rough chastisement.
> (I.i.104-106)

Such hyperhole draws from Richard a metaphor of flight: "How high a pitch his resolution soars!"(I.i.109). Harbage says that "Richard's comment has the detached quality of a connoisseur of style,"16/ while Muir suggests that "the king is uneasy that his own guilt will come to light."17/ Richard can pose, perhaps, as stylistic critic, or worry about the revelation of his own culpability, but, unless we have read Holinshed, we can embrace neither possibility yet. The Abel - Cain allusion, of course, points not at Mowbray but at Richard, Gloucester's close relative. As Sen Gupta says, "Bolingbroke, in defying Mowbray really accuses Richard of shedding the blood of a near kinsman."18/ What seems sheer rant becomes, as Richard recognizes immediately, a threat not merely that he may be exposed, but that he may be supplanted by an avenging relative of "Abel's." But we must reexamine the scene ex post facto, on the basis of Scene ii, to discover Scene i's "hidden meanings."

It seems strange that Shakespeare should begin a play with a scene that must be explained later. We view Claudius's seemingly healthy court against the ominous context of the ghost-watch of the first scene. We see Othello through the obscene filter Iago has set before us. We meet Macbeth with a startling echo of the Weird Sisters on his lips. The later Antony can be seen only in the context of his climactic meeting with Cleopatra, an event that occurs before the play begins, but that Enobarbus provides in detail (II.ii.191-228). Shakespeare seems to suggest that "an event" — like the murder of Gloucester — can be understood only as its meanings ramify. Gaunt in I.ii forces us not merely back into the opening scene, but, as the opening scene has done, back to the murder that triggers Bolingbroke's accusations against Mowbray, who suddenly becomes a stand-in for the guilty king pretending to preside over "justice."

The opening scene suggests, at least, that Richard is not in that "command" he claims for himself (I.i.196). He can bring neither of the adversaries to armistice. Indeed, he admits that he is "no physician" (I.i.154), is unable to cure the illness breaking into the open in his kingdom. He does not possess the power of a Christus, the sanctity of a sacramental king that Richard inherited and insisted upon in his coronation, precisely the power possessed by one of Shakespeare's most sacramental (and neglected) kings, Edward the Confessor:

> How he solicits heaven,
> Himself best knows...and 'tis spoken,
> To the succeeding royalty he leaves
> The healing benediction. With this strange virtue
> He had a heavenly gift of prophecy,
> And sundry blessings hang about his throne
> That speak him full of grace.19/
> (Macbeth: IV.iii.149-159)

One must acknowledge that Macbeth was written some decade after Richard II, that the world of Macbeth is consistently "medieval,"20/ and that the allusions to Edward's healing ability may be a compliment to James I.21/ One must also grant that Richard is helpless before a different strain of "king's evil," this one a product of the king himself, one that links Richard with Macbeth, not Edward. Richard can only "act" as king. His de jure status has already evaporated. While he will die without issue, his legacy will hardly be of healing. Nor will he support, as does Edward the Confessor, a crusade from "Christendom" (Macbeth: IV.iii.192), a crusade Gaunt would have applauded, but that Gaunt's son will be unable to lead, compromised as he is by a king's murder and by the "new world" (IV.i.78) that regicide confirms.

The inefficacy of sacramental values in the world of Richard II is outlined explicitly by Mowbray:

> For you, my noble Lord of Lancaster,
> The honorable father of my foe,
> Once did I lay an ambush for your life,
> A trespass that doth vex my grieved soul;
> But, ere I last received the sacrament,
> I did confess it, and exactly begged
> Your grace's pardon, and I hope I had it.
> (I.i.135-141)

Mowbray has fulfilled the Elizabethan precondition for receiving the sacrament:

> The same order shall the Curate use with those bewixt whom he perceiveth malice and hatred to reigne, not suffering them to be partakers of the Lordes Table, until hee know them to reconciled. And if one of the parties so at variance, bee content to forgive from the bottome of his heart, all that that the other has trespassed against him, and to make amends for that he himself hath offended, and the other partie will not be persuaded to a godly unitie, but remaine still in his frowardness and malice: the Minister in that case ought to admit the penitent person to the holy Communion, and not him that is obstinate.

While we cannot assume Gaunt's fulfillment of the second clause of The Lord's Prayer ("as we forgive them that trespasse against us"), it would be hard to argue against Mowbray's sincerity here. He is, after all, addressing the powerful noble who could impugn Mowbray's testimony.22/ If pardoned by the father, however, Mowbray is accused by the son. If commissioned by the king to commit an anti-sacramental act, Mowbray is banished to fulfill Christian service on foreign strands. Mowbray's case illustrates the essential loss England suffers. Richard has rendered his kingship's sanctity irrelevant, and, in doing so, he has rendered the sacraments irrelevant. It is worth noting that Mowbray's soul is apparently still vexed at his "trespass." He does not feel, it seems, that the precise fulfillment of religious formula has been efficacious. Perhaps he doubts God's grace towards him, although that is a more speculative surmise than it is in the case of Henry V on the eve of Agincourt (IV.i.292-306). Mowbray's example suggests that God's grace is no longer available to England.

Richard cannot encourage his subjects towards a peaceful conclusion and thus cannot fulfill his spiritual function, which would be to reconcile "those betwixt whom he perceiveth malice and hatred to reigne." The guilty party can hardly preside as king-judge or a king-priest. The "invisible power and grace" is no longer his, or England's, to communicate. Signum and res — external form and interior substance — have suffered a basic divorce in England, through Richard's crime, and they will not be reunited again. Truth, we learn, has not been expressed in I.i; it has been suppressed. The movement towards a wholly "political" world has begun, but all of the manifestations of that transition have yet to reveal themselves. Richard, it seems, will be among the first to recognize what he has done. He will exercise his awareness through the devastating pageantry of the Deposition Scene.

One of the first manifestations of England's alienation from Grace is that the trial by combat cannot fulfill its function. The judicium dei, a ritual whereby man brought God into the seat of judgement is simply not available to Richard's kingdom. Instead, justice — or some distorted version of it — is administered behind closed doors and is dictated by the self-protective needs of a fragile monarch. It may be that, as Samuel Schoenbaum says, "at that lists at Conventry, Richard displays as much political acumen as weakness, and that he does not fail but achieves a success necessarily limited by the realities of his situation."23/ Schoenbaum is right to see Richard's complicity in Gloucester's murder as "crucial."24/ The trial can produce no intrinsic justice, since the guilty party — as the principals must know — is presiding. Shakespeare cunningly keeps ambiguous even the question of Mowbray's carrying out of Richard's order to kill Gloucester:

> For Gloucester's death,
> I slew him not; but to my own disgrace,
> Neglected my sworn duty in that case.
> (I.i.132-134)

Thus does Mowbray dismiss, with two fifths of a line and a couplet, the primary charge against him — in contrast to his explicit and detailed denial of Bolingbroke's charges of extortion and other "treasons." In Holinshed, Mowbray claims to have saved Gloucester's life "contrarie to the will of the king." The angry Richard "appointed one of his own servants" to dispatch his uncle. Shakespeare's emphasis is on Richard's guilt. The question of Mowbray's involvement, though raised again by a Bolingbroke intent on posing in IV.i. as "Justicer," is never resolved. Bolingbroke's later guilt and Exton's complicity are made very clear, Shakespeare going to far as so provide Exton with a witness to

Bolingbroke's "Have I no friend will rid me of this living fear?" (V.iv.2). At the end of the play, of course, Bolingbroke is more guilty than Richard was at the beginning. Bolingbroke has killed an anointed king.

On St. Lamberts Day, at Coventry, Richard must maneuver adroitly to banish both men. As Schoenbaum summarizes it: "At a single stroke he manages to rid himself of two embarrassments: his aggressive cousin Bolingbroke, who represents a direct threat, and Mowbray, to whom he owes so much, and who has outlived his usefulness. Had the joust taken place and Bolingbroke triumphed, he would be still more dangerous. If, on the other hand, Mowbray came out on top, he would have an even greater hold on his monarch; the continuing presence of such men is rarely coveted."25/ Schoenbaum is correct, I believe, on Bolingbroke; Richard must blunt the thrust of a cousin assuming a king's prerogatives.26/ While Schoenbaum may utter a political truism about men in Mowbray's position, Mowbray, as characterized, might well have proved a trusty ally in Richard's struggle against the competition Richard has encouraged in England:

> But what thou [Bolingbroke] art, God, thou, and I, do know,
> And all too soon, I fear, the king shall rue.
> (I.iii.203-204)

Suffice it that when Richard throws his warder down, the action reflects what has already happened in England. The judicium dei, endowed in theory with sacramental premises, as Reno brilliantly illustrates,27/ cannot function in practice, since the ritual cannot call "God" into the "quarrel." Sacramental premises are gone. Richard, still endowed with a power he has yet to squander completely, must work out a hasty political solution. He fails, however, to draw the lesson from his need for an extemporaneous politics. Having remarked the height of Bolingbroke's "pitch" in Scene One, having heard Mowbray's warning to him in Scene Three, he can laugh in Scene Four with Aumerle about Bolingbroke's wooing of the populace. And Richard's guilt seems not to trouble him, except as an annoying parenthesis within his capricious reign. Shakespeare does not employ directly the historical fact that Richard was a child-king, but the fact seems implicit in his characterization of a willful "adult" who has not grown into mature capacity. Richard as child seems to be a sub-text for Shakespeare's characterization.28/ Richard seems not to recognize that his murder of Gloucester has erased one of the fundamental premises of the kingship he inherited, that he has, as his own improvisation in I.iii demonstrates, rendered kingship a "political" — or competitive — office. Bolingbroke's imitation of the actions of a man seeking elective office has become less and less a laughing matter.

Richard is king ex opere operatum, "through the objective accomplishment of the sacrament itself," as Reno suggests.29/ Reno goes on to say that "priestly ordination and royal consecration effect a magical change in the very person of the recipient."30/ Kern quotes the priest's words to Gregory the Great: "The grace of God hath this day changed thee into another man, and by the holy rite of unction hath made thee partaker of its divinity."31/ For Kern, anointment is the "tangible rite of consecration, rather than the abstract ideas of preachers or of treatises, that led to the sanctification of the king in the estimation of the people."32/ Thus the historical Richard made his case for divine kingship, and insisted on popular endorsement of the sacred grounds of his sovereignty. Shakespeare's Richard has destroyed one of the premises of his kingship; his tears in the Deposition Scene will merely confirm what has already happened. His interruption of the judicium dei is not merely "political," it is inevitable, a reflection of what happened to England's king and its sacred state once Gloucester's blood was spilled. However much of a threat to Richard may reside in Bolingbroke's allusion to Abel, Bolingbroke points at a fundamental crime that alters man's relationship with God, whether in Genesis, Claudius's Denmark, Macbeth's Scotland, or Richard's England.33/

Richard, however, still wields more than just the illusion of power. Gaunt, the sacramentalist, is reduced to lame similes as he attempts to assuage the impact of Bolingbroke's banishment. But he speaks more realistically when he confronts Richard. The king of a land that possessed and generated sacred energy is now reduced:

> Landlord of England art thou, not king:
> Thy state of law is bondslave to the law.
> (II.i.113-114)

The "shame" of which Gaunt complains (II.i.110) is that Richard has "let this land by lease" (I.i.110), not that Richard has murdered Gloucester. The murder, for Gaunt, is in God's hands, or perhaps it is as irrelevant now as sacrament itself, the invisible and divinely ordained power erased by the murder. Richard has reduced England's sacred soil, one of the manifestations of God's laws, to control by the laws of mere property. Sacramental kingship has decended to the contractual status of "landlord." Richard's position already reflects the status of the kingship Bolingbroke will seize, and predicts the advent of what A. G. Dickens calls "the neo-feudalists of the fifteenth century,"34/ who will conduct the Wars of the Roses on the basis of family, and local loyalty (cf. III Henry VI: III.iii.101-107, and IV.viii.9-18). That allegiances like those of Burgundy and Clarence could shift so easily suggests that expediency rather than basic principle underlay the growth or withering of the roses of Lancaster and York. Reno suggests that, in Richard's England, the land belonged to the crown, as opposed to the king, hence was a "thing quasi-sacred," partaking of the continuum that the crown represented.35/ Richard has become a "king feudal," now subject to the legalities and obligations of feudal practice, thus a reciprocity to which his previous status, as enunciated by the historical, and, later in the play, by the Shakespearean Richard, was not bound. After Gaunt's death, Richard defies the new legal status and the different concept of time he has unwittingly introduced. He will admit his responsibility for the erosion of even feudal values:

> I have...
> Made glory base, and sovereignty a slave,
> Proud majesty a subject, state a peasant.
> (IV.i.248-251)36/

Gaunt warned Richard about the lengths and limits of a king's control of time: "Thy word is current with him for my death,/ But dead, thy kingdom cannot buy my breath" (I.iii.230-231). York admonishes Richard even more specifically after Gaunt's death, because Richard is about to destroy his "secondary position," that of the feudal king who rules only if he observes the precise legalities York details:

> If you do wrongfully seize Hereford's rights,
> Call in the letters patents that he hath
> By his attorneys-general to sue
> His livery, and deny his off'red homage,
> You pluck a thousand dangers on your head,
> You lose a thousand well-disposed hearts,
> And prick my tender patience to those thoughts
> Which honor and allegiance cannot think.
> (II.i.201-208)

Gaunt's England was "under God." York's king is subordinate to "dangers" that are, significantly, rendered in numerical terms. Thus the reduction of England involves a transition from immeasurable quality in which the king participates to measurable quantities that stand threateningly above the king. Richard is pulling "the ground" (III.ii.150) and "the barren earth" (III.ii.153) of the grave metaphor he will employ (III.ii.144 ff.) down on top of himself. Assuming that, as Reno says, the "ancient demense," belonging to the impersonal crown, is the "property of the entire body of the commonwealth and impervious, therefore, to time,"37/ Richard's leasing out of England exposes the commonwealth itself to mortality, and in precisely the monetary terms Gaunt employs ("current" and "buy"). Richard, having erased the sacramental element of his "body politic" in shedding Gloucester's blood, now imposes the mortality of a king's "body natural" upon his state.

Time for Richard is a medium he believes he controls. It is, at least, a rhythm which fulfills his personal goals:

> Now put it, God, in the physician's mind
> To help him to his grave immediately!
> The lining of his coffers shall make coats
> To deck our soldiers for these Irish wars.
> Come, gentlemen, let's all go visit him;
> Pray God we may make haste and come too late!
> (I.iv.59-64)

This anti-prayer shows, as Traversi suggests, that "it is [Richard's] own vocation that he is putting aside."38/ Richard has already disclaimed the role of "physician," and reflects here, in his wish for Gaunt's death, his earlier command for Gloucester's murder.39/ That England's king is no longer a sacred embodiment of God's will is underscored by Richard's easy equation between Gaunt's death and ready cash.40/

Gaunt, however, reemphasizes Richard's sacramental sovereignty, and suggests that Richard, a mal-practitioner himself, has fallen into the hands of quackery:

> Thy deathbed is no lesser than thy land,
> Wherein thou liest in reputation sick;
> And thou, too careless patient as thou art,
> Commit'st thy anointed body to the cure
> Of those physicians that first wounded thee.
> (II.i.95-99)

Richard becomes incensed at Gaunt's warning, claiming that Gaunt's "frozen admonition" (II.i.117) has made "pale our cheek, chasing the royal blood/ With fury from his native residence" (II.i.118-119). But Richard's plurality is again dubious; his physical response to Gaunt's admonitions about Richard's violation of kingship would seem an obvious reflex of Richard's "body natural." He has, after all, rendered his own blood anti-sacramental: "That blood," Gaunt says of Gloucester, "already like the pelican/ Hast thou tapped out and drunkenly caroused" (II.i.126-127).41/ And York will quickly reiterate the point:

> His [Richard's father's] hands were guilty of no kindred
> blood,
> But bloody with the enemies of his kin.
> (II.i.182-183)

York lists yet another instance of Richard's interference with sacrament: "the prevention of poor Bolingbroke/ About his marriage"

(II.i.167-168), a cancellation the sources tell us was "political" (Bolingbroke would have married the French king's cousin), but that Shakespeare includes without motive, giving the action its anti-sacramental emphasis. If sacrament is lost to England, so, immediately, are the more secular premises Richard has embraced:

> Take Hereford's rights away, and take from Time
> His charters and his customary rights,
> Let not tomorrow then ensue today;
> Be not thyself. For how art thou a king
> But by fair sequence and succession?
> (II.i.195-199)

Indeed, Richard has put time out of joint. The timelessness Gaunt celebrated in its sacramental sense is destroyed. Now, even the sequences with which the empirical world moves have been disturbed. History becomes a pattern of events linked, at best, by "cause and effect." As Figgis says of monarchical succession, "this mode of devolution of the crown is in some way superior to the merely human method of election. The birth of an heir is the judgement of God, and the same sanction attended to it."42/ Bodin's emphasis, however, becomes suddenly applicable in both theory and possible practice: "monarchies cannot be distinguished one from another by the method of succession, but only by the way they are conducted."43/ While it is too much to suggest that Richard's failure to produce an heir is a negative judgement of God, he has created a world where "a merely human method of election" is an available alternative, and this after observing Bolingbroke wooing the electorate.44/ By eradicating the premises of kingship, Richard opens even his own selection of an heir to question, as both history and Shakespeare demonstrate.

Richard closes the Confiscation Scene with unconsciously ominous lines: "our time of stay is short" (II.i.223). The "time" of true royal plurality is over, and, indeed, we learn within the scene that follows (still II.i) that Bolingbroke has returned.45/ By erasing principle, the divinity hedging a sacramental king and the laws by which a feudal king governs, Richard has created a vacuum into which can flow only Realpolitik and the attendant ruthlessness of a laissez faire economy. These are the terms of the discussion between the opportunistic Northumberland and Ross and Willoughby. They extend York's forlorn hope that he be "the next that must be bankrout so" (II.i.151) into the general and specific bankruptcy of England. Bolingbroke is duke, says Willoughby, "Barely in title, not in revenues" (II.i.226). Richard has suffered more than merely economic loss because of his fiscal policies:

Ross: The commons hath he pilled with grievous taxes
          And quite lost their hearts. The nobles hath he fined
          For ancient quarrels and quite lost their hearts.

47

Willoughby.
> And daily new exactions are devised
> As blanks, benevolences, and I wot not what:
> But what, a God's name, doth become of this?

Northumberland.
> Wars hath not wasted it, for warred he hath not,
> But basely yielded upon compromise
> That which his noble ancestors achieved with blows.
> More hath he spent in peace than they on wars.

Ross.   The Earl of Wiltshire hath the realm in farm.

Willoughby.   The king's grown bankrout like a broken man.
>   (II.i.246-257)

All this has been done, it would seem, before the Lancastrian seizure, but now it breaks into the open, as if a new equation has been introduced, whereby the world can be comprehended only in monetary terms. Indeed, the king has become a robber:

> He hath not money for these Irish wars,
> His burdenous taxations notwithstanding,
> But by the robbing of the banished duke.
>   (II.i.259-261)

The theme of robbery, so prominent in what follows, is introduced by Richard's action.

As Reno argues, the crown is impersonal under the feudal system; a subject's oath is to it, not to the man wearing it.46/ Oaths to a king who has broken the "social contract," as Richard has done, become as irrelevant as oaths have been in the First Tetralogy (cf. III Henry VI: III.i.72-91, for example).47/ The crown has been employed fraudulently, as Northumberland suggests in wishing to "Redeem from broking pawn the blemished crown" (II.i.293). The crown itself has been lent out at interest, and the only response can be pragmatic, based on power, and expressed in metaphors of commerce. Soon many words will partake of double meanings in England; "crown," "royal," "noble," and "angel" will all become mere coins (as they were, of course) reflecting only ironically their more comprehensive or idealistic meanings.48/ Such is the "reverse-alchemy" Richard engenders. Yet he can discuss all this without any feeling for its implications:

> And for our coffers with too great a court
> And liberal largess are grown somewhat light,

> We are enforced to farm our royal realm,
> The revenue whereof shall furnish us
> For our affairs in hand. If that come short,
> Our substitutes at home shall have blank charters;
> Whereto, when they shall know men are rich,
> They shall subscribe them for large sums of gold.
>
> (I.iv.43-50)

For York, of course, trapped between opposing factions, trying to uphold a "law" that he has seen rendered null and void, the dilemma is absolute: "How shall I do for money for these wars?" (II.ii.104: emphasis on "these," I think, because York refers to Bolingbroke's invasion, not to Richard's Irish adventure). York can provide only empty "armor" (II.ii.107), because he cannot fuse his role as Lord Governor and his own convictions:

> Both [Richard and Bolingbroke] are my kinsmen.
> The one is my sovereign, whom both my oath
> And duty bids defend; the other again
> Is my kinsman, whom the king hath wronged,
> Whom conscience and my kindred bids to right.
>
> (II.ii.111-115)

Those who criticize York for his ineffectuality should recognize that his dilemma is of Richard's making, not York's. York is like so many sub-tragic characters in these plays, trapped "between the fell incensed points of mighty opposites."49/ And those who attempt to ascertain when Bolingbroke "makes his decision" for the throne might better pursue the decisions Richard makes and to which Bolingbroke responds. I do not believe that the play shows us, until Bolingbroke's "In God's name, I'll ascend the regal throne" (IV.i.113), the absolute moment of decision, a moment itself delayed by Carlisle's prophetic objection. To attempt to fix a moment the play doesn't provide is to ignore the process emanating from Richard's fatal decisions. Similarly, in Othello, we witness the Moor's gradual entanglement in the web Iago weaves. In each play we observe a subtle "cooperation" between two characters. In Othello, we watch in horror as a decision is being made, increment by increment, as contrasted to Macbeth's unequivocal placing of each "corporal agent" at the service of the "terrible feat" (I.vii.80). In Richard II, as I will argue, Bolingbroke ends up as much a victim of circumstances as Richard is of his own faulty decisions.50/

The gravitational pull towards quantitative premises for kingship begins with the murder of Gloucester and accelerates with the seizure of Bolingbroke's inheritance. York sends to his sister-in-law for "a thousand pound" (II.ii.91: the first of many times in these plays that that precise figure is used). But the Duchess has died amid the "empty lodgings and unfurnished walls,/ Unpeopled offices, untrodden stones," the poverty of Plashy (I.ii.68-69). One wonders whether she could have provided the money, or would have, considering her championship of "Hereford's spear" (I.ii.47) as agent of revenge for Gloucester. York's hope for a loan from an apparently bankrupt widow, who turns out to have died anyway, reflects England's "progress" under Richard and the futility of trying to stem Bolingbroke's rush on the throne. As for the "commons...their love," as Bagot says, "Lies in their purses, and whoso empties them/ By so much fills their hearts with deadly hate" (II.ii.129-131). The intangible values Gaunt emphasized and Mowbray expressed ("The purest treasure mortal times afford/ Is spotless reputation," for example: I.i.178-179) now equate only with money. England has been reduced from sacrament to tangibility, literally debased. Bolingbroke will protest to York's invocation of "the anointed king" (II.ii.95) that his "rights and royalties" have been "given away/ To upstart unthrifts" (II.iii.119-121), and that his "father's goods are all distrained and sold" (II.iii.130). Willoughby seconds Bolingbroke's plea: "Base men by his endowments are made great" (II.iii.138). The doomed Salisbury summons a metaphor of debasement that Richard will extend in his "Phaethon" speech:

> Ah, Richard! With the eyes of heavy mind
> I see thy glory like a shooting star
> Fall to the base earth from the firmament.
> (II.iv.18-20)

While Aumerle can caution Richard that Bolingbroke "grows great in substance and in power" (III.ii.35), Richard substitutes for the "invisible power and grace" of sacrament a fantasy. The king's return will force "thieves and robbers," who have "range[d] abroad unseen," "murders, treasons...detested sins," and "this thief, this traitor, Bolingbroke" into the revenging "sight of day" (III.ii.39-52). Richard ignores his original sin in murdering Gloucester, the primary treason against sovereign premises, and the robbery that has elicited the response of "this thief, this traitor, Bolingbroke."

Richard's words are now a formula powerless against "the fullest man."51/ He can repeat the premises of his coronation:

> Not all the water in the rough rude sea
> Can wash the balm off from an anointed king;
> The breath of worldly men cannot depose
> The deputy elected by the Lord.
> (III.ii.54-57)

But the premises can be erased. Richard will do so, while demonstrating convincingly that they cannot be reconstituted for Bolingbroke, who has only "hard bright steel and hearts harder than steel" (III.ii.111) to back his claim, if indeed he is making a claim beyond the restoration of his dukedom. York may foresee "the issue of these arms" (II.iii.151), but Bolingbroke simply moves his armor, uttering few words. Bolingbroke wishes to appear, it seems, as Irving Ribner calls him — "a passive instrument of destiny."52/ Richard, after all, is the shaper of a negative destiny, having imposed on his kingdom the "condition of destruction" central to the aristotelian conception of time.53/

Richard's political power, now computable only in military terms, as III.ii makes clear, dwindles to nothing. The manic/ depressive leaps of the scene, a continuation, it seems, of his "late tossing on the breaking seas" (III.ii.3), lead him towards the role he will play so powerfully later:

> Cover your heads, and mock not flesh and blood
> With solemn reverence; throw away respect,
> Tradition, form, and ceremonious duty.
> (III.ii.171-173)

Richard, of course, echoes York's previous warnings to him (II.i.189-207). Body politic erased, both sacramentally and legally, Richard yields to the call of body natural:

> Beshrew thee, cousin, which didst lead me forth
> Of that sweet way I was in to despair...
> A king, woe's slave, shall kingly woe obey.
> (III.ii.204-210)

While Richard makes "woe" king over himself, "unkinged Richard" (IV.i.219) will assert with profound irony and impact the very power that King Richard heedlessly squandered.

One reason why the transition from "Richard's night to Bolingbroke's fair day" (II.ii.218) is difficult to pinpoint is that Richard delivers a superb challenge to Bolingbroke's go-between, Northumberland:

> we thought ourself to be thy lawful king;
> And if we be, how dare thy joints forget
> To pay their awful duty to our presence?
> If we be not, show us the hand of God
> That hath dismissed us from our stewardship;
> For well we know no hand of blood and bone
> Can gripe the sacred handle of our scepter,
> Unless he do profane, steal, or usurp...
> (III.iii.73-80)

While such words may be the "show" of a man who "looks...like a king" (III.iii.67-70), Richard could accept Bolingbroke's public offer (III.iii.35-40), reiterated by Northumberland (III.iii.102-119) at face value, and force either a stalemate or his own "arrest" by Bolingbroke. That alternative seems clear. While rhetoric cannot dissolve steel, Richard, having acceded as he must to Bolingbroke's demands, cues the rest of the scene. He complains to Aumerle that "We do debase ourselves.... To look so poorly and to speak so fair" (III.iii.126-127). But Richard has not, so far, been all that abject; even Bolingbroke has granted him the status of "sun," albeit "blushing and discontented" (III.ii.62). And Aumerle commends Richard's course:

> let's fight with gentle words,
> Till time lend friends, and friends their helpful swords.
> (III.iii.130-131)

At best, "time" can only grant a loan to Richard. He has "profaned" its sacramental and hereditary values, "stolen" from Bolingbroke, thereby obliterating legal principle and encouraging the impulse towards usurpation.

Suddenly, before Northumberland can deliver Bolingbroke's response — one of the most intriguing unuttered speeches in Shakespeare — Richard capitulates in a great flood of language that predicts the tenor and vehicle of the Deposition Scene:

> What must the king do now? Must he submit?
> The king shall do it. Must he be deposed?
> The king shall be contented. Must he lose
> The name of king? a God's name, let it go.
> I'll give my jewels for a set of beads;
> My gorgeous palace for a hermitage;
> My gay apparel for an almsman's gown;
> My figured goblets for a dish of wood;
> My subjects for a pair of carved saints...
> (III.iii.142-151)

Such compulsion will render the king worse than the commerce plying over his corpse:

> I'll be buried in the king's highway,
> Some way of common trade, where subjects' feet
> May hourly trample on their sovereign's head.
> (III.iii.154-156)

The prophecy will be fulfilled. "Dust," as York tells us, "was thrown upon his sacred head" (V.i.30) as Richard rode toward the tower. York suggests the inefficacy of self-imposed martyrdom: "had not God for some strong purpose steeled/ The hearts of men, they must perforce have melted/ And barbarism itself have pitied him" (V.i.34-36). But steel, not God, is the ethic now, and barbarism demands steel to back its strong purpose.

Richard has submitted to the steel. Bolingbroke has displayed it but has not had to impose it. Richard descends to "the base court! Base court where kings grow base/ To come at traitors' calls, and do them grace:/ In the base court, come down" (III.iii.179-181). While Bolingbroke commands that all "Stand...apart/ And show fair duty to his majesty" (III.iii.185-186), Richard responds, "Fair cousin, you debase your princely knee/ To make the base earth proud with kissing it" (III.iii.118-189). Richard, after all, has been the first to suggest Bolingbroke's "motive": "What says King Bolingbroke?" (III.iii.172), calling Bolingbroke "his majesty" (III.iii.172). The rest of the scene is dictated by Richard on that premise, so that perhaps Bolingbroke's movement towards the throne is really Richard's presentation of it to his cousin. Richard, not Bolingbroke, cancels the possibilities for compromise, although it would seem that Richard could hope only to remain a figurehead for the powerful Lancastrian, possibly having to yield to the kind of agreement that Henry VI, who has an heir, accepts in temporarily regaining the throne.54/ Richard's yielding to substance, the armor of Bolingbroke's regiments, is a submission to what Richard himself has insisted upon for England. Even here, however, at Flint Castle, Richard refuses to employ the potency of the intangible power he inherited. He seems now, on the basis of the self-willed wish for martyrdom he exhibited in III.ii, to be reserving that power for the devastating ironies he will inflict on Bolingbroke in the Deposition Scene. While it may seem that Richard plays into Bolingbroke's hands at Flint Castle, the Deposition Scene at Westminister forces us to reevaluate Richard's capitulation.

Richard dictates the steps of Bolingbroke's movement ("Set on towards London, cousin, is it so?: III.iii.206) with a willingness that makes him seem almost as submissive as Henry VI ("Go where you will, the king shall be commanded;/ And be you kings. Command and I'll obey": III Henry VI: III.i.92-93). Richard also dictates the premises of Bolingbroke's reign. Richard, having erased the basis of sacramental kingship, makes sure that the world knows that Bolingbroke cannot enjoy sanctity. The mode of deposition will be that of a religious ceremony, the "anti-ritual" characteristic of the tragedies.55/

> Yet I well remember
> The favors of these men: were they not mine?
> Did they not sometime cry "All hail!" to me?
> So Judas did to Christ: but he in twelve
> Found truth in all but one; I, in twelve thousand, none.

God save the King! Will no man say "Amen?"
Am I both priest and clerk? Well, then, amen.
                    (IV.i.167-173)

Richard's "none" ignores Carlisle, whose argument that Richard be present for his trial reiterates John of Gaunt's thesis to the Duchess of Gloucester:

> shall the figure of God's majesty,
> His captain, steward, deputy elect,
> Anointed, crowned, planted many years,
> Be judged by subject and inferior breath...?
>   (IV.i.125-128)

But Richard's role is that of Christ betrayed, a role valid within the concept of his kingship as Christus, but rendered invalid by Richard's destruction of that concept, his bringing of "Devouring pestilence" (I.iii.283) to England, rather than the healing and restorative functions of monarchy. Richard embraces the role of Eliot's Fourth Tempter, reaching no true martyrdom, but achieving in his pageant of self-pity a political power often overlooked.

Ranald suggests that "Richard takes off his political 'body,' that of the king who never dies, to become the victim who always dies."56/ While Richard intentionally equates himself to Christ, the relationship is not valid merely because he says it is, but because it inheres in kingship itself. Ironically, Richard's insistence on his Christlike qualities helps destroy them for kingship. If, as Bracton suggests, "Christ...willed himself to be under the law that he might redeem those who live under it,"57/ Richard has willed that there be no law. Law becomes what power says it is, as Prince John will demonstrate at Gaultree Forest.

Richard reinvokes the ultimate premises of his kingship, suggesting that the "heavens were over his head" as he was crowned, and that, therefore, anyone deposing him must "oppose himself against God's will":

> God save the king, although I be not he;
> And yet amen, if heaven do think him me.
>   (IV.i.174-175)

While Richard's own willful view of kingship as personal possession rather than Godly stewardship has reduced him to the singularity signalled by the pronouns, that singularity must pertain now to any man who thinks himself king. The scene points ahead not just to Bolingbroke's inability to lead a crusade, but to Claudius's failure to achieve valid repentance (III.iii.37-72), and to the "amen" of Macbeth, which sticks in his throat after he has butchered the sainted Duncan (II.ii.26-32).

We miss the point if we believe that Richard's prominence in the Deposition Scene is due merely to the number of lines he speaks. In the play's first scene, his insecurity was suggested by the few and politically ineffective lines he spoke. The same can be said for Bolingbroke in the Deposition Scene, which is completely Richard's.58/ In one sense, he has nothing to lose, yet in another he can show Bolingbroke what the latter has lost. Richard does not sue here, he commands:

> Give me the crown.
> Here cousin, seize the crown
> (IV.i.180-181)59/

I would suggest that Bolingbroke's fingers, as opposed to Julius Caesar's (as Casca renders them: I.ii.236-240), are very loath to touch the crown, because Richard is forcing him into a pantomime of usurpation. Bolingbroke follows Richard's cue, however reluctantly, and Richard can move the crown in rhythm to his words, coercing the hand of Bolingbroke to follow: "On this side my hand, and on that side yours" (IV.i.182). Richard develops a complicated metaphor that incorporates his own grief, but suggests that Bolingbroke, in mounting fortune's wheel, inherits only a "hollow crown" (III.ii.160):

> Now is this golden crown like a deep well
> That owes two buckets, filling one another,
> The emptier ever dancing in the air,
> The other down, unseen, and full of water.
> That bucket down and full of tears am I,
> Drinking my griefs, whilst you mount up on high.
> (IV.i.183-188)

The machine Richard constructs is also prediction. By the end of the play, Richard's soul (according to his interpretation) will have "mount[ed]...up on high" (V.v.111), while Bolingbroke's "soul" will be "full of woe" (V.vi.45).

Bolingbroke can manage only three lines during all of this, two that attempt to establish Richard's willingness to resign (IV.i.189 and 199). But the question of resignation evokes only magnificent ambiguity from Richard, now warming to his role: "Ay, no; no, ay; for I must nothing be" (IV.i.200). The lines mean, "Yes, no; no, yes; because my identity is erased," as well as, "I know — no I," and "I know no I" — that is, I do not accept the singular pronoun, yet I am forced to: "I know no aye" — I know no way of assenting to what is happening here. Richard's next point is telling: "Therefore no, no, for I resign to thee" (IV.i.201). An emphasis on the singular pronoun would indicate that the crown is not his to give, that, while he resigns personally to Bolingbroke, as he must, the crown as concept cannot be Bolingbroke's. Otherwise, Richard would say "yes," and not "no, for." A singular self surrenders individually to another singular self. That is all that is happening. Richard does what theoretically cannot be done, he denies all premises of kingship, except that of raw power. It is the denial of a profound theory per se, capable of being done only by the individual — the "I" — who has already undone monarchical principle. Richard does not give the objects of kingship and their sacramental powers to Bolingbroke. That cannot be done. In the staging of the scene, the physical objects should probably be handed to a heartbroken York:

> Now, mark me how I will undo myself.
> I give this heavy weight from off my head,
> And this unwieldy scepter from my hand,
> The pride of kingly sway from out my heart;
> With mine own tears I wash away my balm,
> With mine own hands I give away my crown,
> With mine own tongue deny my sacred state,
> With mine own breath release all duteous oaths;
> All pomp and majesty I do forswear;
> My manors, rents, revenues, I forgo;
> My acts, decrees, and statutes I deny:
> God pardon all oaths that are broke to me,
> God keep all vows unbroke are made to thee.
> Make me, that nothing have, with nothing grieved,
> And thou with all pleased, that hast all achieved.
> Long mayst thou live in Richard's seat to sit,
> And soon lie Richard in an earthy pit.
>   (IV.i.202-218)

Richard's paradoxes point at the contradiction in Bolingbroke's position. "Kingly sway" is breathed out, and balm is rinsed away forever by a king's tears. The "sacred state," already denied, is bid a formal farewell. Law itself is erased. Richard creates more than a tabula rasa, however; he shows that oaths are broken to be made to be broken again. Even under a neo-feudal system, "oaths are straws, men's faiths are wafer-cakes," as Pistol will say (Henry V: II.iii.51), pointing at the purely material and explicitly anti-sacramental world which must follow the "undoing" of Richard and of the sacred grounds of English kingship. These premises now are strictly quantitative, as Richard himself will point out to Northumberland: "Thou shalt think,/ Though he divide the realm and give thee half,/ It is too little, helping him to all" (V.i.59-61). Richard's description of the calculus of self-interest predicts the Northumberland faction's quarrel over the map in I Henry IV (III.i). Richard can claim that Bolingbroke has "all achieved" (IV.i.216), but

Richard demonstrates that Bolingbroke has gained nothing:

> God save King Henry, unkinged Richard says,
> And send him many years of sunshine days.
> (IV.i.219-220)

It is not "the king is dead, long live the king" — continuity residing in the office, rather than in the incumbent. Rather, it is the king is alive, although kingship and all its attributes are "undone," and therefore King Henry will not walk in the sun.60/

Richard presses his "Christ metaphor" against Northumberland:

> If thou wouldst,
> There shoudst thou find one heinous article,
> Containing the deposing of a king,
> And cracking the strong warrant of an oath,
> Marked with a blot, damned in the book of heaven.
> Nay, all of you that stand and look upon me,
> Whilst that my wretchedness doth bait myself,
> Though some of you, with Pilate, wash your hands,
> Showing an outward pity: yet you Pilates
> Have here delivered me to my sour cross,
> And water cannot wash away your sin.
> (IV.i.231-241)

But the accusing Richard can hardly avoid his own involvement in this "watery" crime. His own tears become metaphor for his responsibility for the draining away of sacramental value from England. His self-accusation drives the guilt forcefully home to the onlookers, partially because Richard recognizes how far he has gone beyond actions that a man might play:

> Mine eyes are full of tears, I cannot see:
> And yet salt water blinds them not so much,61/
> But they can see a sort of traitors here.
> Nay, If I turn mine eyes upon myself,
> I find myself a traitor with the rest;
> For I have given here my soul's consent
> T' undeck the pompous body of a king.
> (IV.i.243-249)

All this he has done, and the ramifications are both wide and deep. Richard has "Made glory base, and sovereignty a slave,/ Proud majesty a subject, state a peasant" (IV.i.250-251). England itself is "bankrout of its majesty" (IV.i.266), as Richard shows again in employing monetary terms to describe what small prerogative remains his:

> if my word be sterling yet in England,
> Let it command a mirror hither straight.
> (IV.i.263-264)

Bolingbroke, victim of a theatrics that explore a lost reality, can only shrug and accede.

Richard's echoing of Faustus's line to the shade of Helen seems hardly accidental ("Was this face the face.... Was this the face": IV.280 and 282). Richard, as his speech shows, could once muster great power, but that power, as the mirror itself shows, is now a shade. That power represented the king as "body politic," a power that Richard's narcissism — the mirror itself emblematic of self-indulgence — helped destroy. The image in the mirror, obviously a "show" (cf. III.iii.70), reflects the "show" that king and kingship have become. When Richard smashes the mirror down at Bolingbroke's feet,62/ "the moral" is not merely "How soon my sorrow hath destroyed my face" (IV.i.289-290), but that Bolingbroke cannot reassemble the fragments of kingship Richard has disintegrated. All the king's horses and all the king's men will ride only to encounter the rebellions that are inevitable consequences of usurpation and regicide. Bolingbroke will not achieve even the "brittle glory" (IV.i.286) Richard perceives in the mirror-image, a reflection of a body politic that no longer exists in reality.

The anti-sacramental mode of the ex-king's realm deepens beyond his Deposition. Northumberland parts Richard and Isabel:

> Doubly divorced! Bad men, you violate
> A twofold marriage: 'twixt my crown and me,
> And then betwixt me and my married wife.
> (V.i.71-73)

Richard prevented Bolingbroke's marriage (II.i.167-168). Bolingbroke expediently indicted Bushy and Green for making "divorce betwixt [Richard's] queen and him" (III.i.12). The separation of Richard and Isabel becomes, for Richard, an analogue to his "unkinging," an anti-ritual. But if "the breath of worldly men can depose the deputy elected by the lord," such men can, indeed are forced to, ignore other sacramental injunctions: "Those whom God hath joyned together, let no man put asunder." But such distinctions are relegated to "policy" (V.i.84) that overrules "love" (V.i.84), as Richard himself knows.

To emphasize that the divorce is the work of mere men, Richard refuses to complete the anti-ritual himself:

> Let me unkiss the oath 'twixt thee and me.
> And yet not so, for with a kiss 'twas made.
> Part us, Northumberland.
>
> (V.i.74-76)

Again, Richard forces a gesture ("Here cousin, seize the crown") in which another must reluctantly participate in a mime of meaning.

The parting represents a ritual separation of what was fused in marriage. Anti-ritual has become the only mode available to England:

> Queen.   And must we be divided? Must we part ?
>
> Richard.   Ay, hand from hand, my love, and heart from heart.
>
> (V.i.81-82)

Instead of becoming one flesh, they, "two together weeping made one woe" (V.i.86). Again, grief becomes ultimate reality. They marry sorrow and self-destruction, appropriately, since Richard has engendered the inevitable division between king and man, king and kingdom, king and queen, and that union analogous to the fusion of divinity and flesh, "signifying unto us the mistical union that is betwixt Christ and his Churche," between man and wife:

> Come, come, in wooing sorrow let's be brief,
> Since, wedding it, there is such length in grief.
> One kiss shall stop our mouths, and dumbly part;
> Thus give I mine, and thus take I thy heart.
>
> (V.i.93-96)

But hearts, once exchanged to create a new union, are now returned to enunciate a final separation:

> Give me mine own again; 'twere no good part
> To take on me to keep and kill thy heart.
> So, now I have mine own again, be gone,
> That I may strive to kill it with a groan.
>
> (V.i.97-100)

The ceremony that joined them promised that they might "abide in [God's] love unto their lives ende." The anti-ritual parting them ends with the queen's thoughts of death and Richard's "the rest let sorrow say" (V.i.102).63/

59

England falls from grace. The sacrament Mowbray once took as a medium towards pardon now becomes a sanction for regicide, according to no less an authority than the Abbot of Westminster:

> Before I freely speak my mind herein,
> You shall not only take the sacrament
> To bury mine intents, but also to effect
> Whatever I shall happen to devise.
>
> (IV.i.326-334)

The sacrament seals not an oath with God but a conspiracy. A sacred ritual is crucially misdirected towards political ends:

> A dozen of them here have ta'en the sacrament
> And interchangeably set down their hands
> To kill the king at Oxford.
>
> (V.ii.97-99)

Such an oath, according to the Homily against Swearing and Perjury, is "unlawfull and ungodly," but it represents the "woeful division" Carlisle predicts (IV.i.146), here, the opposition of religion and allegiance. England is no longer the "Christian climate" (IV.i.130) for which Carlisle pleaded and John of Gaunt mourned at length.

It may be, as Harbage argues, that "Playing for no audience but himself, Richard plays most honestly."64/ I a more inclined, however, towards Traversi's position that Richard's soliloquy (V.v) is "an academic exercise in poetic pessimism."65/ Richard approaches tragic anaganorisis in "I wasted time, and now doth Time waste me" (V.v.49), but he backs away from the essential truth of what he has wasted:

> The better sort,
> As thoughts of things divine are intermixed
> With scruples, and do set the word itself
> Against the word, as thus: "Come, little ones";
> And then again,
> "It is as hard to come as for a camel
> To thread the postern of a small needle's eye."
>
> (V.v.11-17)

Richard creates a paradox where none exists. It is, after all, the "riche man" who cannot "enter the Kingdome of God" (in Matthew, Mark, and Luke). Richard's inclusion of "riche man" would resolve the seeming paradox between the "little one," symbol of spiritual innocence, and the "riche man," symbol of worldliness and impiety. Christ, indeed, goes further, in the tenth chapter of Mark, a passage familiar to the

Elizabethan by dint of its incorporation into Baptism: "whosoever doeth not receive the kingdome of God, as a lytle chylde: he shall not entre therin." For Richard to penetrate the paradox would be for him to see himself at last, to perceive the impiety that brought him down and to recognize that he must become a little one, must be born again, to achieve spiritual health in his body natural, which is all he has left. Had Richard penetrated the paradox, he would have seen why he, "the proud king," is excluded from his own kingdom, a paradigm of God's kingdom, and why his own incarnation failed. The Elizabethan might have been disturbed enough by Richard's omission of "riche man" to recognize that he does not achieve self-understanding in this soliloquy. Richard's has been a failure of spirit, or spirituality, and the king's failure must ramify into his kingdom, even as it is reflected in the ex-king's musings.

Richard sets the word against the word, his inability to fuse the words, to be a pious king, becomes the plight of his kingdom. His own name is "usurp'd," as he tells us (IV.i.257), another index of the loss of identity suffered by the characters in the play, of the dark, indistinguishable world into which they plunge, no matter what they do, no matter which of the play's kings they follow. Mowbray's is the choric voice:

> thus I turn me from my country's light,
> To dwell in solemn shades of endless night.
> (I.iii.176-177)

Bolingbroke exiles Exton with similar words:

> With Cain go wander through shades of night,
> And never show thy head by day nor light.
> (V.vi.43-44)

Richard becomes "lesser than [his] name" (III.iii.136) even as his kingdom lapses toward the vague destiny the queen perceives:

> But what it is, that is not yet known; what,
> I cannot name; 'tis nameless woe I wot.
> (II.ii.39-40)

Aumerle becomes
> Aumerle that was,
> But that is lost for being Richard's friend;
> And madam, you must call him Rutland now.
> (V.ii.41-43)

Northumberland's "Richard" (III.iii.6) draws a rebuke from York. Northumberland delivers the modernistic excuse that "only to be brief/ Left I his title out" (III.iii.10-11). "The time hath been," York responds, that "your whole head's length" would have paid for such brevity (III.iii.11-14). Between that time and the moment of the interchange has come the erasure of Bolingbroke's "impresse" (III.i.25), the effort to deny Bolingbroke's existence, an action predicating and predicting the elimination of Richard's title. Gaunt has defined Richard's activity: "thou dost seek to kill my name in me" (II.i.86).66/ The king cannot engage in such activity with impunity. Northumberland suggests that words are to be measured against efficiency. The word as index of ritualistic meaning is lost, but the principal "traitor" (IV.i.248) is Richard, not Northumberland. The kingdom does not plunge into namelessness, but some names are lost, some changed, many become negative — Richard a "traitor with the rest" (IV.i.248). Nobles loyal to the king-that-was become, in the new dispensation, "dangerous consorted traitors" (V.vi.15), a churchman becomes a "grand conspirator" (V.vi.19). Exton become "Cain" (V.vi.43), as Bolingbroke attempts to assign him "the guilt of conscience" (V.vi.41) that is Bolingbroke's.

The deep schism the world of Richard II experiences is suggested by the constant appeal to ancestry and to familial ties made, usually, by characters who oppose Richard. The Duchess of Gloucester makes the appeal to Gaunt, as the Duchess of York does to York (V.ii.90-110). Gaunt berates Richard for dividing father and son (II.i.80) and for refuting his own ancestry:

> O, had thy grandsire with a prophet's eye
> Seen how his son's son should destroy his sons,
> From forth thy reach he would have laid thy shame,
> Deposing thee...
> (II.i.104-106)

York extends the argument, invoking Richard's father and grandfather:

> when [thy father] frown'd, it was against the French
> And not against his friends. His noble hand
> Did win what he did spend and spent not that
> Which his triumphant father's hand had won.
> His hands were guilty of no kindred blood,
> But bloody with the enemies of his kin.
> (II.i.178-183)

York goes on, of course, to suggest that Richard compounds his own defection from heritage by denying Bolingbroke's right of inheritance. Richard, typically, plays with the idea, expressing the altered lines of inheritance he has encouraged by disrupting the sequence of Bolingbroke's succession:

> Cousin, I am too young to be your father,
> Though you are old enough to be my heir.
> (III.iii.202-203)

York, painfully aware that Bolingbroke is his "kinsman.... Whom conscience and my kindred bids to right" (II.ii.114-115), is therefore susceptible to Bolingbroke's attempt to rouse York's "father instinct":

> You are my father, for methinks in you
> I see old Gaunt alive. O, then, my father,
> Will you permit that I shall stand condemn'd
> A wandering vagabond...?
> (II.iii.117-120)

> You have a son, Aumerle, my noble cousin;
> Had you first died, and he been thus trod down,
> He should have found his uncle Gaunt a father
> To rouse his wrongs and chase them to the bay.
> (II.iii.125-128)

Having acquiesced in this argument, or, perhaps, in the impossibility of his situation, York, in turn, must attempt to condemn his own son and rob his wife of _her_ identity:

> wilt thou pluck my fair son from mine age,
> And rob me of a happy mother's name?
> Is he not like thee? Is he not thine own?
> (V.ii.92-94)

York's actions, she suggests, reflect a denial of all levels of meaning in matrimony, ultimately a denial of York himself:

> thou dost suspect
> That I have been disloyal to thy bed,
> And that he is a bastard, not thy son,
> Sweet York, sweet husband, be not of that mind.
> He is as like thee as a man may be...
> (V.ii.104-108)

York can be loyal to the new king only by betraying his son. He too "sets the word itself against the word" (V.iii.121). According to the duchess, a wife divided against her husband, York engages in false prayers, the linguistic contradiction that the divided world forces upon those who would endow their words with religious resonance:

He prays but faintly and would be deni'd;
We pray with heart and soul and all beside...
His prayers are full of false hypocrisy;
Ours of true zeal and deep integrity.
Our prayers do out-pray his; then let them have
That mercy which true prayer ought to have.
                                    (V.iii.103-110)

Bolingbroke's granting of her prayer hardly makes him a "true king." The plot was devised by Richard's party, representing a deposed king still alive, and thus emphasizing Bolingbroke's dilemma. The Duchess of York praying for pardon creates a disjunctive analogue to the Duchess of Gloucester begging for revenge, but both imply the unnatural choices Gaunt and York have made:

and though thou liv'st and breath'st,
Yet art thou slain in him.
                                    (I.ii.24-25)

Is he not like thee? Is he not thine own?...
He is as like thee as any man may be.
                                    (V.ii.94-108)

To be loyal to one king is to ignore a brother's murder; to be loyal to another is to demand a son's death. York's indictment of Aumerle is a distant echo of Gaunt's judgement against Bolingbroke in I.iii. The word against the flesh — into such profoundly anti-sacramental dilemmas are the characters thrust who inhabit Richard's world, a world divided against itself since Gloucester's murder.

Regicide does occur, but not the murder of Bolingbroke. Richard's murder completes the play's movement away from sacramentality:

Exton, thy fierce hand
Hath with the king's blood stained the king's own land.
                                    (V.v.109-110)

As full of valor as of royal blood!
Both have I spilled. O, would the deed were good!
For now the devil that told me I did well
Says that this deed is chronicled in hell.
                                    (V.v.113-116)

Exton, I thank thee not, for thou has wrought
A deed of slander with thy fatal hand
Upon my head and all this famous land.
                                    (V.vi.34-36)

The land, already a "peasant," descends to infamy. The "blood" that "sprinkle[s Bolingbroke] to make [him] grow" (V.vi.46) infuses his spirit with no grace, no regeneration. Instead, his "soul is full of woe" (V.vi.44). He, too, must "kingly woe obey" (III.ii.210).

The "crusade" Bolingbroke would lead is led instead by the Archbishop of York, who does not lend a religious countenance to a unified English effort, but enlists his authority in a rebellion against Bolingbroke. Morton claims that the Archbishop is "a man/ Who with a double surety binds his followers...the bishop/ Turns insurrection to religion.../ And doth enlarge his rising with the blood/ Of fair King Richard, scraped from Pomfret stones;/ Derives from heaven his quarrel and his cause" (II Henry IV: I.i.190-206).

Insurrection and religion, like regicide and the Eucharist must be at odds, no matter what smooth rationalizations Morton, and later, the Archbishop, may make (I.iii.87-108, for example). Sacred blood simply has no efficacy; it could be invoked sacramentally only when it flowed in Richard's veins, and, then, only before he became guilty of a kinsman's blood, before he spilled Gloucester's "precious liquor" (I.ii.19), which is Richard's own in both familial and sacramental senses.67/ By the time of II Henry IV, we have entered a world where religion may clothe military action, but where military action cannot enjoy the intrinsic arbitration of a judicium dei, and where "sacred" objects are endowed with no more energy than are the relics of Chaucer's Pardoner.

Richard's world lives on in II Henry IV, but only as parody. Sacramental value attempts to emerge, but it can do so only as a rebellion which moves not merely against the king who has spilled Richard's blood, but also counter to the negative "nature of things" Richard dictated in spilling Gloucester's blood. Sacred blood cannot be re-introduced into England. Its truth — as insurrection shows per se — can only be untruth, as Prince John deftly demonstrates. The deep oxymoron of the Archbishop's "crusade-rebellion" shows us Bolingbroke's "crusade" in the same warped mirror. No sanctity resides behind the image. Richard has shattered the linkage between image and reality.

If Richard learns the nature of the world he inherited, he does so only to employ that knowledge in a devastating demonstration that that world is forever gone. Neither the original confrontation between Mowbray and Bolingbroke nor the meeting at Gaultree Forest between the rebels and Prince John comes to combat. Each is deflected by politics; the first by Richard's desperation, the second by John's cunning in a world where machiavellian means have long since displaced sacred premises. It is not so much that "the word 'rebellion,'" as Morton argues of Hotspur and his followers at Shrewsbury, divided "The actions of their bodies from their souls" (II Henry IV: I.i.194-195), but that such basic division has already occurred in England. Anyone who acts on premises of the "unity" of body and soul, that is, on sacramental grounds, is doomed. The Archbishop, as John demonstrates, is a political anachronism, and "a traitor with the rest," as Richard admitted himself to be (IV.i.247). Anyone pursuing Richard's cause must share the treason Richard has introduced to England's "blessed plot."

Endnotes: Chapter II

1. I am indebted, hic et ubique, to Ernst Kantorowitz's seminal study, The King's Two Bodies (Princeton University Press, 1957).

2. J. N. Figgis, The Divine Right of Kings (Cambridge, England, 1934), p. 79.

3. The French reaction to Richard's deposition, as reported by Holinshed, emphasizes the importance they placed on anointment: "When the news of king Richards deposing was reported in France, king Charles and all his court wondering, detested and abhorred such an injurie doone to an annointed king, to a crowned prince, and to the head of a realme...". (my ital.). Cf. the order of the declaration of Edward IV's title: "enoynted, coroned, and consecrate," Select Documents of English Constitutional History, ed. S. B. Chrimes and A. L. Brown (London, 1961), p. 322. The significance of Richard's coronation qua coronation can hardly be over-emphasized, for, as Margaret Loftus Ranald says: "Holinshed['s]... account of the crowning of Richard II is considered the definitive statement of the ceremony." "The Degradation of Richard II: An Inquiry into the Ritual Backgrounds, " English Literary Renaissance #2 (Spring, 1977), 170-196.

4. Henry VI will hear the following: "Thy place is filled, thy scepter wrung from thee,/ Thy balm washed off, wherein thou wast anointed" (III Henry VI: III.i.16-17). How easy is it then!

5. Fritz Kern, Kingship and the Law in the Middle Ages, tr. S.P. Chrimes (Oxford, 1948), p. 52.

6. Figgis, The Divine Right of Kings, p. 79.

7. Percy E. Schramm, A History of the English Coronation, tr. Leopold Legg (Oxford, 1937), p. 10. Schramm's argument validates Roy Strong's assertion that "Festivals... are in reality much more a branch of political history and thought [than] a curious ancestor of the theater." Splendor at Court: Renaissance Spectacle and the Theater of Power (Boston, 1973), p. 248. See also Sidney Anglo, Spectacle, Pageantry, and Early Tudor Policy (Oxford, 1969), and David Bergeron, English Civil Pageantry (London, 1971).

8. Quoted in Kantorowicz, The King's Two Bodies, p. 216.

9. Some actors pause on the word "rain," which comes at a line ending: "... whilst on the earth I rain/ My waters" (III.iii.58-59). The effect of such a pause is that Bolingbroke has savored the pun on "reign," then completed his metaphor as a hasty afterthought. While Bolingbroke is not one of those Shakespearean subjects characterized as having a

67

punning habit, here the word "rain" would betray almost conscious intention. To argue "almost conscious intention" would be fallacious, of course, unless it could be shown on stage.

10.   Raymond Reno, From Sacrament to Ceremony (unpublished ms.), p. 26.

11.   Schramm, A History of the English Coronation, p. 172.

12.   Shakespeare seems very conscious of the royal plurality. Henry V, a character who observes the distinction between the "king's two bodies" ("Touching our person, seek we no revenge": II.ii.174), is manifestly unfair in his use of the royal plurality in charging Williams: "It was ourself thou didst abuse" (IV.vii.49).   Williams responds correctly, I believe: "Your majesty came not like yourself" (Iv.vii.50) Julius Caesar signals his fatal error in responding to Artemidorus: "What touches us ourself shall be last served" (II.i.8) The effect of humility is undercut by Caesar's failure to recognize that what touches Caesar qua Rome should be served immediately.   Lear betrays a characteristic obliviousness to the "king's two bodies" when he uses the royal plural to refer to the "body natural" that, even in kings, does die: "while we/ Unburthened crawl toward death" (I.i.40-41).

13.   Gaunt must also be uneasy, torn as he is, and as so many characters will be, between his oath to his king and his loyalty to a closer relative. We must infer from Scene ii that Gaunt knows the precise nature of Bolingbroke's appeal, and that he has been very cautious with Richard in Scene i.

14.   An ominous prediction per se, even before we encounter the play's consistent tug-of-war between royal and familial loyalties.

15.   Richard's use of singular and plural here is curious. He says " our sacred blood," appropriately (if ironically, when we hear the Duchess of Gloucester use the same modifier for her husband's blood: I.ii.12 and 17) and "my upright soul," again appropriately, since an individual soul is individual, but again ironically as we learn from I.ii. Yet, he uses first person singular in talking of "kingdom" and "scepter," suggesting perhaps that he views them as personal possessions. He should be warned by "one but flatters us" (I.i.25), which implies a split or rupture beneath the embrace of royal plurality.   The line, and, as we learn, the underlying fact that Richard is complicit, contradict Richard's assumption of royal plurality.   Richard's "one but flatters us" points ahead nicely to his "I have a king here to my flatterer" (IV.i.307).

16.   Alfred Harbage, Shakespeare: A Reader's Guide (New York, 1963), p. 122.

17.   Kenneth Muir, "Richard II" (Complete Signet Shakespeare, New York, 1972), p. 446 n.

18.   S. C. Sen Gupta, Shakespeare's Historical Plays (Oxford, 1964), p. 119.

19.   "The healing benediction" would seem to have leaped over Richard II, to land on James I, who claimed Edward's "strange virtue" for himself.

20.   The admixture of machiavellianism Malcolm reveals in his testing of Macduff (IV.iii) seems a necessary addition to the traditional virtues Malcolm shares with Duncan as requisite to effective rule.   Unlike the England of the Second Henriad, the Scotland of Macbeth is restored to "the grace of Grace" (V.viii.72), although under a leadership alert enough to probe "the mind's construction" (I.iv.11) that Macbeth's "false face" (I.vii.82) concealed from Duncan. The Polanski film provided a ludicrous "modern" ending, wherein Donalbain sought out the Weird Sisters, thereby suggesting a recycling of evil into a world that, in Shakespeare's version, has witnessed a convincing restoration of order. In the recent BBC production, Malcolm read his final speech coolly, suggesting that he would be wary about letting any of his thanes and kinsmen get too close to him.   That interpretation was consistent with the negative lesson Malcolm has learned from his father's example.   The recent R.S.C. production showed Malcolm and his kinsmen as exhausted, enervated, as if, in defeating Macbeth, they had destroyed a great motive power, an energy partly their own.   That ending seemed appropriate to an extremely intense production, even for Macbeth.

21.   Cf. Henry N. Paul, The Royal Play of 'Macbeth' (New York, 1950).

22.   Gaunt's case invites intriguing speculations, however.   He is cautious with Richard about Bolingbroke's motives: "As near as I could sift him on that argument,/ On some apparent danger seen in him/ Aimed at your highness, no inveterate malice" (I.i.12-14).   Again, the second pronoun, referring to Mowbray, finds its more immediate antecedent in the "him" referring to Bolingbroke.   Yet we learn in I.ii that Gaunt knows of Richard's complicity.   Are we to infer that Gaunt, having discussed the matter with his son, has not confided in Bolingbroke? I don't believe so. Are we then to infer that Gaunt has encouraged Bolingbroke to indict Richard, however indirectly, through Mowbray? Bolingbroke's lines to Gaunt before the trial by combat could be interpreted to suggest that Gaunt has encouraged Bolingbroke in his enterprise: "O thou, the earthly author of my blood,/ Whose youthful spirit in me regenerate/ Doth with a twofold vigor lift me up/ To reach at victory above my head" (I.iii.69-72).   But against that interpretation, we have Gaunt's "God's is the quarrel," although Gaunt would see the trial-by-combat as falling within the will of God. I believe that we must take Gaunt at face value here, as caught unwillingly in a power struggle between the two young "pretenders."   Certainly the question can be

answered in at least three different ways: Gaunt, knowing of Richard's guilt, encourages Bolingbroke; Gaunt, knowing of Richard's guilt, discourages Bolingbroke, who goes ahead anyway; or, Gaunt, knowing of Richard's guilt, says to Bolingbroke, "I can't stop you, but be careful." Where the evidence of the play is ambiguous at best, one must rely on intuition. Mine is that Gaunt would scrupulously avoid any involvement in a conspiracy against Richard. This feeling is backed by Gaunt's ability to act as "judge" in his son's case, rather than as "father" (I.iii.236-237), by his rejoinder to the Duchess of Gloucester who would urge him into an anti-Richard position, and by the speech in II.i, which cannot be interpreted as some politic attempt to convince his audience, the Duke of York, who clearly agrees with Gaunt's sentiments. Like so many of the play's characters, York included, Gaunt is trapped into an equivocal position between familial and monarchical loyalties by Richard's basic defection from sovereignty. While speculation about Gaunt's "motive" in his son's accusation goes beyond the "dramatic evidence," Shakespeare invites such probing in a play where motives are so consistently obscured. Some evaluation of Gaunt's motivation would be a necessary sub-text, I believe, for the actor playing the role. In the recent and excellent BBC-TV production of Richard II, Mowbray's hope for pardon was directed at John Gielgud's Gaunt. The later nodded, giving this stalwart Mowbray a powerful refutation against yet another of Bolingbroke's accusations.

23. Samuel Schoenbaum, "Richard II and the Realities of Power," Shakespeare Survey, 28 (Cambridge, England, 1975), 10. Cf. Colley: "Once Richard throws his warder down to prevent the combat... he signals the end of one era and the dawn of another. For in his interrruption he allows personal political motives to reshape a traditional means of determining the rights and wrongs of a dispute. The trial scene is merely symbolic of a number of offenses that Richard perpetrates upon his own crumbling political order." "The Economics of Richard II?" 161.

24. Schoenbaum, "Richard II and the Realities of Power, " 10, n4.

25. Schoenbaum, "Richard II and the Realities of Power, "12.

26. This interpretation is consistent with Froissart, whose Richard comes to Bolingbroke after the sentencing: "At the erles departynge, the kynge humyled hym greatly to his cosyn of Derby, and said As Godde helps me, it right greatly displeaseth me, the wordes that hath been bytwene you and Erle Marshalle. But the sentence that I have gyven is for the beste, and for to apease therby the people, who greatly murmured on this matter. Wherfore cosyn, yet to ease you somwhat of your payne, I release my Judgement fro tenne yere to syxe yere." In Holinshed, Bolingbroke's banishment is reduced later: "The Duke of Hereford tooke his leave of the king at Eltham, who there released foure yeares of his banishment." Sen Gupta suggests that Richard reduces

Bolingbroke's sentence "out of pity for [Gaunt], and not with an eye to the public." Shakespeare's Historical Plays (Oxford, 1964), p. 116. Schoenbaum, responding to Sen Gupta, says "The seeming clemency of the reduced sentence is a gesture of politic magnanimity that costs Richard nothing — why worry about what will happen in six years? — but serves as a sop to Gaunt." "Richard II and the Realities of Power."

27.   Reno, From Sacrament to Ceremony, pp. 41 ff.

28.   That Richard's reign as depicted by Shakespeare represents that of a child king, regardless of Richard's chronological age, is suggested by The Homily "against willfull Rebellion": "Againe the Scriptures, of undiscreet and evill Princes, speake thus, woe be to thee (O thou land) whose King is but a child, and whose Princes are early at their bankets. Againe, when the wicked doe raigne, then men goe to ruine. And againe, A foolish Prince destroyeth the people, and a covetous King undoeth his subjects."   "A child," here, is equatable with a bad prince.   Alan Howard's brilliant Stratford, England performance of Henry VI depicted a child king quite willfully creating a vacuum of power.   Howard conveyed the child's technique of manipulating God-like adults through tantrums and refusals.   Howard's Henry VI seemed to be saying, "I could rule, but I would prefer not to, and I rather enjoy the trouble I am causing."   Lear is, in a sense, a Richard II grown old, someone who has always been a king, thus has maintained the psyche of a child.   Lear, however, will learn more than Richard does.   See my "The Death of Cordelia: A Jungian Approach," in The Hebrew University Studies in Literature, VIII #1 (Spring, 1980), 1-12, on Lear's "education."

29.   Reno, From Sacrament to Ceremony, p. 10.

30.   Reno, From Sacrament to Ceremony, p. 13.

31.   Kern, Kingship and the Law in the Middle Ages, p. 37.

32.   Kern, Kingship and the Law in the Middle Ages, p. 52.

33.   Edenic imagery is employed in both Hamlet (I.v.38-40 and III.iii.36-39, for example) and Macbeth (I.v.65-66, for example) to describe regicide.

34.   A. G. Dickens, "The Dimensions of the English Reformation," The English Tradition, I, p. 196.

35.   Reno, From Sacrament to Ceremony, pp. 76-80.

36.   "State" as "peasant" personifies kingship, land, and law (all encompassed by "state") negatively.

37.   Reno, From Sacrament to Ceremony, p.77.

38. Derek Traversi, Shakespeare: From Richard II to Henry V (Stanford, California, 1957), p. 20.

39. The other brother, York, wishes that, "So my untruth had not provoked him to it —/ The king had cut off my head with my brother's" (II.ii.101-102).

40. Richard seems almost a character out of Thackeray: cf. the new Sir Pitt: " 'I'll clear the estate now with the ready money,' he thought, and rapidly calculated its incumbrances and the improvements which he would make. He would not use his aunt's money previously, lest Sir Pitt should recover, and his outlay be in vain." Vanity Fair (New York, Rinehart Edition, 1958), p. 425.

41. The concept of the Eucharist corrupted by drunkenness is developed through Cassio (Othello: II.iii) and Caliban (The Tempest: II.ii and III.ii). See my discussions on the plays in Christian Ritual and the World of Shakespeare's Tragedies (Bucknell, 1976) for an extension of the thesis.

42. Figgis, The Divine Right of Kings, p. 36.

43. Jean Bodin, Six Books of the Commonwealth, abridged and trans. M. J. Tookey (New York, 1955), p. 66.

44. The precise nature of Richard's violation of feudal law is described by Clarkson and Warren: "Now, when John of Gaunt died, King Richard was entitled to primer seisin in such lands as Gaunt held as tenant in capite; and Henry, Gaunt's heir, being of full age, would be entitled, after doing homage and paying his relief, to sue his livery" (that is, prove his title and procure his inheritance). The Law of Property in Shakespeare and the Elizabethan Drama (Baltimore, 1942), p. 30. Richard denies Bolingbroke any legal redress to the seizure, a point Bolingbroke stresses: "I am denied to sue my livery here,/ And yet my letters patents give me leave... I am a subject;/ And I challenge law; attorneys are denied me;/ And therefore personally I lay my claim/ To my inheritance of free descent" (II.iii. 128-135). One has to ask what recourse Bolingbroke has.

45. The scene would seem to be a dramatic foreshortening of events. I do not believe that the scene suggests that Bolingbroke is returning before he learns of his father's death and the confiscation of the Lancastrian estates. That interpretation would make Bolingbroke more of a gambler than I believe he is — and it would make his thrust at the crown itself more obvious then he allows it to be. The ambiguity of time itself, however, suggests Richard's destruction of sequential rhythms based on more than "action and reaction." The question of time subtly raises the issue of Bolingbroke's "true motive." We see him, for example, almost immediately accepting homage from Hotspur (II.iii.41-

50). For discussion of time in Richard II, see the Variorum Edition, pp. 401-404. The recent BBC-TV production showed the scene between Northumberland, Ross, and Willoughby at Gaunt's funeral. Time, then, had passed since Gaunt's death.

46. Reno, From Sacrament to Ceremony, p. 89.

47. Shakespeare appears, in the Second Tetralogy, to be "writing ahead" to that segment of history he has already explored. He is able in the Second Tetralogy to explore the causes of the fragmented world he has depicted in the First Tetralogy.

48. Shakespeare anticipates the Jacobean tendency of writers like Donne and Jonson to pun on coins. For an article suggesting that Donne was heavily indebted to Shakespeare and Elizabethan drama, see H. M. Richmond, "Donne's Master: The Young Shakespeare," Criticism, XV (1973), 126-144.

49. Cf. Queen Isabel, The Duchess of Gloucester, Humphrey of Gloucester in Henry VI, Ophelia, Desdemona, Lady Macduff and family, King Lear's Gloucester and Albany, and Enobarbus, although the latter could be granted a full tragic configuration.

50. Yet even when his nemesis faces him, backed by a silent army, Richard will reveal his own self-destructive nature by altering mythology to justify himself: "Down, down I come, like glist'ring Phaethon,/ Wanting the manage of unruly jades" (III.iii.177-178). The myth points at Richard's inadequacy on the throne, but Richard's interpretation of it tends to blame the horses, not the hubristic charioteer. In "wanting the manage" (i.e. " lacking the ability to control"), however, Richard admits that his shortcomings contributed to cosmic disaster.

51. The line is Thidias's, of course, referring to Octavius Caesar (Antony and Cleopatra: III.xiii.87). Octavius, not inhibited by the sanctions Bolingbroke must violate, gathers a Bolingbrokean momentum in his movement against an Antony who, like Richard, allows his body natural to over-rule political considerations, and who, like Richard, suffers massive defections from his ranks, until he is "plucked" (III.xii.3: cf. "plume-plucked Richard": IV.i.108).

52. Irving Ribner, The English History Play in the Age of Shakespeare (Princeton, 1957), p. 164.

53. Aristotle, Physica, trans. R. P. Hardie and R. K. Gaye, The Basic Works of Aristotle, ed. Richard McKeon (New York, 1942), p. 298.

54. As Charles VI disinherits Lewis, the Dauphin, in Henry V. That Lewis refuses to remain disinherited is one reason why poor Henry VI must deny the heredity of Edward, Prince of Wales. For an excellent article treating "mirror scenes" and parallelisms, particularly the Mortimer claim to the throne in both tetralogies, see Karl P. Wentersdorf, "The Conspiracy of Silence in Henry V," Shakespeare Quarterly, Vol. 27 #3 (Summer, 1976), 264-287.

55. Pater is predictably sensitive to this motif in Richard II: "In the Roman Pontifical, of which the order of Coronation is really a part, there is no form for the inverse process, no rite of 'degradation,' such as that by which an offending priest or bishop may be deprived, if not of the essential quality of 'orders,' yet, one by one, of its outward dignities. It is as if Shakespeare had in mind some such inverted rite, like those old ecclesiastical or military ones, by which human hardness, or human justice, adds the last touch of unkindness to the execution of its sentences, in the scene where Richard 'deposes' himself, as in some long, agonising ceremony..." Appreciations (1889), p. 205. For a similar, though less Pateresque view of the scene, see my Christian Ritual and the World of Shakespeare's Tragedies, p. 73-77. See also Ranald, "The Degradation of Richard II," for a demonstration that "accounts of chivalric, military, and ecclesiastical degradations were readily available to Shakespeare and his contemporaries" (170).

56. Margaret Loftus Ranald, "The Degradation of Richard II: An Inquiry into the Ritual Backgrounds," 170.

57. Henry Bracton, Bracton on the Laws and Customs of England, ed. George E. Woodbine, trans. with revisions and notes, Samuel E. Thorne, 2 vols. (Cambridge, Mass., 1968), II, p. 33.

58. To equate elaborate language with powerlessness, terseness with strength is a mistake in Richard II, though the contrast between Bolingbroke's brief, brutal III.i and Richard's self-indulgence in III.ii would seem to suggest that brevity is the soul of strength. But against that simplistic thesis, we have Bolingbroke's powerful and lengthy indictment in I.i, and Richard's potent "undoing" of himself and Bolingbroke in IV.i. See Lois Potter, "The Antic Disposition of Richard II," Shakespeare Survey 27 (1974), 33-41.

59. Here, the crown begins to become "a plaything of forces it could not control," as G.R. Elton describes its instability during the Wars of the Roses, in England Under the Tudors (London, 1957).

60. While Harold F. Folland calls Richard's a "pallid victory" in the Deposition Scene, Folland is accurate in describing Richard's strategy: "the scene is dramatically powerful, and much of its power comes... from the way Richard, behind and through his apparently helpless self-dramatization, continues to fight his case against Bolingbroke so as to

achieve a moral victory which has enduring political consequences. And in passing the royal power on to Henry, Richard subtly alters its character by dimming its 'numinous light.'" I would qualify this by saying that Richard demonstrates that the "numinous light" has been already extinguished. Folland continues with a nice parallelism: "As [Richard] learns that forms and symbols are futile when they are empty, his opponent will learn that power without formal sanctions is not enough either." Yes — although the Deposition Scene and Richard's management of it show that power is all there is. The Deposition Scene demonstrates and reiterates the erasure of "formal sanctions." "King Richard's Pallid Victory," SQ XXIV #4 (Autumn, 1973),

61. Here is "the rough rude sea" (III.ii.54) that, in Richard's previous metaphor, could not "wash the balm off from an anointed king" (III.ii.55). That sea — archetypally symbolic of the unconscious — ultimately resides within Richard, springing from "the unseen grief/ That swells with silence in the tortured soul,/ There lies the substance..."(IV.i.296-298). Ranald compares Richard's tears to the "anti-Baptism" aspect of the chivalric degradation: "he thus 'baptizes' himself into his new 'unkinged' identity... Shakespeare has Richard declare himself someone who has never existed as a legal person" (192-193). Such personal eradication is an ultimate extension of Richard's attack on legality and "legitimacy." For an analysis of Shakespeare's use of Baptism as "anti-ritual," see my "Ophelia's Doubtful Death," Christianity and Literature, XXVII #3 (Spring, 1978), 28-31.

62. In the recent grotesque R.S.C. production, Richard wore the smashed mirror around his neck. It became a tumbled-down crown of thorns, as well as an albatross.

63. On the human plane, and in spite of Richard's self-pitying posturing and the rhyming couplets, husband and wife recognize with piercing pathos what they might have had together — now that it is too late. That belated recognition, reflecting much that happens in the play, should, I believe, be the subtext of the "Divorce" scene.

64. Harbage, Shakespeare: A Reader's Guide, p. 138.

65. Traversi, Shakespeare: From Richard II to Henry V, p. 47. Richard's discussion of "waste," for example, involves only a quantitative assessment of what he has done to a personal "I."

66. Cf. C.L. Barber: "The historical view expresses life as drama. People in drama are not identical with their names, for they gain and lose their names, their status and meaning — and not by settled ritual: the gaining and losing of names, of meaning, is beyond the control of any set ritual sequence... The people [in Shakespeare's plays] try to organize their lives by pageant and ritual, but the plays are dramatic precisely because the effort fails." Shakespeare's Festive Comedy: A Study of

Dramatic Form and Its Relation to Social Custom (Princeton, Princeton University Press, 1959), p. 193. While I believe that "pageantry" can work in the Second Henriad, particularly as produced by Henry V, "ritual," which I take to be a valid means of contacting God, cannot work, as Henry V seems to recognize as he pleads with God not to allow his father's usurpation to inhibit his own effort at Agincourt (Henry V: IV.i.289-306).

67. Christopher Morris offers this interesting point about royal blood as expressed by the Tudor Homilies: "extreme as they are, it is worth noting what [they] do not say. Although they are couched at times in almost mystical terms, they contain no mysticism about the sanctity of the blood royal — possibly because Tudor legitimacy was not quite unchallengeable — nor yet about the sanctity attaching to the Lord's Anointed as such. In other words they did not preach a full-blooded theory of the divine right of kings." Political Thought in England: Tyndale to Hooker (Oxford, 1953), pp. 66-67.

III

Bolingbroke's England

In Bolingbroke, Shakespeare characterizes a pragmatist, not a doctrinaire. One method of characterization is to keep such a character's motivation obscure. Bolingbroke defines his steps only as he takes them. His actions, however, from before the play begins and even through the Deposition Scene, are responses to Richard's actions. Bolingbroke, an ambitious nobleman trapped within a medieval world endowed with sacred and inviolable premises, can move only when Richard undermines the premises and shakes the hierarchy to its base. Whatever terse pieties Bolingbroke utters in public, he is characterized as a "politician" (I Henry IV: I.iii.239, and Richard II: I.iv), a word with perhaps even more negative associations to the Elizabethan ear than recent history has made it to ours,1/ and as a literalist (I.iii.293-302).

In one sense, Bolingbroke's vision dictates the nature of any kingdom he might rule. He sees things "as they are," with no regard for intangibles,2/ and would agree with Theseus that darkness can work the fearful imagination to make "a bush" seem "a bear" (A Midsummer-Night's Dream: V.i.22) and with Bacon that "Men fear death as children fear to go in the dark." That Bolingbroke should be involved in the strange cooperation that confirms the destruction of sacramentalism in England is both appropriate to his literalism and doubly ironic, first because he poses as a traditionalist in I.i. A "traditionalist" who challenges traditional authority, however, must accept the second irony — once he has helped erase sacred values, he cannot reconstitute them. And he will destroy, as Reno points out brilliantly, the very basis of his "new world". Left with neo-feudalism as the only version of government available, Bolingbroke will insist on absolute rule, and will thus intensify the opposition to his rule.

Whatever his "motives," Bolingbroke sets up a new feudal system in England even as he conveys his limited intentions to his sympathizers and to York. His intentions are neatly expressed and obscured in the cogent contractual agreements of feudalism. In seconding Bolingbroke's claim, Northumberland tells York that

> The noble duke hath sworn his coming is
> But for his own; and for the right of that
> We all have strongly sworn to give him aid:
> And let him never see joy that breaks that oath.3/
> (II.ii.147-150)

Northumberland's oath is that of fealty in response to the reciprocal oath of a feudal lord. Bolingbroke's "Oath of Doncaster," made on his return to England, will reemerge with increasing specificity to haunt him (I Henry IV: V.i. 41-71). Even before York appears to challenge him, we observe Bolingbroke conducting a feudal ceremony with the younger Percy:

Percy.   My gracious lord, I tender you my service,
                                Such as it is, being tender, raw, and young,
                                Which elder days shall ripen and confirm
                                To more approved service and desert.

Bolingbroke.   I thank thee, gentle Percy, and be sure
                                I count myself in nothing else so happy
                                As in a soul rememb'ring my good friends;
                                And as my fortune ripens with thy love,
                                It shall be still thy true love's recompense:
                                My heart this covenant makes, my hand thus
                                seals it.

                                       (II.iii.41-50)

The reciprocal nature of the feudal oath, the service and reward equation, is clearly outlined. Growth is anticipated on each side of the equation ("as my fortune ripens with thy love"). Bolingbroke would seem to be building a base of power extending beyond the possibility of his regaining a dukedom. The relative proximity of Lancashire to Northumberland would not permit Bolingbroke to make much of a case for a merely "local arrangement," subordinate to an encompassing loyalty to the crown. Bolingbroke repeats the formula with Ross and Willoughby, this time extending the metaphor of "fortune" into the full-fledged commercial language that will define the "ethic" of his version of feudalism:

Bolingbroke.   Welcome my lords, I wot your love pursues
                                A banished traitor. All my treasury
                                Is yet but unfelt thanks, which more enrich'd
                                Shall be your love and labor's recompense.

Ross.   Your presence makes us rich, most noble lord.

Willoughby.   And far surmounts our labor to attain it.

Bolingbroke.   Evermore thank's the exchequer of the poor,
                                Which till my infant fortune come to years
                                Stands for my bounty.
                                 (II.iii.59-67)

The contract is based on explicitly material rewards — "a percentage of the take" — and it predicts that, should Bolingbroke ignore his contractual obligations — as he will — England will be reduced to the "mere anarchy" of a commercial ethic run amuck. Bolingbroke encourages the "social darwinism" that will motivate many of his former followers, chiefly Northumberland, and that will be one of the characteristics of the debased nobleman, Sir John Falstaff, who will enter the histories only after sacramental relevance has evaporated from England, although he will be dismissed in Henry V's first ceremonial.

In Act II, Scene Three of <u>Richard II</u>, Bolingbroke enunciates a radically different concept of power than that conferred by the anointment of Richard, but a concept to which Richard has already unwittingly descended. Power no longer comes "from above." It is rather the product of the gathering of material wealth which can become "more enriched." Sovereignty extends outward from the man who controls the allegiance of the most troops, and who can thus encourage his infant exchequer to maturity. Here "the ripeness is all," as is "the readiness," but on strictly quantitative terms. Bolingbroke plans to be no "upstart unthrift" (II.iii.121). He would seem to know — well before Richard's submission at Flint Castle — that his power will not incorporate sacramental sanctions. York is correct to chide Bolingbroke: "that word 'grace'/ In an ungracious mouth is but profane" (II.iii.87-88). Bolingbroke's insistence on the "profane" formulas of feudal contract has been forced upon him by the prior conditions Richard has established — the draining of sacred essence from the crown, the leasing out of sacred soil, and the law-shattering confiscation of the Lancastrian estates. While Bolingbroke is shrewd enough to understand and to exploit these conditions, they are not of his making. It is as if he is pulled into a power vacuum ("the absent time": II.iii.79) and must obey the imperative of the revised "rules of the game," in fact, must extemporize new rules.

But such rules as dominant ethic return to plague their promulgator. While Bolingbroke can project a crusade to the Holy Land, he finds his own strategy employed against him in his own realm by the Archbishop of York. While Bolingbroke can plan a medieval pageant to celebrate the restoration of English values, a rival faction, also espousing "value," would have regicide the chief event of the Oxford festival. While Bolingbroke can condemn Bushy and Green for having "fed upon [his] signories" (III.i.22), he discovers that his own son seems to embody all that Bolingbroke would have extirpated from England:

Can no man tell me of my unthrifty son?
'Tis full three months since I did see him last.
If any plague hang over us, 'tis he.
I would to God, my lords, he might be found:
Inquire at London, 'mongst the taverns there,

> For there, they say, he daily doth frequent
> With unrestrained loose companions,
> Even such, they say, as stand in narrow lanes,
> And beat our watch and rob our passengers;
> While he, young wanton and effeminate boy,
> Takes on the point of honor to support
> So dissolute a crew.
>
> (V.iii.1-12)

Bolingbroke has spawned, it seems, precisely what he returned to England to eliminate, prodigality and criminality that extend the commercial metaphor to its logical negative conclusion. The words "taverns," "narrow lanes," "watch," and "passengers" introduce a new area of England that Henry IV's accession has suddenly made visible.

The Prince's attitude towards the Oxford tourney is described by young Percy:

> His answer was, he would unto the stews,
> And from the commonest creature pluck a glove,
> And wear it as a favor, and with that
> He would unhorse the lustiest challenger.
>
> (V.i.16-19)

While we receive here an outline of Hal's career — " the lustiest challenger" will be first Hotspur (Percy, here), then Falstaff — and while Shakespeare neatly sets up his next play — the conflicts between Hal and Henry IV and Hal and Hotspur — the scene has its impact within the play. "This new world" extends to the underside of London, where Marlowe can be murdered over a tavern reckoning, where robbers lurk in lanes and princes sneer at chivalric exercise, making dissoluteness the standard of "honor."

Almost immediately, York will make similar accusations about his son:

> So shall my virtue be my vice's bawd,
> And he shall spend my honor with his shame,
> As thriftless sons their scraping father's gold.
>
> (V.iii.66-68)

Again, the metaphor is debasement. While Bolingbroke can joke:

> Our scene is alt'red from a serious thing,
> And now is changed to "The Beggar and the King."
>
> (V.iii.78-79)

his allusion points at several truths. His reign will not be the "serious thing" Richard's was. Though no comedy, Bolingbroke's reign will be marked by an often ineffective theatricality. Having helped reduce the world to its lowest common denominator —mere materialism — Bolingbroke will introduce several "counterfeit" (I Henry IV: V.v.33) kings to the field at Shrewsbury; "royal" and "noble" become real only as they equate with coinage. He will tell his son, finally, that "All my reign hath been but as a scene/ Acting that argument" (II Henry IV: IV.v.197-198). His has been a play with but a single scene, the acting out of a role he did not achieve by straight, direct ways. If Richard "made state a peasant" (IV.i.251), Bolingbroke has married the beggar-state, as King Cophetua, in the ballad, married the beggar-girl. The Duchess of York's "A god on earth art thou" (V.iii.135) can only be placed against the truth — that that is precisely what Bolingbroke is not.2/ The King may be principal, but he is no long principle. Berkeley's accusation that Bolingbroke "frights our native peace with self-borne arms" (II.iii.80) carries the pun of "self-born," or "self-created." Bolingbroke's is a successful version of Laertes's rebellion:

> as the world were now but to begin,
> Antiquity forgot, customs not known,
> The ratifiers and props of every word,
> They, cry, "Choose we! Laertes shall be king!"
> (Hamlet: IV.v.104-107)

Bolingbroke's "marriage" will partake of no "mystical incorporation." He will fulfill his feudal obligations to the variety of noblemen who report the series of crown-confirming successes:

> We thank thee, gentle Percy, for thy pains,
> And to thy worth will add right worthy gains.
> (V.vi.11-12)

> Thy pains, Fitzwater, shall not be forgot:
> Right noble is thy merit well I wot.
> (V.vi.17-18)

The couplets aim at the "effect" of royalty, but underline the contractual obligations of feudalism, and remind us of the scene in which Bolingbroke bought Aumerle's loyalty with pardon. To burnish his royal image, Bolingbroke magnanimously pardons Carlisle:

> Carlisle, this is your doom:
> Choose out some secret place, some reverend room,
> More than thou hast, and with it joy thy life.
> So as thou liv'st in peace, die free from strife;

For though mine enemy thou hast ever been,
High sparks of honor in thee have I seen.
(V.vi.24-29)

While Bolingbroke can emphasize that he appreciates the qualities of even an adversary, he can requite the necessary Exton only with the "guilt of conscience" for his "labor/ But neither my good word, nor princely favor" (V.vi.41-42). Bolingbroke finds himself in a position analogous to Gaunt's after the latter had voted to sentence his own son: "you gave leave to my unwilling tongue/ Against my will to do myself this wrong" (I.iii.244-245). Bolingbroke's couplets to Exton do not convey the easy formulae of those to Percy and Fitzwater. The negatives define the limits of kingly power, limits once outlined to Richard by Gaunt. Bolingbroke must become "a traitor with the rest," never to make his "voyage to the Holy Land,/ To wash this blood from off [his] guilty hand" (V.vi.49-50). Instead, that very blood will become an element in a crusade against him. No "grace" can really accrue to his "mournings" (V.vi.51), however sincere he is as an individual, because he has helped reduce the king from "grace" to individual. As he mourns for Richard, Bolingbroke acts out the role Poins attributes to Hal, grieving over his father's illness: "a most princely hypocrite" (II Henry IV: II.ii.52). Hypocrisy at a profound level is now part of kingship, since each scene can now only act the "argument" of kingship, not its intrinsic reality. Bolingbroke's argument will not be the intangible qualities of "grace," but the ethic Bolingbroke confirms in seizing the crown, an ethic like the crown itself, now to be measured only in quantitative terms. At the end of Richard II, sovereignty is a "shadow," and "substance" is a "woe" that fills the "soul" of the new king (V.vi.45). The substance of Bolingbroke's ascension is captured in York's description of the shallowest of ceremonials: "all the walls/ With painted imagery . . . said at once,/ 'Jesu preserve thee! Welcome, Bolingbroke!'" (V.ii.15-17). In one vital sense, Bolingbroke's command for Richard's funeral is mere "painted imagery." The intrinsic links with God that ritual represents have become the display of ceremony, designed merely to impress men, not framed to contact God.

Bolingbroke continues to preside over scenes that demonstrate response to action, rather than initiation of it. We discover, at the beginning of I Henry IV, that a year has passed since the murder of Richard, yet no crusade is toward. Bolingbroke opens with a long piety about "new boils/ To be commenced in stronds afar remote":

As far as to the sepulcher of Christ —
Whose soldier now, under whose blessed cross
We are impressed and engaged to fight —
Forthwith a power of English shall we levy,
Whose arms were molded in their mother's womb,
To chase these pagans in those holy fields

Over whose acres walked those blessed feet
Which fourteen hundred years ago were nailed
For our advantage on the bitter cross.

(I.i.3-27)

Such piety seems uncharacteristic of the Bolingbroke we have observed marching towards the throne, with only blithe lip-service to God on his tongue. He seems to wish to return to Gaunt's England ("This teeming womb of royal kings"). But England equates more to the Duchess of York, whose "teeming date [is] drunk up with time" (V.ii.91). And the motive for the crusade has shifted during the year's delay. Atonement for Richard's murder is not mentioned. Instead, the crusade would replace "the intestine shock/ And furious close of civil butchery" (I.i.12-13). One war, a united effort, will absorb the "war [that] like an ill-sheathed knife,/ . . . cut [s] his master" (I.i.17-18). The motivation for the crusade has become political, subsuming or ignoring the personal guilt Bolingbroke expressed at the end of <u>Richard II</u>. One reason for the shifting, possibly the widening, of the motive for the crusade is, of course, that Bolingbroke is speaking as king, a position in which he must at least appear to express "the good of England."

We learn, however, that the opening 27 lines have all been propaganda.5/ Bolingbroke tells his nobles that "Therefor we meet not now" (I.i.30), which would <u>seem</u> to say, "You haven't gathered here merely to hear me talk of my crusade again." Actually, since Bolingbroke already knows the outcome of the battle of which Westmoreland is doubtful (I.i.61), and has already learned of the problems raised by the success of <u>his</u> forces in the battle (I.i.62-75 and 91-94), he also knows that "our business for the Holy Land" has <u>already</u> been interrupted. His "therefor we meet. . . now" refers to "the tidings of this broil" (I.i.47), the battle in Northumbria, not his crusade. As happens so often in these plays, the meaning of a line becomes clear only as subsequent events clarify it.6/ The "time" of the court is now measured only as response. The court is no longer the generator of original activity. Henry IV will complain that he is "a common 'larum-bell" (<u>II Henry IV</u>: III.i.17), the focal point of emergency. The king can only react in alarm. "And for this cause," he says, "awhile we must neglect/ Our holy purpose to Jerusalem" (I.i.101-102). Such "neglect," which will last for the duration of Henry IV's reign, signals again the shift from the "sacred" time of Gaunt's speech, where wars were chivalric exercises in France or forays on "stubborn Jewry."

No "holy purpose" can be fulfilled during the reign of Henry IV. The world John of Gaunt described, already anachronistic as he spoke, has faded into a distant past. "This cause" facing Henry IV is Hotspur's withholding all prisoners from the king "but Mordake, Earl of Fife" (I.i.94). Mordake, being of royal blood, would be the only prisoner Hotspur would <u>have</u> to surrender, under the <u>quid pro quo</u> agreements of feudal law. But Henry IV seems to believe that all that is won is in his name is "an honorable spoil.../ A gallant prize" (I.i.74-75).7/ Having seized the crown, his attitude seems suddenly like Richard's. He seems to ignore the specific and narrow definitions of his throne, far more circumscribed than the sacred premises of Richard's monarchy. As Reno suggests, "feudal law is natural in that it governs man as he is a denizen of this world only."8/ Bolingbroke seems consciously to wish to free his throne of feudal obligation, an effort that can only reduce "this world" to a jungle. Bolingbroke's apparent thrust for absolutism will, as Reno says, "spawn a host of imitators who [will mimic] his strategies — now for their own ends rather than his."9/

That his kingship is personal — the crown having been stripped of its mystical incorporation — seems evident in Bolingbroke's confrontation with Northumberland, Worcester, and Hotspur: "I will from henceforth rather be myself,/ Mighty and to be feared" (I Henry IV: I.iii.5-6). One might expect an expression of king qua king to be couched in the royal plurality. Worcester, however, reiterates the feudal contract, employing an ironic plurality expressing the baronial support that has backed Bolingbroke and that continues to be his basis of power:

> Our house, my sovereign liege, little deserves
> The scourge of greatness to be used on it —
> And that same greatness to which our own hands
> Have holp to make so portly.
> (I.iii.10-13)

Bolingbroke reads this only as a threat. The rewards he promised before he became king are now reserved for a king who will not "endure/ The moody frontier of a servant brow" (I.iii.17-18). The contract is broken. As Henry IV sees things, service is an automatic response to kingship, not the fruit of a contract stipulating that a portion of the "prize" or "spoils" be retained by the loyal subject.

Northumberland seems willing to compromise on this point, excusing the withholding of "Those prisoners in your highness' name demanded/ Which Harry Percy here at Holmedon took" (I.iii.22-23). Northumberland suggests that the king's demand — not necessarily the "legality" of that demand — was respected, and that Hotspur's response has been misrepresented, as Hotspur makes engagingly clear (I.iii.26-65). Hotspur hopes that King Henry will view him still as true coinage, still working in the king's interest:

> And I beseech you, let not his report
> Come current for an accusation
> Betwixt my love and your high majesty.
> (I.iii.66-68)

It would seem that Henry IV <u>can</u> have it "his way," that his powerful barons are willing to yield on the question of feudal obligation, indeed are ready to reaffirm their loyalty to him.

But the truth underlying the quarrel emerges. Hotspur has compromised the king unknowingly:

> Why, yet he doth deny his prisoners,
> But with proviso and exception,
> That we at our own charge shall ransom straight
> His brother-in-law, the foolish Mortimer;
> Who, on my soul, hath willfully betrayed
> The lives of those that he did lead to fight
> Against that great magician, damned Glendower.
> ... Shall our coffers, then,
> Be emptied to redeem a traitor home?
> Shall we buy treason, and indent with fears
> When they have lost and forfeited themselves?
> No, on the barren mountains let him starve!
> For I shall never hold that man my friend
> Whose tongue shall ask me for one penny cost
> To ransom home revolted Mortimer.
>
> (I.iii.76-91)

This patent piece of self-serving places the question of Mortimer squarely within the market-place metaphor that Bolingbroke's version of feudalism has introduced. In condemning Mortimer, however, Henry IV must ignore the testimony of an eye-witness (I.iii.92-116), and must exile a nobleman who, according to Hotspur, fought <u>for</u> the king and fell off only "by the chance of war" (I.iii.94). But the angry king, having called Hotspur a liar, assumes the prerogative of granting Northumberland a "license [for] departure with your son" (I.iii.121), seemingly making up the rules as he goes. Having cancelled hope for Mortimer's ransom, Henry IV reiterates his demand, adding a threat: "Send us your prisoners, or you will hear of it" (I.iii.122). The royal plurality emerges only from the will of the individual now wearing the crown. Henry IV seems as preemptory here as Richard was in seizing Bolingbroke's inheritance.

The technique Shakespeare employed in <u>Richard II</u> — a "private" scene that reveals the meaning of the "public" scene we have just witnessed (cf. I.ii) is used again in <u>I Henry IV</u>. While we have learned in <u>Richard II</u> that Bolingbroke is not Richard's heir, we learn here — with Hotspur — that the heir is Mortimer. Worcester "cannot blame" Henry IV for "Trembling even at the name of Mortimer," for Mortimer was "proclaimed/ By Richard that dead is, the next of blood..." (I.iii.142-144). We learn, suddenly, that Bolingbroke has been as compromised in his meeting with Worcester, Northumberland, and Hotspur as Richard had been as he stood in the crossfire between Mowbray and Bolingbroke. Henry IV's dismissal of Worcester (I.iii.14-20) is analogous to Richard's banishment of Bolingbroke and Mowbray — and equally ineffective, again the product of a desperate, extemporaneous politics that cannot dispell either the murder of Gloucester or the nomination of Mortimer. As Richard cut kingship from its sacramental bonds, Bolingbroke breaks the new, worldly contract. The result can only be a new sequence of ad hoc agreements and alliances, a splintering off from the king of parties bound to him only by a contract with a reciprocity clause:

> ... yet time serves where in you may redeem
> Your banished honors and restore yourselves
> Into the good thoughts of the world again;
> Revenge the jeering and disdained contempt
> Of this proud king, who studies day and night
> To answer all the debt he owes to you
> Even with the bloody payment of your deaths.
> (I.iii.178-184)

So much for Henry's fulfillment of his obligations. Time become a medium for a kind of "commercial revenge"; Hotspur will answer Henry IV quid pro quo:

> I'll keep them all.
> By God, he shall not have a Scot of them!
> No, if a Scot would save his soul, he shall not.
> I'll keep them, by this hand.
> (I.iii.213-215)

A "scot," of course, is "a small payment." Hotspur's oath defines how things are measured now in England, and how things will be won or lost — by hand, or power, regardless of what rhetoric is summoned to justify Realpolitik. And, of course, any rhetoric that does not recognize the basis of power as power, any rhetoric that serves abstractions like "honor" will be downright dangerous, if employed unironically, as Hotspur uses it (I.iii.193-206), ignoring the truth latent in his metaphors of debt and payment.

Worcester counters Hotspur's vehemence with a pragmatism that persuades him to "Deliver [his] Scottish prisoners... up without their ransom straight" (I.iii.256-257). Worcester knows that

> The king will always think him in our debt,
> And think we think ourselves unsatisfied,
> Till he hath found a way to pay us home.
> (I.iii.282-284)

The only recourse is "To bear our fortunes in our own strong arms" (I.iii.294).

Henry IV, then, in attempting to secure power to his throne, has only incited rebellion. Having introduced a kingship based on a series of rapid transactions in which the terms are not always clearly delineated ("I come but for my own": Richard II III.iii.194), but in which the quantitative premises were always clear, even to Richard (V.i.59-61), and compromised by the presence of an heir who begins to "stir/ About his title" (I Henry IV: II.ii.82-83), the king attempts to assert more power. In doing so, however, he snaps his links with the northern faction, and encourages his barons "to line [Mortimer's] enterprise" (I Henry IV: II.ii.84). Having promoted the premise that power alone wins the prizes — crown included — the king discovers that power alone can hardly stamp the idea out. The exercise of mere power invites a response in kind. Whatever Henry could have done, he has fomented rebellion, perhaps an inevitable consequence of usurpation and regicide, but certainly a result of the king's rejection of the premises of his authority, or, conversely, of the king's continued exercise of the means whereby the end has been achieved. Not the least of the ironies of Henry IV's situation is that Mortimer, heir both by descent (Lionel being Edward's third son, Gaunt, his fourth) and by royal decree, has fought in the ranks of Henry IV. By willfully misconstruing Mortimer's combat against Glendower, the new king has given Mortimer more than a pretext on which to stir about his title. And Henry has encouraged an alliance that, were it ever to gather to a single "head," might well topple him. But, as Bolingbroke cannot gather England into the unity of a crusade, the rebels prove unable to draw their puissance towards a single decisive conflict. England becomes a jungle in which the social darwinists seek for profit and power, climb and fall upon the wheel of fortune, and eradicate England's links with any larger, intangible auspices. Admittedly, England does not descend to the nightmarish confusion of conflicting loyalties and betrayals that Britain suffers after Lear sunders the realm, not merely by dividing it, but by giving the land to the daughters (the map), the power to the sons-in-law (the coronet), and by insisting on all the perquisites of kingship but none of the obligations.

Having engendered a "spoils system," and having rejected "the agents or base second means" (I.iii.163) whereby he attained the office, the king encourages the kind of independent power-play that Lear also foments — in Edmund, for example, who decides to prosper in the unsettled state. The tripartite division of I Henry IV never makes it from map to landscape, but the scene is a prototype for the first scene of King Lear. "Shall we divide our right," Glendower asks, "According to our threefold order taken?" (III.i.69-70). "Right" here — with the exception of Mortimer's claim, now shrunken by two thirds — is based on power, on winning a battle yet to be fought. The "indentures tripartite" are to be "sealed interchangeably" (III.i.79-80), but lack even the dubious sanction that the Oxford conspirators assumed when they took "the sacrament/ And interchangeably set down their hands/ To kill the king" (Richard II: V.ii.97-99). Perhaps the ethic of power is clearer under Bolingbroke. Henry IV, having broken his contractual agreements, has forced his "servants" into the formation of new charters. Remarkably, Mortimer does not bother to make a formal claim, instead, he agrees to the political fragmentation of the realm. That the rebellion is based on feudal premises is made clear by Mortimer's instructions to Glendower:

> Within that space [of two weeks] you may have drawn together
> Your tenants, friends, and neighboring gentlemen.
> (III.i.88-89)

Henry IV's version of kingship rises against him. Reno suggests that the Percies "acknowledged no obligation to Henry other than the strictly feudal, and no one, not even among the king's supporters, seemed to feel there was any special sacrilege involved in their revolt."10/ The question of "sacrilege" can scarcely emerge into a world where it has been rendered irrelevant. Indeed, Hotspur emphasizes the ethic underlying this new world in arguing that the Trent "shall not wind with such a deep indent/ To rob me of so rich a bottom here" (III.i.103-104). While the language is that of robbery and richness, aspects of the "nature" Bolingbroke has introduced. Hotspur argues "against nature," as even Glendower, no literalist, can tell him in the next line ("You see it doth": III.i.105). The conflict suggests Hotspur's profound misunderstanding of the kingdom he inhabits. He operates on outmoded premises that doom him, even as he seems to recognize that England is now a place of mere "getting and spending":

> I do not care. I'll give thrice so much land
> To any well-deserving friend;
> But in the way of bargain, mark ye me,
> I'll cavil on the ninth part of a hair.
> (III.i.133-136)

Hotspur's mad quest after "honor" requires only the merest pretext for a quarrel. Such potentially valuable energy has been cut loose from national purpose, cannot be enlisted in a crusade or French campaign. Hotspur becomes the anarchy that must be destroyed by the powers-that-be — if they are to remain in power. At first, enlisted by the "robber-king," then alienated by him, Hotspur can only be a "criminal." He has, according to his wife, "given my treasuries and my rights of thee/ To thick-eyed musings and cursed melancholy" (II.iii.45-46). He mutters in his sleep "of prisoner's ransoms. . ./ And all the currents of a bloody fight" (II.iii.54-55). His currency with the king totally depreciated, largely through Henry IV's failure to ransom Mortimer, Hotspur's power can only flow against the king. If Richard produced

Henry IV, Henry IV produces Hotspur. While Lady Percy may be amused at his antics, she is correct to call him a "thief" (III.i.232). As anti-sacrament becomes the mode under a king who eradicates his sacredness, robbery must become the way of the world under a king who has seized the crown and then, as Reno says, attempts "to conduct himself as though he were independent of the baronial and popular support he had invoked to gain the crown."11/

Hotspur cannot properly define his role. While he uses the new language of profit, his actions rest on an honor that can have no meaning in a world divorced from contact with intangible principle. Hotspur is like the cartoon character who takes several steps over the edge of a cliff before he recognizes his contravention of the law of gravity, held in momentary abeyance by the liberties of animation. His own leaping and diving metaphors tell us as much (I.iii.199-206). He would "redeem" (I.iii.204) honor, but that cannot be done in a world where "redemption" equates only with some fifteenth-century version of green stamps. "What is that honor?" Falstaff asks. "Air — a trim reckoning!" (V.i.135). Honor is the thin air on which Hotspur treads, and he will be called to a shrewd "reckoning" by the Prince of Wales at Shrewsbury.

Hotspur's speech to his army before Shrewsbury captures the play's suggestion that whatever Hotspur represents, his quality has already been consumed. He brushes aside the letters a messenger brings:

> I cannot read them now —
> O gentlemen, the time of life is short!
> To spend that shortness basely were too long
> If life did ride upon a dial's point,
> Still ending in the arrival of an hour.
>
> (V.ii.81-84)

Henry IV creates Hotspur in one sense, but in forcing Hotspur into disloyalty and rebellion — the attempt to steal already stolen goods — Henry IV destroys the essential Hotspur long before Shrewsbury. But Richard has destroyed the opportunity for man to participate in essence long before Henry IV. Hotspur lives merely "to be spent," because, as Hal explains to his father,

> the time will come
> That I shall make this northern youth exchange
> His glorious deeds for my indignities.
> Percy is but my factor, good my lord,
> To engross up glorious deeds on my behalf;
> And I will call him to so strict account
> That he shall render every glory up,

Yea, even the slightest worship of his time,
Or I will tear the reckoning from his heart.
(III.ii.144-152)

Hal, seeming to "spend that shortness basely," knows, as Hotspur does not, what time it is. Hotspur is merely Hal's banker. Honor is mere currency, as Hal sees it. Hotspur will surrender a "reckoning" to Hal's "strict account," as Hotspur himself says, recognizing the medals and campaign ribbons he surrenders at Shrewsbury:

O Harry, thou hast robbed me of my youth!
I better brook the loss of brittle life
Than those proud titles thou hast won of me.
(V.iv.75-77)

The "honorable spoil" and "gallant prize" (I.i.74-75) that had been Hotspur's, now revert to Hal, by robbery if we accept Hotspur's word. It is, at any rate, the commercial exchange typical of the world of Henry IV. Falstaff is right — to "counterfeit" is "to die," and "to conterfeit dying when a man thereby liveth, is to be no counterfeit, but the true and perfect image of life indeed" (V.iv.113-117). The coining metaphor suggests that true "currency" equates to pragmatic or political success. Falstaff's "catechism" (V.i.141) on honor accurately defines the "religion" of this new world. As Henry IV says before the battle: "Then with the losers let us sympathize,/ For nothing can seem foul to those that win" (V.i.7-8). The bad weather, however, might suggest that there are no real winners in a civil war, only survivors.12/

Henry IV can chastize Worcester for not bearing "true intelligence... like a Christian... Betwixt our armies" (v.v.9-10), but the battle is not endowed on either side with "Christian" premise or purpose. Henry IV's is perhaps the briefest exhortation to an army in all of Shakespeare, but typical of the king's terse reaction to necessity:

Hence, therefore, every leader to his charge;
For, on their answer, will we set on them;
And God befriend us as our cause is just.
(V.i.118-120)

The lines anticipate the rebels' rebuff of Henry IV's terms and mouth a politician's platitudes about God and justice. The cause of the confrontation has nothing to do with God and little to do with any concept of intrinsic justice. Justice is what power says it is. Bolingbroke's seizure of the crown and subsequent neglect of obligations reflect back at him from the conspirators' spokesman, Worcester:

> From this swarm of fair advantages
> You took occasion to be quickly wooed
> To gripe the general sway into your hand;
> Forgot your oath to us at Doncaster;
> And, being fed by us, you used us so
> As that ungentle gull, the cuckoo's bird,
> Useth the sparrow — did oppress our nest...
> Whereby we stand opposed by such means
> As you yourself have forged against yourself
> By unkind usage, dangerous countenance,
> And violation of all faith and troth
> Sworn to us in your younger enterprise.
>
> (V.i.55-71)

Again, as so often in these plays, Worcester recreates that past in the matrix of the present. In the Henry IV plays, Richard's actions seem to fade into a benevolent haze, while Bolingbroke's take on the sharp edges of revisionist interpretations. Having grabbed the "general sway," Bolingbroke would maintain it — obviously — but in securing his own nest, he would destroy others. His dilemma, as Reno suggests, is that he has made the crown "available to anyone... strong enough and ambitious enough — and ruthless enough — to challenge it."13/ Even Worcester admits — alone among the rebels — that the problem began with Richard, "the absent king" and "the injuries of a wanton time" (V.i.49-50). Bolingbroke can only respond to Worcester with an indictment of "surface" that defines his own kingship (cf. York: "all the walls/ With painted imagery..." Richard II: V.ii.15-16). Henry IV accuses Worcester of facing

> the garment of rebellion
> With some fine color that may please the eye...
> And never yet did insurrection want
> Such water colors to impaint his cause,
> Nor moody beggars, starving for a time
> Of pell-mell havoc and confusion
>
> (V.i.74-82)

The "moody frontier of a servant brow" (also Worcester's: I.iii.18) descends to "moody 'beggary'." But the "age of penury" is not wholly of Bolingbroke's making, nor of Worcester's . It is the condition into which England has fallen, and the issues of that condition can be met only with power. The prize to be taken or retained at Shrewsbury is the crown; the metaphors of the contest reflect the solely quantitative debate at Shrewsbury. "We must, " says Hotspur, transmuting battle into coinage, "Have bloody noses and cracked crowns/ And pass them current too"

(II.iii.92-93). For Hotspur, Douglas is a "noble Scot" (a double pun on money), "As not a soldier of this season's stamp/ Should go so general current through the world" (IV.i.1-5).

Hal can tell Falstaff that "thou owest God a death," and Falstaff can respond, "'Tis not due yet: I would be loath to pay him before his day" (V.i.126-128). But even the cost of counterfeiting can be high, as Sir Walter Blunt learns, albeit posthumously: "A fool go with they soul, whither it goes!/ A borrowed title hast thou bought too dear" (V.viii.22-23). Douglas's words point also at Henry IV who, like Claudius, can afford no jester in his court,14/ who has brought only insurrection with his "borrowed title." That "the king hath many marching in his coats " (V.iii.25) suggests not merely that Henry IV is a "player king acting an argument" (cf. II Henry IV: IV.v.197-198), but also that "true" kingship has splintered off into false fragments.15/ When Douglas meets the "true king," the Scot suspects that Henry IV may be "another counterfeit" (V.iv.33). Hal intervenes to make sure that the exchange of kingships (his included) is not consummated: "It is the Prince of Wales that threatens thee,/ Who never promiseth but he means to pay" (V.iv.40-41). Thus does Hal "redeem... [his] lost opinion" (V.iv.46), significantly identifying himself as heir apparent. Again, a commercial exchange; a coin is driven off to preserve a more valuable commodity. Had Henry IV not counterfeited through the alter-egos of Shirley, Stafford, and Blunt, all killed by Douglas, the king might not have escaped, as Falstaff also has: "'twas time to counterfeit, or that hot termagant Scot had paid me scot and lot too" (V.iv.111-112). Falstaff might have had to pay in full the debt he never promised. His reference to parish taxes ("scot and lot") again suggests the state of "religion" in England. Falstaff reminds us that Henry IV's failure to pay has brought on the insurrection, indeed endowed it with its sole rationale.

Blunt has told Hotspur that "you shall have your desires with interest" (IV.iii.49). Percy's reply is that "The king is kind, and well we know the king/ Knows at what time to promise, when to pay" (IV.iii.51-52). But Bolingbroke has counterfeited, bearing on his "face/ This seeming brow of justice" (IV.iii.82-83), and has allowed

> his kinsman March
> (Who is, if every owner were well placed,
> Indeed the king) to be engaged in Wales,
> There without ransom to lie forfeited.
> (IV.iii.93-96)

If Richard violated Bolingbroke's "ownership," Bolingbroke's response has confused the issue of the owner of the crown itself. Matters in England have descended not merely to the "law of property," but to basic confusion about whose property is whose, and from thence to armed conflict. In not paying for Mortimer, Bolingbroke pays in another way.

Hotspur defines the conflict correctly, although with a gambler's overconfidence, as a contest for merely material gains:

> Were it good
> To set the exact wealth of all our states
> All at one cast? To set so rich a main
> On the nice hazard of one doubtful hour?
> It were not good; for therein should we read
> The very bottom and the soul of hope, 16/
> The very list, the very utmost bound
> Of all our fortunes.
>
> (IV.i.45-52)

> I am on fire
> To hear this rich reprisal is so nigh,
> And yet not ours.
>
> (IV.i.116-118)

His corpse will become Falstaff's prize, as Hal necessarily deflects a portion of the "honor" he has won:

> Come, bring your luggage nobly on your back.
> For my part, if a lie will do thee grace,
> I'll gild it with the happiest terms I have.
>
> (V.iv.154-156)

Falstaff follows with his stolen goods "for reward" (V.iv.160), the sequence representing a macabre reduction of the value Gaunt recalled as part of England's recent past. Hal's "lie," of course, cannot confer "grace" on Falstaff, but it, and the other "honorable bounty" (V.iv.26) he gives away, are necessary cancellations of his equally necessary, but premature, redemption. The sequence with Hotspur's corpse represents a complicated reversal of Gad's Hill, and of the roles Hal and Falstaff played there. At Gad's Hill, Falstaff accomplished the robbery only to be robbed again by Hal. At Shrewsbury, Hal robs Hotspur of his youth and is robbed of his prize by Falstaff. In each case the kingship as material is involved. Bardolph says, just before the Gad's Hill robbery, "There's money of the king's coming down the hill; 'tis going to the king's exchequer" (II.ii.53-54).17/

The king closes the play with a couplet appropriately commercial and ironic: "And since this business so fair is done,/ Let us not leave till all our own be won" (V.vi.43-44). Having "won" the crown,18/ Bolingbroke must keep winning it. He is the successful gambler who cannot quit the game he has begun, or, to use his own metaphor, the now respectable thief who cannot escape his criminal past:

I stole all courtesy from heaven,
And dressed myself in such humility
That I did pluck allegiance from men's hearts,
Loud shouts and salutations from their mouths
Even in the presence of the crowned king.

(III.ii.50-54)

Hal has temporarily "redeemed [his] lost opinion" (V.iv.46), 19/ but Bolingbroke has perpetrated a theft "from heaven," and must continue as counterfeit king, even as he played "pretender." "Humility" was the ironic cloak of raw ambition. While Richard began separating England from sacramental premises, Bolingbroke confirms the rift, and has no choice but to continue to confirm it within a world of Realpolitik of which he has been at once victim and creator. Bolingbroke's presence may have been "like a robe pontifical," as he says (III.ii.55), but the proliferation of kingly clothes on the field of Shrewsbury suggests that mere simile, and not the deeper fusion of sacrament, is Henry IV's neccessary mode.

One critic finds the end of I Henry IV a garble: "the aftermath of battle is equally puzzling. Having made a garland of Hotspur's budding honors, the Prince swiftly drops the whole matter and signs over the honors to Falstaff, who strikes us as a rather disproportionately unworthy recipient."20/ But honor is a "mere scutcheon" (V.i.140), as both Falstaff and Hotspur have proved, Falstaff by surviving without it, Hotspur by dying with it. And Hal also knows its value. He is not yet the king who can employ the term when it seems rhetorically appropriate (cf. Henry V: IV.iii.18-33), but still prince-in-waiting. He must submerge again into Falstaff's world, as his gesture in making his victory ludicrous demonstrates. His resubmergence may be reluctant, but it is necessary. Honor now would conflict with the grand strategy Hal has dictated in order to succeed as king as his father cannot.

1.   Hotspur's "politician" is modified by "vile," Lear's by "scurvy" (IV.vi.171).   Hamlet's "politician... would circumvent God" (V.i.78-79). "Politics," of course, was not yet a "profession," so it is not, contrary to popular belief, the world's oldest.   "Politic," in Shakespeare, can mean "well-ordered," as in Beatrice's "so politic a state of evil" (Much Ado About Nothing: V.ii.63), and Parolles's "it is not politic in the commonwealth of nature to preserve virginity" (All's Well That Ends Well: I.i.129-130).   The context of these examples, however, seems to tinge the word "politic" with the irony, as does Malvoilio's, "I will read politic authors" (Twelfth Night: II.v.156).   "Politic" also means "cunning," as the Third Servant suggest in Timon of Athens: "The devil knew what he did when he made man politic" (III.iii.34).   The most frequent meaning of "politic" would seem to be "prudent," as in Mortimer's use of it in I Henry VI (II.v.101), Desdemona's in Othello (III.iii.13), and Goneril's in King Lear (I.iv.323).   "Prudent" would also seem to apply to the contrast in Sonnet 124 between faithless self-interest and the nature of love: "It [i.e. 'love,' but with sexual punning] fears not Policy, that heretic,/ But all alone stands hugely politic" (10-11).   In Twelfth Night, "politician" is used twice, both times for "intriguer" or "schemer" (II.iii.75 and III.ii32).

2.   Bolingbroke's response to banishment is curious and vaguely menacing: "That sun that warms you here shall shine on me,/ And those his golden beams to you here lent/ Shall point on me, and gild my banishment" (I.iii.145-147).   The sun that Richard can claim as his (and does: III.ii.37-53) on the basis of divine kingship, is to Bolingbroke an object merely lent to Richard, something which adorns ("glid") but which is not intrinsic to kingship, as it is in Richard's theory. Bolingbroke's sun "points on" him, as if England were "in reversion his" (I.iv.35).   Later, Richard will see himself as "a mockery king of snow,/ Standing before the sun of Bolingbroke,/   To melt [himself] away in water drops!" (IV.i.259-261).   The recent Royal Shakespeare production made a mockery of that metaphor by inducing a sheeted "snowman" to melt behind York's Speech (V.ii.7-40).   One could not tell whether the carrot nose and coal-lump eyes had wandered in from another play or whether York's speech was being superimposed on a literal rendition of Richard's metaphor, or what. But then, it did not matter.

3.   Again, an ambiguous pronoun, appropriately encompassing Bolingbroke.

4.   I am aware, of course, of the homiletic parellel between God and earthly king, but the equation is by analogy only, as in the "Sermon Against Willful Rebellion":   "And as God himselfe, being of an infinite Majestie, power, and wisedome, ruleth and governeth all things in heaven and earth, as the universall Monarch and onely King and Emperour over

all, as being onely able to take and beare the charge of all: so hath hee constituted, ordeyned, and set earthly Princes over particular kingdomes and Dominions in earth, both for the avoyding of all confusion, which els would be in the world, if it should be without governours, and for the great quiet and benefite of earthly men their subjects, and also that the Princes themselves, in authoritie, power, wisedome, providence, and righteousnesse in governement of people and contreys committed to their charge, should resemble his heavenly governance, as the majestie of heavenly things may by the basenesse of earthly things bee shadowed and resembled. And for that similitude, that is betweene the heavenly Monarchie, and earthly Kingdomes well governed, our Saviour Christ is sundry parables saith, that the Kingdom of heaven is resembled unto a man, a king: and as the name of the king, is very often attributed and given unto God in the holy Scriptures, so doeth God himselfe in the same Scriptures sometime vouchsafe to communicate that his Name with earthly Princes, terming them gods: doubtlesse for that similitude of government which they have or should have, not unlike unto God their King." Cf. Portia in The Merchant of Venice (IV.i.187-201), and Isabella in Measure for Measure (II.ii.75-80, and 110-123).

5. While perceiving "psychology" through "style" can be a tricky business, Mary Olive Thomas makes some telling suggestions about Bolingbroke's rhetoric in this scene: "When Henry speaks of civil war his elaborately counterpointed clauses suggest concentration and concern. When he speaks of Christian warfare, however, his syntax goes slack and the thought diffuses...". Strangely, Ms. Thomas goes on to claim that "if style is an index to imaginative involvement, Henry has directed his thoughts and feelings away from England." Being an often laconic literalist, Bolingbroke would seem to have his "thoughts" where his "concentration and concern" is. Ms. Thomas goes on to suggest that "Henry's motive is that of the politic ruler who, as Machiavelli advised, employs religion in the service of policy." "The Elevation of Hal in I Henry IV," Studies in the Literary Imagination V #1 (April, 1972), 83.

6. Prince John comments on the way the plays unfold their meanings: "You are too shallow, Hastings, much too shallow,/ To sound the bottom of the after-times" (II Henry IV: IV.ii.50-51). What is true for the characters is true for the audience. We discover what Hastings discovers — that the immediate after-time includes his execution. We should note, however, that Hastings, like Carlisle before him, has predicted the Wars of the Roses. John's words point ahead, of course, to the rejection of Falstaff, in the company of the "Justice" who was to be "my Lord Shallow," as endowed by "fortune's steward," Falstaff (II Henry IV: V.iii.134-135). H. Ax notes that "the reason why the holy purpose to Jerusalem could not be performed was already existent in the king's knowledge before he uttered his very first words, and these therefore cease to appear any longer sincere." Quoted in the Variorum Henry the Fourth, Part I, ed. S.B. Hemingway (Philadelphia and London, 1936), p. 23n.

7. Ventidius recognizes the premises under which he fights. The "politic" subordinant, having defeated the Parthians for the first time, will "humbly signify what in [Antony's] name,/ That magical word of war, we have effected" (Antony and Cleopatra: III.i.29-30). Antony is no feudal monarch.

8. Reno, From Sacrament to Ceremony, p. 108.

9. Reno, From Sacrament to Ceremony, p. 231.

10. Reno, From Sacrament to Ceremony, pp. 126-127.

11. Reno, From Sacrament to Ceremony, p. 111.

12. Although the same meteorological conditions pertain before Bosworth Field (Richard III: V.iii.278-288). Since Richard III can no longer see his shadow in the sun, however, the gray skies portend alone the fall of Richard.

13. Reno, From Sacrament to Ceremony, pp. 89-90.

14. Hal commands "Peace, chewet, peace!" (V.i.29) to a jesting Falstaff, who is later admonished for lugging sack onto so vital a battlefield ("What, is it a time to jest and dally now?": V.iii.57) as Shrewsbury. Henry V's rejection of Falstaff suggests that the new king does not wish the services of a jester: "How ill white hairs become a fool and jester" — we do not see a younger jester replace the old, nor is the old allowed to launch a joke: "Reply not to me with a fool-born jest" (II Henry IV: V.v.49 and 55). Richard III, of course, has no fool, but one consequence of not allowing an external alter-ego is that the truth-sayer emerges from within Richard, precisely as a "Fool" (V.iii.193).

15. Although Henry's practice at Shrewsbury seems to have been common. Cf. Richard III, V.v. Richmond does the same thing at Bosworth Field.

16. The line anticipates John of Lancaster's "You are too shallow, Hastings, much too shallow,/ To sound the bottom of the aftertimes" (II Henry IV: IV.ii.50-51) and Falstaff's "I do see the bottom of Justice Shallow" (III.ii.306-307).

17. I believe that Norman Rabkin is more accurate than Sherman Hawkins on Hal's iconographic modelling at Shrewsbury. Hawkins suggests that "As [Hal] stands at last upright between the prostrate bodies of his rivals, those alternate and extreme possibilities of the self, he is also an emblem of triumphant virtue with its opposed vices fallen at his feet." "Virtue and Kingship in Shakespeare's Henry IV," English Literary Renaissance 5 (1975), 313-343. Rabkin sees Hal as far less of a character in an allegory or morality play: "Hal's famous schematic

stance between the appropriately dead Hotspur and a Falstaff equally appropriately feigning death indicates not so much a compromise between their incompatible values as the difference between Hal's ability to thrive in a world of process by employing the time as an instrument and Hotspur's and Falstaff's oddly similar unwillingness to do so." "Rabbits, Ducks, and Henry V," SQ 28 #3 (Summer, 1977). 281. John F. Sisk argues that Hotspur surrenders policy for honor, Falstaff honor for policy, but that Hal represents a more comprehensive eutrapelia — neither over-earnestness nor frivolousness. "Prince Hal and the Specialist," SQ 28 #4 (Autumn, 1977), 523.

18. Cf. Hal's "You won it, wore it, kept it, gave it me": Part II: IV.v.221, where "possession" (II: IV.v.222) can be in physical terms only.

19. In the Welles film, Falstaff's heroic pose worked. Henry IV (played by Sir John Gielgud) was disgusted that the likes of Falstaff had fought honorably and well, and was therefore the more outraged at his scapegrace son. In the film, Hal's strategy worked perfectly; he achieved his pragmatic and potentially contradictory goals of defeating Hotspur and avoiding credit for the deed.

20. Anthony La Branche, "Private and Public Virtue in I Henry IV, Shakespeare Quarterly, XVII (Autumn, 1966), 380.

IV

Prince Hal's England: I Henry IV

While the career of Henry IV can be isolated politically from much of the Prince Hal - Falstaff subplot, since Hal, except upon emergent occasions, absents himself from the court, the world of Windsor cannot be viewed dramatically in isolation from that of Eastcheap. For purposes of organization and emphasis, I have done just that, and I confess to a distortion of the way Shakespeare's play unfolds. Hal's understanding and organizing of his world is as important dramatically to the two parts of Henry IV as is the king's political struggle.

The political world of Henry IV consists of broken contracts, duplicity, politic calculation and miscalculation, prizetaking and robbery, angry parley, and pitched combat. Over it all presides a player - king who would be otherwise. The "underworld" of the play reveals the same characteristics, though depicted in petty, often burlesque and parodic, rather than explicitly monarchical terms. Its master, however, is a player - prince who has chosen his part consciously, and who discerns a positive monarchical issue in his role. Bolingbroke strives to be a strong king and fails in the exercise of anything but strength, a result partly inevitable, partly of his own making. Hal appears to ignore his position as heir apparent, but, in doing so, prepares to become a strong king who will at least appear to exercise more than mere strength. The subplot is marked by more calculation than the main plot; in the former, Hal, although he may lose in skirmishes with Falstaff, asserts an ultimate control his father cannot achieve, no matter how successful Henry IV may be in responding to insurrection and in maintaining the unity of "modern England."

Our entrance into Hal's world in Richard II (V.iii.1-12) has suggested his apparent defiance of the ceremonial and legal trappings of kingship his father would perpetuate. Time, in Hal's world, seems to be measured only by gluttony and lust:

> What a devil hast thou to do with the time of the
> day? Unless hours were cups of sack, and minutes
> capons, and clocks the tongues of bawds, and dials
> the signs of leaping houses, and the blessed sun
> himself a fair hot wench in flame-colored taffeta,
> I see no reason why thou shouldst be so superfluous
> to demand the time of the day.
>
> (I Henry IV: I.ii.6-12)

While Hal's speech is an indictment of Falstaff, we discover the prince in the very world of which his father has complained, the reality of which Percy has confirmed in Richard II. The Prince of Wales apparently accepts the valuation Richard and Bolingbroke have cooperated to place on England, where, to say the least, time seems out of joint, where "men of good government... sleep upon benches after noon," but "take purses... by the moon" (I.ii.4.14.27-28). But both "natural" and "man-made" laws pertain to such "thieves," as Hal says, placing Falstaff's willful perversion of "societal value" back into a conventional frame:

> for the fortune of us that are the moon's
> men doth ebb and flow like the sea being governed
> as the sea is by the moon. As, for proof now: a
> purse of gold most resolutely snatched on Monday
> night and most dissolutely spent on Tuesday
> morning; got with swearing "Lay by," and spent
> with crying "Bring in"; now in as low an ebb as
> the foot of the ladder, and by and by in as high a
> flow as the ridge of the gallows.
>   (I.ii.31-39)

Immediately, we sense Hal's role in all of this. Regardless of his pose and of the considerable wit of his retort, he represents "law and order." He can claim, however, to be the spendthrift prince:

Falstaff.   Well, thou has called her [the Hostess] to a reckoning many a time and oft.

Prince.   Did I ever call for thee to pay thy part?

Falstaff.   No; I'll give thee thy due, thou hast paid all there.

Prince.   Yea, and elsewhere, so far as my coin would stretch; and where it would not, I have used my credit.
                                        (I.ii.49-55)

Falstaff asks Hal whether there will "be gallows standing in England when thou are king?" (I.ii.58-59). Reno suggests that Falstaff means that "should Hal... prove hard on thieves, he would be rejecting his inheritance,"1/ Falstaff driving a shrewd thrust at Henry IV. And this suggestion is valid, as Falstaff has already implied: "God save thy grace — majesty I should say, for grace thou wilt have none" (I.ii.17-18). While Falstaff plays with the idea of a prayer before a meal ("prologue to an egg and butter": I.ii.21), the lines suggest the deeper truth that Henry V's kingship, while it may be "majestic," will not partake of "grace," which is no longer communicated with the succession. Falstaff senses profit in the kingship of Henry V, not as a judge, or as a courtier ("For obtaining of suits": I.ii.71), but as a hangman, who inherits the clothes of his victims and therefore "hath no lean wardrobe" (I.ii.73). Falstaff believes, as he will tell us, that he "will turn diseases to commodity" (II Henry IV: I.ii.251). Here he wishes he knew "where a commodity of good names were to be bought" (I Henry IV: I.ii.83-84). Names are a commercial entity, ushered in, we infer, by the likes of "this base man," "all too base," as Aumerle calls Bagot (Richard II: IV.i.20.28).2/ Falstaff, the counterfeit at Shrewsbury who claimed victory over Hotspur, will call himself "Sir John with all Europe" (II Henry IV: II.ii.133).

The opening scene of Hal's world suggests not merely a reversal of normal "time" — however the play will come to define time — but a reversal of conventional "value" as well, although, admittedly, the question of value per se has become equivocal. Falstaff claims Hal has corrupted him and that he will be "damned for never a king's son in Christendom" (I.ii.98). As soon as Hal suggests taking a purse, however, Falstaff replies, "An I do not, call me a villain" (I.ii.102), to which Hal responds, "I see a good amendment of life in thee — from praying to purse-taking" (I.ii.103-104).3/ Falstaff perverts the Puritan ethic to his own use: "Why, Hal, 'tis my vocation, Hal. 'Tis no sin for a man to labor in his vocation" (I.ii.105-106). The bandying reiterates lightly the debasement of religious terms, employed here to express normally irreligious activities like purse-taking. Poins pursues the theme, suggesting that Falstaff has made as paltry a bargain as did Dr. John Faustus:

> What says Sir John Sack and Sugar? Jack, how
> agrees the devil and thee about thy soul, that,
> thou soldest him on Good Friday last for a cup
> of Madeira and cold capon's leg?
>
> (I.ii.114-117)4/

The allusion to Good Friday suggests betrayal, of course, and Falstaff's violation of the spirit of a day of atonement and fasting. Falstaff has attributed his fall to Hal:

> Thou hast done much harm upon me Hal — God
> forgive thee for it! Before I knew thee, Hal, I
> knew nothing; and now am I, if a man should speak
> truly, little better than one of the wicked.
>
> (I.ii.92-96)

Richard II was a parody of Christ, but his "martyrdom" carried with it a concept of kingship that made his demonstration in IV.i devastatingly effective. The parody here is broader, though each parody echoes the fundamental inversion of values represented by Good Friday, on which, according to the Collect for Good Friday, "our Lord Jesus Christ was contented to be betrayed, and given up into the hands of wicked men." The Second Collect for Good Friday underlines the irony Falstaff consciously develops; it hopes that "all estates of men in thy holy congregation... every member of the same in his vocation and ministrie, may truely and godly serve thee."

While the first tavern scene represents a burlesquing of religious values, unlike the more profound farewell to sacrament bade by Richard, it suggests again what has happened to "value" in England. Even damnation — probably more of an issue for the Sixteeenth Century because of the Reformation emphasis on the "inward man" and the specific Puritan rejection of good works, a subject to be employed dramatically in Hamlet, Othello, and Macbeth — is here an evoker of wit:

> Prince.   Sir John stands to his word, the devil
> shall have his bargain; for he was
> never yet a breaker of proverbs. He
> will give the devil his due.
>
> Poins.   Then art thou damned for keeping thy
> word with the devil.
>
> Prince.   Else he had been damned for cozening the
> devil.
>   (I.ii.118-124)

Richard's dying words ("Mount, mount, my soul; thy seat is up on high": V.v.111), Exton's sudden sense "that this deed is chronicled in hell" (V.v.116), and Bolingbroke's penitent final speech seem distant anachronisms. The talk in I Henry IV, in the taverns at least, is profane, and , in its specifically Puritan vocabulary, "Elizabethan." Falstaff can play the theme of damnation against Bardolph's nose, finding in its luminosity an economy which spares a robber's expense and drunkard's cost in moving from pub to pub:

> I make as good use of it as many a man doth
> of a death's-head or a memento mori. I never see
> thy face but I think upon hellfire and Dives that
> lived in purple; for there he is in his robes,
> burning, burning. If thou wert any way given to
> virtue, I would swear by thy face; my oath should
> be "By this fire, that's God's angel." But thou
> art altogether given over, and wert indeed, but
> for the light in thy face, the son of utter dark-
> ness. When thou ran'st up Gad's Hill in the night
> to catch my horse, if I did not think thou hadst

been an ignis fatuus or a ball of wildfire, there's
no purchase in money. O, thou art a perpetual
triumph, an everlasting bonfire-light! Thou hast
saved me a thousand marks in links and torches,
walking with thee in the night betwixt tavern and
tavern; but the sack that thou hast drunk me would
have bought me lights as good cheap at the dearest
chandler's in Europe. I have maintained that sala-
mander of yours with fire any time this two and
thirty years. God reward me for it!

(III.iii.31-51)<u>5</u>/

Falstaff will later profit by forming a platoon composed of "slaves as
ragged as Lazarus in his painted cloth" (IV.ii.25-26), but Falstaff will not
link himself to Dives.

The motive of the tavern world, as in the "royal world," is
profit: "There are pilgrims going to Canterbury with rich offerings, and
traders riding to London with fat purses" (I.ii.126-128). These pilgrims,
unlike Chaucer's, seeking "the holy blissful martyr," are merely the
agents bringing profits to thieves. Their pilgrimage is to be interrupted,
like Bolingbroke's crusade, by those who, like Hotspur, "hear this rich
reprisal is so nigh" (IV.i.117). The Gad's Hill robbery, we learn, is of
"money of the king's... going to the king's exchequer" (II.ii.53-54). The
robbers have received more accurate information about the loot,
apparently from the Chamberlain, who knows that the party includes "a
kind of auditor [revenue officer], one that hath an abundance of charge,
too..." (II.i.59-60). The robbery, then, represents on a smaller scale
precisely what Hotspur and his confederates would perpetrate. The
character Gadshill's commentary applies to both "worlds" of the play, his
punning suggesting the profound transition England has made since the
times remembered by Gaunt:

> I lie, for they pray continually to their
saint, the commonwealth, or rather not pray to
her, but prey on her, for they ride up and down
on her and make her their boots... We steal as
in a castle, cocksure.

(II.i.81-88)

"Sainthood" has been reduced to the tangibility of a mere political
entity, itself further debased by heedless exploitation. Henry IV, himself
having "stolen a castle," has tendered thieves the security of
battlements and drawbridges, since England itself is a theft. Not
engaging in robbery becomes, for Poins, a hanging offense: "If you will
not, tarry at home and be hanged" (I.ii.132-133).<u>6</u>/ "We may do it as

secure as sleep," Poins argues (I.ii.131), and Falstaff pursues the attack, directing it at the prince who will not be "a thief... by my faith" (I.ii.138):

> There's neither honesty, manhood, nor good
> fellowship in thee, nor thou com'st not of the
> blood royal if thou darest not stand for ten
> shillings.
>
> (I.ii.139-140)

The "blood royal" is no longer that quasi-sacramental liquor spilled in Gloucester's murder, then in Richard's (V.v.110.112-113; V.vi.50). It is the blood of a thief. "Royal," like "crown," now equates to coinage; a "royal" being worth precisely the "ten shillings" Falstaff mentions. Falstaff at once inverts and reflects the "reality" of the world of Henry IV, which incorporates Eastcheap, by delivering to Hal a parody of Puritan sermon:

> Well, God give thee the spirit of persuasion
> and him the ears of profiting, that what thou
> speakest may move and what he hears may be be-
> lieved, that the true prince may (for recreation
> sake) prove a false thief; for the poor abuses of
> the time want countenance.
>
> (I.ii.151-156)

Upon Falstaff's exit, however, we learn that the scene is enclosed by the more comprehensive plan Poins outlines to Hal: "when they have the booty, if you I do not rob them, cut this head from off my shoulders" (I.ii.164-165).

And when Poins leaves, we learn that the robbery, and the trap laid for the robbers, are merely part of a larger strategy, calculated by the prince:

> I know you all, and will awhile uphold
> The unyoked humor of your idleness.
> Yet herein will I imitate the sun,
> Who doth permit the base contagious clouds
> To smother up his beauty from the world,
> That, when he pleases again to be himself,
> Being wanted, he may be more wond'red at
> By breaking through the foul and ugly mists
> Of vapors that did seem to strangle him.
> If all the year were playing holidays,
> To sport would be as tedious as to work;
> But when they seldom come, they wished-for come,

And nothing pleaseth but rare accidents.
So when this loose behavior I throw off
And pay the debt I never promised,
By so much shall I falsify men's hopes;
And, like bright metal on a sullen ground,
My reformation, glitt'ring o'er my fault,
Shall show more goodly and attract more eyes
Than that which hath no foil to set it off.
I'll so offend to make offense a skill,
Redeeming time when men think least I will.
(I.ii.191-214)7/

Here is Hal's "faith" — a faith in political expendiency, a purely machiavellian strategy emerging from an open-eyed awareness of the pragmatic and material calculus of power now applicable in England. That "baseness" introduced to England by Richard and confirmed by Bolingbroke has the utilitarian value of "foil." Hal will "imitate" the sun much as Falstaff says he will: "Shall the blessed sun of heaven prove a micher and eat blackberries?" (II.iv.412-414), pretending that "the blessed sun himself" is no more to him than "a fair hot wench in flame-colored taffeta" (I.ii.9-10). He will allow "base contagious clouds" to seem to "smother up his beauty from the world," for the sake of a political "profit" that depends on the seamy contrast the tavern world will provide to kingship. The sun as "concept" is itself useful in a political _mimesis_ that can no longer partake of the truth of Richard's appearing

As doth the blushing discontented sun
From out the fiery portal of the East,
When he perceives the envious clouds are bent
To dim his glory, and to stain the track,
Of his bright passage to the Orient.
(Richard II: III.iii.61-66)

While Bolingbroke's words enter a sequence in which Richard's "glory" is to become "a shooting star," falling "to the base earth from the firmament" (II.iii.19-20), Richard inherited the intrinsic links with the supernature that Gaunt celebrated for England, however much Richard encouraged the envious clouds to extinguish his glory, and regardless of his willful drive to become "Phaethon." Hal knows that the holy metaphor is sundered, that he will inherit a dubious throne, and, that while he cannot control the duration of his waiting to become king, he can manage that time by consciously gathering the stain of dishonor around his "majesty." In a world where value itself has virtually lost its meaning, he will assert "value" only by seeming to become absolutely debased. His necessary emergence at Shrewsbury predicts the ultimate impact of his strategy, as Vernon describes him to the envious ears of

Hotspur: "As full of spirit as the month of May/ And gorgeous as the sun at midsummer" (I Henry IV: IV.i.100-101). Hal's metaphor is not that of his father, who, "like a comet... was wond'red at" (III.ii.47). Hal, "being wanted" will "be more wond'red at" (I.ii.198), not like a comet. The comet is a sign of cosmic disorder: "the meteors of a troubled heaven," as Bolingbroke has also said (I.i.10), or the "exhaled meteor,/ A prodigy of fear, and a protent/ Of broached mischief to the unborn times" (V.i.19-21).7/ The disorder Bolingbroke has encouraged, with the cooperation of the "shooting star," Richard, reflects back at Henry IV within the vehicle of his own metaphor of power. Worcester will not "move in that obedient orb again/ Where [he] did give a fair and natural light" (V.i.17-18). While "cosmic harmony" does not reflect its disruption through natural disorder in the play, as it will in Macbeth, the concept of discord is captured in images only, images that define Bolingbroke as completely as they do those who oppose him. That no great storm rages over England suggests that Shakespeare is dealing with historical dilemmas rather than with the metaphysics of cosmic evil, that the career of Henry IV represents "an inextricable tangle of right and unright," to use Bradley's useful phrase about Richard II.8/ Even if God had not been virtually dismissed by Richard and were somehow brooding over the world of these plays, He could manifest himself only in a storm as ambiguous as that in King Lear or in weather as equivocal as that on the morning of Shrewsbury. After Richard's fall, most references to the cosmos in these plays are political rhetoric.

Hal's behavior, Bolingbroke suggests, can "Afford no extraordinary gaze,/ Such as is bent on sunlike majesty/ When it shines seldom in admiring eyes" (III.ii.78-80). Even for Bolingbroke, kingship and the sun from only a simile. But Bolingbroke does not account for Hal's not yet being a king. Nor can Henry IV understand that Hal's association with the court of a "robber-king" would, as Falstaff has implied, tarnish rather than enhance his "image." Hal will seem to take the world as its basest valuation, the better to control a situation that cannot be reversed. Like his father, Hal will achieve a kind of invisibility. He, too, understands the value of "seldom": "But when they seldom come, they wished-for come" (I.ii.203). By being too much seen, Hal will be seen as something other than what he is, and will "attract more eyes" than his father did, when Hal pleases "again to be himself." Bolingbroke also contrived to seem other than what he was, although he did not fool Richard (Richard II: I.iv.). Bolingbroke's rationed appearances seemed to deny his ambition (III.ii.39-54), even as Hal's over-exposure veils his serious intent. Hal transforms his father's strategy into a different tactic, but the goal of popular support remains the same.9/

Hal will "pay the debt he never promised" (I.ii.206) in exchange for all debts he has incurred in Eastcheap, the latter "reckonings" a counterfeit which "falsi[fies] men's hopes" (I.ii.208) and makes possible the temporary redemption of time-political, the only "real time" there is in England. Hal permits what his father warns against. Men will look at Hal as Bolingbroke claims they looked at Richard. They "rather drowsed and hung their eyelids down/ Slept in his face, and rend'red such aspect/ As cloudy men use to their adversaries" (III.ii.81-83). While Richard, as king, should hardly have encouraged such response, Hal is not king yet. Bolingbroke, of course, does not comprehend that Hal controls the clouds by his very knowledge of who and what they are, and will wave them away when the time is right, on a day of which Henry IV receives a glimpse at Shrewsbury. While Bolingbroke had a plan, his literal mind cannot penetrate Hal's strategy.10/ Hal explicitly embraces the advice Gaunt gave to Bolingbroke:

> The sullen passage of thy weary steps
> Esteem as foil wherein thou art to set
> The precious jewel of thy home return.
>
> (Richard II: I.iii.264-266)

"Before God, I am exceeding weary," he will say (II Henry IV: II.ii.1), during his self-imposed exile in Eastcheap. While England will never again be "This precious stone set in the silver sea" (Richard II: II.i.46), Hal has worked out an effective plan for the imitation of a king's value, and will thus allow England to borrow during his reign a reflected and premeditated "glory." Alone among the characters of this play, Hal knows what time it is — when to promise and when to pay, when a commodity of good names can be bought — though he will quickly surrender the titles he robs from Hotspur — and how to turn seeming diseases to actual commodity. His chief "foil," Falstaff, will be his "tutor," if not the "feeder of [his] riots." Hal has far more to learn in Eastcheap than in the emergency-ridden and deeply tainted court of his "other father," Henry IV.

The robbery at Gad's Hill predicts the battle of Shrewsbury. Falstaff complains about "thieves [that] cannot be true to one another" (II.ii.27-28), and shouts "Give me my horse, you rogues! Give me my horse and be hanged !" (II.ii.29-30). He objects to walking, even for profit:

> Sblood, I'll not bear mine own flesh so far
> afoot again for all the coin in thy father's ex-
> chequer. What a plague mean ye to colt [i.e.
> trick] me thus?
>
> (II.ii.35-37)

In a play which projects double meanings, both verbally and strategically, Hal responds, "thou liest... thou art not colted, thou are uncolted" (II.ii.38-39). Hal will "uncolt" Falstaff again before Shrewsbury:

Prince.	I have procured thee, Jack, a charge of foot.
Falstaff.	I would it had been of horse. Where shall I find one that can steal well? O for a fine thief [i.e. horse thief, I assume] of the two and twenty thereabouts! I am heinously unprovided.

(III.iii.194-198)

Just before this colloquy, Falstaff has asked Hal to "Rob me the exchequer the first thing thou doest" (III.iii.191-192), and at Shrewsbury, again, on foot, Falstaff will lumber under the corpse of Hotspur, "for reward" (V.ii.160) from the king's exchequer, the crown making for Falstaff a consistent equation with money. Hal will be content at Shrewsbury to have removed the anarchic energy of Hotspur, achieving the political goal but avoiding the "credit," indeed debasing his feat by attributing it to Falstaff. But Falstaff, pressing the debasement of England to the exteme that Hal has pretended to represent from his introduction in Richard II onward, will be the ultimate dangerous energy that Henry V — not Hal — must excise from England.

Falstaff's sudden fear at Gad's Hill — "Zounds, will they not rob us?" (II.ii.64) — does not occur to Hotspur before Shrewsbury. Yet each is robbed. The barons who divide the map of England in advance (III.i) are thwarted by Hal's defeat of Hotspur, the "robbery of youth." The robbers, Falstaff, Gadshill, Bardolph, and Peto, are driven off by Hal and Poins, even as the robbers divide the "booty" (II.ii.105.s.d.). Hal will say after this re-robbery, that "The thieves are all scattered, and possessed with fear so strongly that they dare not meet each other" (II.ii.108-109). After Shrewsbury, Hal will describe Douglas, "The noble Scot" who, "when he saw/ The fortune of the day quite turned from him.../ Upon the foot of fear, fled with the rest" (V.iv.17-20), an action paralleling Falstaff's: "They all run away, and Falstaff, after a blow or two, runs away too" (II.ii.105. s.d.). While Hotspur's force has dwindled as he approaches battle, helping assure his defeat by swelling his lust for honor,11/ the forces facing Falstaff grow in his epic account, allowing him a self-conscious and verbal "victory." Falstaff admits that he was defeated by the mere appearance of the "heir apparent" (II.iv.272), his action evidence of absolute loyalty. Hotspur will die at the hands of a prince protecting his right, the death itself predicting what will happen to Falstaff when "King Hal" becomes an oxymoron. The complex mosaics of Gad's Hill, Shrewsbury, and Westminster (Part II: V.v) contain many similar pieces.

In each instance, Hal's stance is that of "law and order." At Shrewsbury, he fights on the side of a de facto kingship that had promised redress to the rebels "with interest" (IV.iii.49). The interest accrues to Hal, who rapidly transfers it to Falstaff. The Gad's Hill booty is returned by the prince: "The money shall be paid back again with advantage" (II.iv.552),12/ and later, the transaction completed, "The money is paid back again" (III.iii.186). In each case, Hal guards the king's exchequer, the inheritance he will confirm in banishing Falstaff outside Westminster. That quantity is all that remains to be retained is the inevitable consequence of Richard's actions, particularly his act of confiscation and Bolingbroke's response to it, a cause-and-effect sequence that ratifies the descent of England from sacramental to commercial premises. After his coronation, Henry V will be "law and order," as his speech to Falstaff and to England makes clear.

Indebtedness, robbery, promises to pay and failures to pay, devaluation — commodity — are the measurements of Bolingbroke's kingdom. The Prince Hal sub-plot provides so many reflections of the political main-plot, that they can scarcely be itemized. That there is a sub-plot, opening out into the stinking streets, taverns, and brothels of an actual London, is itself significant; it is the world of "real people" ("draymen," Richard II: I.iv.28.31.32), that Bolingbroke, however reluctantly, has invited into the purview of his kingdom. It is the world we glimpse in Richard — not through allegorical Gardeners — but through the brief visit of Richard's loyal groom, where the inversion of rank ("Thanks noble peer!" and "Tell me, gentle friend": Richard II: V.v.67 and 81) testify to the shift from hierarchical and inherited values to a more egalitarian and self-initiated politics.13/

In I Henry IV, England suffers from inflation, a devaluation of even monetary value: "Poor [Robin Ostler] never joyed since the price of oats rose; it was the death of him" (II.i.12-13). Part of Falstaff's company will include those who survived the economic - physical death of poor Robin: "Ostlers trade-fall'n" (IV.ii.29-30). War — civil war — is hardly "a boost to the economy": "Worcester is stol'n away tonight," says Falstaff, "you may buy land now as cheap as stinking mack'rel"14/ (II.iv.361-363). Hal responds in kind to this theory of economics, which would make a bargain of what loses its value in time, particularly in time of civil war, when men go off to die: "Why then, it is like, if there come a hot June, and this civil buffeting hold, we shall buy maidenheads as they buy hobnails, by the hundreds" (II.iv.364-366). The knightly contests at Oxford, which Hal promised to win wearing a glove "from the commonest creature" (Richard II: V.iii.17),15/ have descended to become England itself. Hal can emerge from an England of humorous idleness and civil buffeting because he recognizes it for what it is. A man unillusioned — as opposed to disillusioned — will be in a position to create illusions around a court whose value is expressed in the props of "a play extempore" (II.iv.282), which is the status Richard wished on the crown with the murder of Gloucester:

> Falstaff. This chair shall be my state, this dag-
> ger my scepter, and this cushion my crown.

```
Prince.          Thy state is taken for a joined stool,
                 thy golden scepter for a leaden dagger,
                 and thy precious rich crown for a piti-
                 ful bald crown.
                                         (II.iv.380-385)
```

While the objects at Westminster and Windsor have more "market value,"
they _are_ as at Eastcheap, mere objects without intangible signification,
props in the extemporaneous reign of Henry IV.   Even this early,
however, Prince Hal is learning how to make the objects seem like more
than they are: "Dost thou speak like a king?" he demands of Falstaff
(II.iv.438).   Hal knows that it is speaking _like_ a king, achieving a
convincing similitude of monarchy, that counts in a world devoid of
Gaunt's values.

Falstaff can instruct Hal "Never [to] call a true piece of gold a
counterfeit" (II.iv.496-497), not wishing to be turned over to the sheriff
and the watch at the door.   "Thou are essentially made without seeming
so" (II.iv.497-498), Falstaff continues, imputing the same essence to Hal
as to himself.   But the metaphor of coinage is itself suspect in its sheer
tangibility, and Falstaff misconstrues Hal, who is seeming _not_ to be a
prince the better to seem a king.   Actually, Hal is learning the art of
counterfeiting from Falstaff, who can stimulate Hotspur (" A plague of
all cowards, I say": II.iv.115), Henry IV ("Shall the son of England prove
a thief and take purses?": II.iv.414-415), Hal ("My lord, the man I know":
II.iv.469)16/ and, if darkness serve, a slender young man ("They hate us
youth," "young men must live":   II.ii.86.92-93) robbing fat men
("Baconfed knaves!":   "gorbellied knaves," and "fat chuffs": II.ii.85-
86.90.91), and, of course, a corpse to avoid the debt ("death") that is "not
due yet" (V.i.126).   When the Hostess announces that "a nobleman of the
court" would speak with Hal (II.iv.290-291), Hal flips her a coin: "Give
him as much as will make him a royal man, and send him back again"
(II.iv.293-294).   Hal enhances the man's "value" by something less than
four shillings, a royal being worth ten shillings, a noble six (shillings) and
eight (pence).   The metaphor is money, not royalty or nobility, but Hal's
increasing the value predicts the "glittering reformation" (I.ii.210) he
plans, an augmentation which can be expressed only in the material
terms reflective of "value"in England.

Hal's cruel catechism of Francis, however, reveals another
intrinsic quality, inarticulate beneath the commercial ethic, a quality
that will respond, when the time is right, to an effective imitation of
kingship. Hal gives Poins a "pennyworth of sugar" (II.iv.23) that Francis
has given the prince. Francis has learned only the new language of
England: he is "one that never spake other English in his life than 'Eight
shillings and sixpence'" (II.iv.24-26). "His industry is upstairs and
downstairs, his eloquence the parcel of a reckoning" (II.iv.101-103). Hal

asks Francis whether he would dare "be so valiant as to play the coward with thy indenture and show it a fair pair of heels and run from it?" (II.iv.47-49).17/ The breaking of such a contract would be analogous on the level of apprenticeship to the sundering of feudal contracts by both Richard and Bolingbroke. If Hal is administering a loyalty test, however, Francis passes it:

> Prince. For the sugar thou gavest me — 'twas a
>   pennyworth, was it not?
>
> Francis. O Lord! I would it had been two!
>   (II.iv.60-61)

Hal promises Francis "a thousand pound for it" (II.iv.62), a debt he may promise but cannot mean to pay, then asks the bewildered drawer whether he will "rob this leathern-jerkin, crystal-button, not-pated, agate-ring, puke-stocking, caddis-garter, smooth-tongue, Spanish-pouch?" (II.iv.70-72). Francis does not recognize Hal's description of the petit-bourgeois inn-keeper: "O Lord, sir, who do you mean?" (II.iv.73). Francis, it would seem, will neither run from his indenture nor rob his master.   Whatever Hal is doing with Francis — and even Poins is confused (II.iv.91-93) — Hal has proved that "your brown bastard is your only drink" (II.iv.74-75), that is, that Francis must remain a tapster. With Poins as his uncomprehending accomplice, Hal plays a manipulative game for his own amusement, "to drive away the time till Falstaff come" (II.iv.28-29), a game whose terms again are those of commerce, but one that reveals in Francis a loyal heart with which Hal merely toys.   We perceive perhaps that the subject of the approaching game, Falstaff, will end with "His heart... fracted and corroborate" (Henry V: II.i.125). but we perceive as well the latent potentiality of this prince to sway the hearts of his countrymen as king.   There is a spirit in England that Hal can "command... when [he is] King of England" (III.iv.13-14). That command can only be asserted, however, if Hal learns "how to handle" Falstaff (II Henry IV: II.iv.318).

But before that moment can come, Hal must also deal with Hotspur:

> I am not yet of Percy's mind, the Hotspur of
> the north; he that kills me some six or seven dozen
> of Scots at a breakfast, washes his hands, and says
> to his wife, "Fie upon this quiet life! I want
> work." "O my sweet Harry," says she, "how many hast
> thou killed today?" "Give my roan horse a drench,"
> says he, and answers "Some fourteen," an hour af-
> ter, "a trifle, a trifle."18/
>   (II.iv.103-110)

Hal knows them both — Hotspur and Falstaff — and predicts in his parody of Hotspur the very inflation of opponents Falstaff soon introduces. Hal's victory over Hotspur will be assisted by the diminution of Percy's force. One of Hotspur's other errors, of course, will be to underestimate his opponent. While Hal may seem to Hotspur "so wild a liberty" (V.ii.71), we see him from the first engaged in manipulations of Falstaff, efforts that usually fail, but that sharpen the skills Hal will need when he "suddenly" becomes Henry V. In one sense, of course, his reign arrives with little notice, but in another sense he has been preparing for it since the first mention of him in Richard II.

The world Henry V will have to control is embodied in Falstaff, a "globe of sinful continents" (II Henry IV: II.iv.291), whose financial situation can be enhanced only by lies, evasions, and abuse of office. While Hal calls those who have defamed him to his father "smiling pickthanks and base newsmongers" (III.ii.25) — a bit sanctimonious perhaps, in view of the public record Hal has promoted — the prince himself picks Falstaff's pocket, and pulls forth a tavern reckoning whose largest item is five and eight for two gallons of sack (II.iv.542). Falstaff's values, at least, are revealed clearly: "O monstrous! But one halfpenny worth of bread to this intolerable deal of sack!" (II.iv.545-546). Hal can probe "beneath the surface" of England and find merely confirmation of what it shows on the surface:19/

> If there were anything in thy pocket but
> tavern reckonings, memorandums of bawdy houses, and
> one poor pennyworth of sugar candy to make thee
> long-winded — if thy pocket were enriched with any
> other injuries than these, I am a villain.
>   (III.iii.165-170)

Falstaff's evasion of his debt to the Hostess will rest on his demand that she discover "who picked my pockets" (III.iii.57). She responds with perfect naivete: "Do you think I keep thieves in my house?" (III.iii.59), and turns his "pick" against him: "You owe me money, Sir John, and now you pick a quarrel to beguile me of it. I bought you a dozen shirts to your back" (III.iii.70-72). Falstaff's ragged crew, of course, will steal shirts "from my host at St. Albans, or the red-nose innkeeper of Daventry," and, beyond that, "will find linen enough on every hedge" (IV.ii.46-48). While he will lead a band of bare-backed robbers through the inns and lanes of England, Falstaff responds to the Hostess with a one-way contractual agreement, demanding the privileges due a guest:

> Shall I not take mine ease in mine inn but I
> shall have my pocket picked? I have lost a seal-
> ring of my grandfather's worth forty mark.
>   (III.iii.85-87)

Falstaff parallels Henry IV, obtaining the crown through contractual agreements then complaining when the debts come due. Falstaff puts a monetary value on heredity, as if the old world is re-viewed from the stance of a new theory. The Hostess responds to Falstaff's valuation with Hal's word "that the ring was copper" (III.iii.89), which Hal substantiates: "A trifle, some eight penny matter" (III.iii.110). The Hostess further attacks Falstaff with a debt Hal never promised, although the same amount Hal "promised" to Francis:

> Hostess.   he... said this other day you ought him
>   a thousand pound.
>
> Prince.   Sirrah, do I owe you a thousand pound?
>
> Falstaff.   A thousand pound, Hal? A million! Thy
>   love is worth a million, thou owest me
>   thy love.
>
>   (III.iii.141-145)

We know that Hal has never owed Falstaff the money, and that Hal will not pay Falstaff in the currency of "love" either.

Instead, Hal berates Falstaff for his profligacy:

> But, sirrah, there's no room for faith, truth, nor
> honesty in this bosom of thine. It is all filled
> up with guts and midriff. Charge an honest woman
> with picking thy pocket?
>
>   (III.iii.161-164)

Falstaff adroitly has Hal "confess" to the pocket-picking and magnanimously forgives the hostess with a pious homily:

> Hostess, I forgive thee, go make ready breakfast,
> love thy husband, look to thy servants, cherish
> thy guests. Thou shall find me tractable to any
> honest reason.
>
>   (III.iii.178-181)

The "Money" Falstaff receives for his "charge" (III.iii.209-210) becomes, of course, a "pocket[ing] up of wrong" (III.iii.170-171). The only element Falstaff does not misrepresent is the "bottle of sack" (IV.ii.2) Falstaff orders Bardolph to purchase, a non-counterfeit to be bought apparently with Bardolph's own money:

> Bardolph.   Will you give me money, captain?

Falstaff.	Lay out, lay out.
Bardolph.	This bottle makes an angel.
Falstaff.	And if it do, take it for thy labor; and if it make twenty, take them all; I'll answer the coinage.

(IV.ii.4-8)

Falstaff magnanimously allows Bardolph to keep the Midas-bottle that mints money, although it would seem that Bardolph has reminded Falstaff of the money Falstaff owes him. Falstaff has already placed his "charge" in his own pocket:

> I have misused the king's press damnably. I
> have got, in exchange of a hundred and fifty
> soldiers, three hundred and odd pounds. I press
> me none but good householders, yeomen's sons; in-
> quire me out contracted bachelors, such as had been
> asked twice on the banns — such a commodity of
> warm slaves as had as lief hear the devil as a
> drum... and they have bought out their services.

(IV.ii.12-23)

Here the sacrament of matrimony is neatly employed by Falstaff for profit. His pose as military man is nicely turned by Hal:

Westmoreland.	The king, I can tell you looks for us all, we must away all night.
Falstaff.	Tut, never fear me: I am as vigilant as a cat to steal cream.
Prince.	I think, to steal cream indeed, for thy theft hath already made thee butter.

(IV.ii.56-62)

Westmoreland's comment that Falstaff's company is "exceeding poor and bare, too beggarly" (IV.ii.69), draws the response that "for their poverty, I know not where they had that, and for their bareness, I am sure they never learned that of me" (IV.ii.70-72). Yet, in one sense, their beggarly quality has enriched Falstaff and their bareness has fattened him. He has conscripted only men too poor to buy their way out. Their staggering progress towards Shrewsbury also suits Falstaff: "Well, to the latter end of a fray and the beginning of a feast fits a dull fighter and a keen guest" (IV.ii.79-81). Falstaff's blade is honed primarily for a meal.

He will lead his "food for powder" (IV.ii.66) to "where they are peppered" (V.ii.36), and leave them to die so that he can collect their pay. He himself will survive the possibility of becoming the feast himself:

Prince.   Death hath not struck so fat a deer today,
Though many dearer in this bloody fray.
Emboweled will I see thee by-and-by;
Till then in blood by noble Percy lie.

Falstaff.   Emboweled? If thou embowel me today, I'll give you leave to powder me and eat me too tomorrow.
                    (IV.ii.56-62)

Falstaff's resurrection, as counterfeit as Hal's will be when he becomes Henry V, serves Hal neatly. Falstaff's threat to "make [anyone who would deny his triumph over Hotspur] eat a piece of my sword" (V.iv.150-151) is met by Hal's granting Falstaff credit for Hotspur's death. Falstaff's role in the Shrewsbury episode suggests how far England has moved from the England recalled by Gaunt, yet the historical time is only some fifty years.

In I Henry IV, Hal manages to destroy the anachronistic anarchy of Hotspur. The patient bider-of-time masters the impetuous leaper into doomsday. The final sword fight would reflect the personalities of the two young men — Hotspur rushing aggressively at his rival, on fire to extinquish Hal, Hal parrying defensively until Hotspur leaves himself open. A short thrust and it is over.

But Hal must still associate with Falstaff. The latter's "rising again" at Shrewsbury is necessary to the prince's redemption. Hal has planned a version of the Parable of the Prodigal son that demands Falstaff as actor in the interlude. The chaos Falstaff represents, imaged in metaphors of indebtedness, appetite, and disease, is yet another threat the prince must be capable of controlling once he becomes Harry, King of England. If Hal is to achieve "value" as Henry V, he must seem to link himself to the seamy underside of England which shows the "devaluation" that the court attempts to obscure beneath royal rhetoric and majestic posturing. Hal's "counterfeit" is the only method available for "redeeming" whatever value may still reside in kingship. With intrinsic quality evaporated from king and crown, "seeming" is all that is left. Hal will seem to be one thing the better to simulate another. Falstaff and the "Falstaff ethic" — a dangerous exaggeration of the standards Bolingbroke has introduced — must survive Shrewsbury, to be banished for good at Westminster.20/

1. Reno, From Sacrament to Ceremony, pp. 196-197.

2. We are reminded that it was Richard, again, who introduced "baseness" to the monarchy, hence to England. Cf. Fabyan: "The rumor... ranne upon him, that he had letten to ferme the revenues of the crowne, to Busshey, Bagot, and Grene, which caused as well the noble men of the realm to grudge against him..." The Chronicles (London, 1559), p. 343.

3. Cf. the Communion exhortation: "with full purpose of amendment of life."

4. The text of Dr. Faustus makes the point within itself, of course, as in the scene between Wagner and the Clown, to which Shakespeare seems to refer:

> Wagner.   Alas, poor slave. See how poverty jesteth
> in his nakedness: the villain is bare and out of
> service, and so hungry that I know he would give
> his soul to the Devil for a shoulder of mutton,
> though it were blood-raw.
>
> Clown.   How, my soul to the Devil for a shoulder of
> mutton, though it were blood-raw?   Not so, good
> friend: by'r Lady, I had need have it well roasted,
> and good sauce to it, if I pay so dear.
>   (IV.8-17)

5. Falstaff's final joke is reported by the Boy in a colloquy that hearkens back to Falstaff's disquisition on Bardolph's nose:

> Boy.   Do you not remember 'a saw a flea stick
> upon Bardolph's nose, and 'a said it
> was a black soul burning in hell?
>
> Bardolph.   Well, the fuel is gone that maintained
> that fire: that's all the riches I got in
> his service
>   (Henry V: II.iii.37-41)

Falstaff betrays a certain preoccupation with damnation, even as he mocks religion generally and Puritanism specifically.

6. The line looks ahead to King Henry V's rewarding of Williams after Agincourt: "Here, uncle Exeter, fill this glove with crowns,/ And give it to this fellow" (IV.viii.57-58). The similarity of the lines supports Harold

Goddard's thesis that "the Battle of Agincourt was the royal equivalent of the Gadshill robbery." The Meaning of Shakespeare (Chicago, 1951), p. 260.

7.   In a persuasive and often illuminating essay, Sherman Hawkins responds to Hal's soliloquy by saying that Hal "is still of all humors, an accomplished mimic who can play any role but his own — in short, as my students instantly recognize, a young man in search of himself." But Hal knows what he will be — a king — something that Mr. Hawkin's students know they will not be, even with a Wesleyan education. Furthermore Hal's role as madcap is basic to the sudden transition he purposes. I believe Mr. Hawkins is simply wrong to suggest that Hal recognizes that "his initial choice [in consorting with Falstaff] has been mistaken." Hal's soliloquy, quite simply, argues that Hal has not "chosen" Falstaff, but is using Falstaff for Hal's purposes. "When we choose the wrong way of life at first, Cicero counsels, we should change it by degrees, as we gradually dissolve a friendship that is no longer pleasing to us. So it will be with Hal and Falstaff."   Even assuming Cicero's advice to be applicable (it seems very bad advice to me), the effect Henry V produces on Falstaff and within the world of the play is precisely as Hal had predicted — a sudden and dramatic change. I admit that we, privy to Hal's soliloquy, may sense a gradual withdrawal of Hal from Falstaff after Shrewsbury.   While Falstaff may be, as Mr. Hawkins argues, "a deliberate and comic inversion of the ideal master described by Erasmus and others," Falstaff is a brilliant, if unconscious tutor, giving Hal the training for precisely the trap Henry V springs on Falstaff at the end of Part II. Mr. Hawkins claims that the "society with whom [Hal] consorts at the Boarshead is worse than 'unlettered' — these drunkards, whores, thieves, and parasites, are exactly the sort of dangerous company forbidden future rulers by every educator from Plato to Shakespeare's own day." "Educators" may indeed utter such pieties and may well eschew such low company, but the Boarshead represents a segment of that England Henry will temporarily fuse into one for the invasion of France. Falstaff is demonstrably not unlettered. To discard him thus moralistically is to ignore Hal's recognition that he, as prince, exists in a world whose basic premises he cannot alter but whose dynamic he can understand and possibly control.   The world of the two parts of Henry IV and of Henry V is one in which Aristotle is a better mentor for a prince than Plato.   Machiavelli would be the best candidate for the highest place on Hal's reading list, but Machiavelli is unnecessary, since Falstaff is demonstrably there, in the play, and since the results of Falstaff's tutoring of Hal are demonstrably present from the rejection scene onward. Mr. Hawkins inexplicably exludes Machiavelli in the discussion of a very literal "mirror" of those Christian princes to whom the cardinal virtues of justice, valor, fortitude, temperance, and (as of Agincourt) piety must, it seems, pertain.   I deeply doubt the validity of Mr. Hawkins's assumptions about Shakespeare's attitude toward Hal/Henry V. "Virtue and Kingship in Shakespeare's Henry V," English Literary Renaissance V (1975), 313–343.

7. As one would expect, the metaphor is picked up in the sub-plot, through Bardolph's ubiquitous nose, whose "meteors" and "exhalations" (II.iv.322-323) portend, says Hal, "Hot livers and cold purses" (II.iv.326). Hal's light words illuminate again the commercial zone his father has made of England. Hotspur, "on fire/ To hear this rich reprisal is so nigh" (I Henry IV: IV.i.115-116) will soon become "Coldspur" (II Henry IV: I.i.50). The recent BBC-TV Production of I Henry IV suggested neatly that Henry IV's insecurity in the opening sequences of the play emerges from his fears of Mortimer's claim — thus the King's over-emphasis on his position as King, his sudden and unwarranted use of an "absoluteness" that no longer pertains to his contractual position. Jon Finch's Bolingbroke nicely paralleled Derek Jacobi's initial insecurity as Richard II. The plays themselves, of course, make the point, but good productions enforce it. By the time of Henry IV, a king's concerns have become purely political, however much the king may prate of crusades.

8. A. C. Bradley, "The Rejection of Falstaff," Oxford Lectures on Poetry (London, 1909), p. 255.

9. Cf. James Winney: "As though taking his lead from the King, who hides his dishonorable record behind a front of kingly authority, the Prince masks his nobility and respect for law by putting on the appearance of contempt for order and justice, so inverting the moral paradox presented by his father." The Player King (London, Chatto & Windus, 1968), p. 137.

10. In each scene in which the "father-figures" advise Hal, Falstaff and Bolingbroke seem to talk more of themselves than of Hal (II.iv.422-436 and III.i. 39-59). This self-concern signals insecurity, although that insecurity emerges from different sources. Certainly Henry IV has some right to feel concern about his heir. Although the monarchy is hereditary, Bolingbroke himself has proved the exception to the rule, and has yet "To fight with... the Earl of March" (V.iv.40) by the end of the play. Shakespeare explores the problems of succession, of course, in both histories and tragedies. In at least two cases, kings name heirs to elective kingships; Claudius in I.ii, although Hamlet will complain that Claudius "popped in between the election and my hopes" (V.ii.65), and Duncan (I.iv), an action that startles Macbeth. For a discussion of the latter sequence, see Joseph Q. Adam's edition of Macbeth (Boston, 1931), pp. 139-141.

11. Hotspur at Shrewsbury contrasts, of course, with Henry V at Agincourt. Henry V makes excellent use of the concept of honor (IV.iii.21-29) in the face of a diminished English army, translating the danger into a cause for celebration and the pretext for a quasi-religious holiday which will resound into the future. Henry V has the crucial advantage of being a representative, the representative, of a united England.

12. The word "advantage," employed by Hal in its strictly commercial sense, casts irony on Henry IV's piety, as he talks of "those blessed feet/ Which fourteen hundred years ago were nailed/ For our advantage on the bitter cross" (I.i.25-27). Even Christ, it seems, is a party to the accrual of "interest."

13. The recent R.S.C. production made some point about Bolingbroke's conscience and underscored the topsy-turviness of England by making Bolingbroke the groom, but such ingenuity seemed directed at some "shock of recognition" — on Richard's part and ours when Bolingbroke drew back his hood and revealed himself — and obscured other dramatic issues, as this production did with consistent perversity.

14. The line, of course, reaches back to Richard's leasing out of the quasi-sacred soil of the realm. His seizing of the Lancastrian property leads directly to the sequence of events that has rendered real estate temporarily valueless. England's unsettled status is described by Dr. Johnson in his comment on the line: "In former times the prosperity of the nation was known by the value of the land as now by the price of stocks. Before Henry the seventh made it safe to serve the king regnant, it was the practice at every revolution for the conqueror to confiscate the estates of those that opposed, and perhaps of those who did not assist him. Those, therefore, that foresaw a change of government, and thought their estates in danger, were desirous to sell them in haste for something that might be carried away." Johnson: Prose and Poetry, ed. Mona Wilson (Cambridge, Massachusetts, 1951), p. 562.

15. Our introduction to Hal foreshadows the exchange of gloves between Henry V and Williams before Agincourt. Shakespeare seems to pick up the idea of a future dramatic sequence from his own work. The scene between Richard and the groom (V.v), for example, predicts Falstaff's clever perversion of hierarchy as he outflanks Hal in II Henry IV, II.iv.

16. Cf. "I know you all..." and "I know thee not, old man..."

17. Francis contrasts with Falstaff at Gad's Hill, Douglas at Shrewsbury, and the "revolted tapsters" who nevertheless find themselves in Falstaff's platoon (IV.ii.29), but Francis compares with the surprising Feeble (II Henry IV: III.ii.159-160).

18. Fredson Bowers equates Hotspur and Francis: "Hotspur's slaughter of the Scots in private pursuit of the mere word 'honor'... is fundamentally no more rational or noble an occupation than Francis' treading the staircase in his endless round... Percy has been placed in his right perspective beside Francis, whose industry was 'upstairs and downstairs' and 'his eloquence the parcel of a reckoning,' no different from the itemizing of a parcel of some fourteen Scots." Such a case

puts perhaps a heavier weight on Hal's parody of Hotspur than it warrants. "Hal and Francis in King Henry IV, Part I, Renaissance Papers 1965, ed. G. W. Williams (Durham, N.C., 1966), 19-20.

19.　Although one must grant the contrast between "noble" Falstaff and "base men" like Francis, Feeble, and Williams.　After Richard II, the "nobility" of England resides only in "base men," a reality Richard encouraged.　Hal seems to recognize as much, and Henry V will take full advantage of that recognition at Agincourt.

20.　Curiously, Hawkins objects to Hal's return to Eastcheap after Shrewsbury: "Why... at the beginning of Part II does [Hal] shun his dying father?　How does he find his way back to the Boarshead and to Falstaff?　Hal himself has no clear answers to such questions" (333).　Hal needs none.　His "clear answer" remains his soliloquy in Part I.　In each case the answer is that Hal in not yet King.　Since Mr. Hawkins objects to Hal's association with Falstaff et.al. on moral grounds, the clear political motives for Hal's shunning of Windsor and Westminster and his return to Eastcheap will not suffice for Mr. Hawkins — though that is the answer the play provides.　To permit one's own priggishness to condition one's response to Hal is to risk missing the entire point of his tutorial with Falstaff.

V

Falstaff's England: II Henry IV

The England of II Henry IV sinks even below the baseness represented by a purely commercial ethic. Falstaff's "I will turn diseases to commodity" (I.ii.251) could almost be translated into the "disease of commodity." The relentless materialism that has marched into every corner of England is imaged consistently as disease: "I can get no remedy against this consumption of the purse. Borrowing only lingers it out, but the disease is incurable" (I.ii.239-241).

The king, wasting away during the final days of his bankrupt reign, does not appear until the Third Act, although he is mentioned earlier, as if he has inherited only Plashy: "the unfirm king ['s] coffers sound/ With hollow poverty and emptiness" (I.iii.73-75). The same is true of the rebels, now bereft of the Hotspur who "lined himself with hope,/ Eating the air and promise of supply" (I.iii.27-28). Lord Bardolph is correct to warn "that the cost of the erection [i.e. mounting yet another insurrection]. . . outweighs ability" (I.iii.44-45). When the project fails, it will leave, in Lord Bardolph's architectural metaphor, a "part-created cost/ A naked subject to the weeping clouds/ And waste for churlish winter's tyranny" (I.iii.60-62), lines that remind us of Richard, the weeping king obscured by the cloudy Bolingbroke. Northumberland, "crafty-sick" (Induction. 37) when Hotspur died at Shrewsbury, guilty of a defection from any concept of "honor," decides at last that "my honor is at pawn/ And, but my going [i.e. into battle], nothing can redeem it" (II.iii.7-8). But honor is pawned again, and Northumberland reflects the dominant code of a world he has helped shape by retiring to Scotland "to ripe his growing fortunes" (IV.i.13). He will be defeated ultimately by a mere provincial sheriff (IV.iv.97-99), an appropriately ironic end for a nobleman who has assisted in the overturning of hierarchy in England.

The play represents the "ling'ring act" (I.i.156) of Northumberland's career, a lingering act of disease that also eats away Falstaff's pretensions to power and Bolingbroke's kingship, at least the life of the man beneath the guilty crown. While Warwick assures Henry IV that "Rumor doth double, like the voice and echo/ The numbers of the fear'd" (III.i.96-97), and that the "powers that you already have sent forth/ Shall bring this prize in very easily" (III.i.100-101), such predictions do no more to cure the king's insomnia than the toast of reconciliation erases young Mowbray's intuitive apprehension at Gaultree Forest: "You wish me health in very happy season,/ For I am, on the sudden, something ill" (IV.iv.79-80). A malignant malaise pervades the kingdom.

Prince John of Lancaster can claim that the Archbishop has taken up

> Under the counterfeited zeal of God,
> The subjects of His substitute, my father,
> And both against the peace of heaven and him
> Have here upswarmed them.
> (IV.ii.26-30)

The lines echo Gaunt's to the Duchess of Gloucester long before, but here they are mere political rhetoric, achieving no contact with even a living past. Bolingbroke has helped to begin the long erosive action we witness; now virtually his very promise to Richard at Flint Castle comes from the Archbishop of York, who says that "With grant of our most just and right desires ... true obedience, of this madness cured," will "Stoop tamely to the foot of majesty" (IV.i.40-42). Richard began a seemingly endless process of grievances, endless, at least partly because Bolingbroke, in redressing wrong, substituted himself for God's substitute.

Dr. Johnson finds Prince John's handling of the rebellion dastardly: "It cannot but raise some indignation to find this horrible violation of faith passed over so slightly by the poet, without any note of censure or detestation."1/ Any assumption of "faith" in any transaction, however, allows one party, Falstaff with a commission from the king, Pistol as "sutler . . . Unto the camp" (Henry V: II.i.111-112), or, in this case, Prince John, to translate faith into commodity. The "ethic" is success, and success at the smallest possible expense. This Prince John achieves consummately. He raises expectations, only, as Norman Holland suggests, to "mock" them.2/ The point is that "it works."3/ If we, as spectators, feel uncomfortable or outraged, then that is our reaction to the world of the play, like it or not as we will. And we may not enjoy participating in a political tour de force, particularly when "the poet" does not build in a response for us. John can claim, with whatever thin legality, that he "pawned" no "faith" to the rebels (IV.ii.113), and can then blithely attribute the "victory" to higher powers, as his brother will do after the military contest at Agincourt. "God, and not we," says Prince John, "hath safely fought today" (IV.ii.122). But this "God" is a god of necessity and expediency, a pagan god of this world, to be employed as an adjunct to political success. And we can expect a Falstaffian commentary, perhaps the "note" Dr. Johnson seeks for in vain. Falstaff will produce a ballad, "with mine own picture on the top of it, Coleville kissing my foot" (IV.iii.48-49), a parody of the Archbishop's promise to "Stoop tamely to the foot of majesty" (IV.ii.42), but finding instead the "block of death" (IV.ii.123). Falstaff's ballad will make of him a heavenly body, significantly the one beneath which thieves ply their trade:

To the which course if I be enforced, if you
do not all show like gilt twopences to me, and I
in the clear sky of fame o'ershine you as much as
the full moon doth the cinders of the element,
which show like pins' heads to her, believe not
the word of the noble.
                         (IV.iii.49-54)

"The word of the noble" is that of the counterfeit coin; a "gilt two-pence" piece would pass for a gold half-crown, as Falstaff would pass for "the hook-nosed fellow of Rome, " Julius Caesar (IV.iii.40-41). Falstaff suggests that Gaultree Forest shows not perfidy, faithlessness, or dishonor — such negative qualities have no positive context against which to be portrayed — but a commodity that is itself based on the counterfeit standards of Bolingbroke's kingship. Since he _is_ king, however, those who oppose him must reflect a "zeal " as "counterfeited" (IV.ii.27) as John's promise to "perform with a most Christian care" (IV.ii.116) the "redress of these same grievances" (IV.ii.114). No grievances can _be_ redressed until the source of grievance, Bolingbroke, is removed from the throne, either by rebellion, which would replace one grievance with another, as Shakespeare shows in his depiction of the Wars of the Roses, or by death. And while Bolingbroke's death will remove a major grievance, it cannot restore a sacramentalism that died with Richard.

The sub-plot shows us again the ethic of the political plot. It, too, is shadowed by imagery of approaching death. Falstaff's shrewdness is never more in evidence than in his handling of the prince, whom he calls "A good shallow young fellow" (II.iv.241), and of Justice Robert Shallow of Gloucestershire. The prince's "face is a face-royal" (I.ii.23), says Falstaff, but, unlike a bottle that mints angels, a face on which hair won't grow will bring no profit: "He may keep it still at a face-royal, for a barber shall never earn sixpence out of it" (I.ii.24-26), unless, of course, it was a clipped coin — a meaning Falstaff may be glancing at. Falstaff himself cannot purchase "satin" without "security" (I.ii.29-33), hence the tailor must be "damned like the glutton! Pray God his tongue be hotter!" (I.ii.34-35). The allusion to the Dives/ Lazarus story allows Falstaff to place himself conveniently on the Lazarus side of the equation. His inability to obtain garments reminds us of the "slaves as ragged as Lazarus" he led to Shrewsbury (I Henry IV: IV.ii.25). The very Hostess he has so often cheated, however, will consign him to "Arthur's bosom" (Henry V: I.iii.9-10), not "Abraham's," where Lazarus rests in Luke, a wonderfully ironic quicklyism that links Falstaff with the heroic legends of Britain. Falstaff's career, however, links him all too solidly with the thievery, profit-taking, and spiritual poverty which is England's post-heroic heritage.

I agree with those commentators who discern in Falstaff increasingly unpleasant and disturbing characteristics. These characteristics are best defined through Falstaff's gradual immersion in the "commercial ethic," whose seamy side he has always contacted, but of which he was once also chief satirist. The Falstaff of II Henry IV seems more the subject of satire, finally of a cold political allegory designed by the prince (or, Il Principe), than the puncturer of the very poses he himself assumes, although some of his conscious satire still obtains. We observe Falstaff sinking heavily into the morass Richard and Bolingbroke have cooperated to create:

> I bought him in Paul's, and he'll buy me a
> horse in Smithfield. And I could get me but a
> wife in the stews, I were manned, horsed, and
> wived.
>   (I.ii.52-54)4/

That a great cathedral is now a market-place for servants is hardly Falstaff's fault, of course, but it is yet another index of the "spiritual state" of England, of which Falstaff becomes a gross exaggeration.

Falstaff's command of the ironies of his own situation, a consistent characterization in I Henry IV, is less sure, a decline in perception that allows us to anticipate his rejection. The "former Falstaff" emerges in his self-dictated "pure and immaculate valor" (IV.iii.37) in capturing Coleville, and in his superb posturing as he leaves the tavern for war: "You see, my good wenches, how men of merit are sought after. The undeserver may sleep when the man of action is called on" (II.iv.381-384). The lines occur, however, after Falstaff has commanded his Page to "Pay the musicians, sirrah" (II.iv.380). Does Falstaff provide the coin? The moment might be staged with the Boy shrugging and plucking the money from his own purse.

The Chief Justice accosts Falstaff because he is "in question for the robb'ry" (I.ii.60-61) - - another example of the past returning in very specific terms to inhabit the stage of the present. Falstaff conveniently mistakes the Chief Justice's Servant for a beggar, and extends his error into a sober concern about the unsettled state of England:

> What! A young knave, and begging! Is there
> not wars? Is there not employment? Doth not the
> king lack subjects? Do not the rebels need
> soldiers? Though it be a shame to be on any side
> but one, it is worse shame to beg than to be on
> the worst side, were it worse than the name of re-
> bellion can tell how to make it.
>   (I.ii.73-79)

Having feigned deafness (II.ii.67), Falstaff attributes illness to the Chief Justice and exhibits a solicitous concern for both the Chief Justice and King Henry, launching into a long disquisition on the syndrome of Bolingbroke's disease - - all efforts to "turn diseases to commodity" (I.ii.251), in this case by evading the question of Gad's Hill. Falstaff suggests that the only cause for his incarceration might be his impoverished status: "I am as poor as Job, my lord, but not so patient. Your lordship may minister the potion of imprisonment to me in respect of poverty..." (I.ii.127-129). The images of disease and poverty intermingle here, as they will throughout the play, and the second scene predicts Falstaff's final incarceration. Fortunately for him, however, the false coinage of his exploit at Shrewsbury has helped revalue his night-work at Gad's Hill: "Your day's service at Shrewsbury hath a little gilded over your night's exploit on Gad's Hill. You may thank th' unquiet time for your quiet o'erposting that action" (I.ii.150-154). The Chief Justice accepts Falstaff's argument that service to "the land" is of more immediate relevance than action against the crown (the robbery having been of the king's funds): Falstaff ignored a summons from the Chief Justice because "As I was then advised by my learned counsel in the laws of this land-service, I did not come" (I.ii.136-137). The lines suggest that elements once in harmony in England - - land, crown, and law - - are now in collision. A robbery directed against the king is excused by service in defense of the same king, exploits we know to be false but that Falstaff's genius has promulgated as true. That service, and the continued civil wars that Falstaff has cleverly emphasized to the Servant override the law. But "the laws of England" that Falstaff believes to be at his "commandment" (V.iii.140-141) wait in ambush for him, as he waited for the unwary travellers at Gad's Hill.

While Falstaff's remarkable skills emerge completely in his confrontations with the Chief Justice, the theme is consistently the debasement of England. As he often does, Falstaff affects to deplore what he knows he represents: "Pregnancy is made a tapster, and hath his quick wit wasted in giving reckonings" (I.ii.172-173). Falstaff describes his own career, indeed the contents of his own pockets, accurately, but ascribes it to the spurns that patient merit - - his pose now, in spite of his prior contrasting of himself to Job - - of the unworthy must absorb. He swings the Chief Justice's allusion to the morality play quickly into a pun on false coinage, again underlining England's transition from "religious" to "commercial" premises:

Chief Justice.   You follow the young prince up and down like his ill angel.

Falstaff.   Not so, my lord. Your ill angel is light, but I hope he that looks upon me will take me without weighing. (I.ii.165-168)

Falstaff claims to be no "clipped coin" but a "true and perfect image"
(I Henry IV: V.iv.117), with a weight undervalued in "these costermonger
[i.e. huckster] times" (I.ii.171). Falstaff's pretense of youth under the
darkness of Gad's Hill now becomes a blatant assertion of youth; he is
old only in that he is poor:

> To approve my youth further, I will not. The
> truth is, I am only old in judgment and understanding;
> and he that will caper with me for a thousand
> marks, let him lend me the money, and have at him!
> (I.ii.191-195)

He ends the scene by forcing the Chief Justice into the monetary mode:

Falstaff.   Will your lordship lend me a thousand
                              pound to furnish me forth?

Chief Justice.   Not a penny, not a penny. You are too
                              impatient to bear crosses [i.e. afflic-
                              tions, and coins marked with a cross].
                              (I.ii.226-229)

Falstaff must know that the Chief Justice will never lend him one
thousand pounds, but he leaves the Chief Justice in the position of
having refused a soldier of the king.

The "unquiet time" (I.ii.152), which must continue as long as
Henry IV lives, continues at Falstaff's service. The poverty of England is
reflected in the penury Falstaff has imposed upon the Hostess: "A
hundred mark is a long one for a poor lone woman to bear, and I have
borne, and borne and borne, and have been fubbed off, and fubbed off
and fubbed off, from this day to that day, that it is a shame to be
thought on. There is no honesty in such dealing, unless a woman should
be made an ass and a beast, to bear every knave's wrong" (II.i.30-37).
Falstaff's arrest on the Hostess's charge is interrupted by the Chief
Justice:

Hostess.   O my most worshipful lord, and't
                              please your grace, I am a poor
                              widow of Eastcheap, and he is arres-
                              ted at my suit.

Chief Justice.   For what sum?

Hostess.   It is more than for some, my lord, it
                              is for all I have. He hath eaten me
                              out of house and home; he hath put

126

all my substance into that fat belly
of his.
(II.i.68-74)

To Falstaff's claim that "she was in good case, and the truth is, poverty
hath distracted her" (II.i.105-106), the Chief Justice responds with a
more direct truth: "You have, as it appears to me, practiced upon the
easy-yielding spirit of this woman, and made her serve your uses both in
purse and in person" (II.i.113-116). Falstaff is ordered to "Pay her the
debt you owe her and unpay the villainy you have done with her. The one
you may do with sterling money, and the other with current repentance"
(II.i.118-121). Even in the Chief Justice we notice the easy punning on
religious terminology. Falstaff responds by confusing the issue of debt
and stressing his office:

> My lord, I will not undergo this sneap with-
> out reply. You call honorable boldness impudent
> sauciness. If a man will make curtsy and say noth-
> ing, he is virtuous. No, my lord, my humble duty
> rememb'red, I will not be your suitor. I say to
> you, I do desire deliverance from these officers,
> being upon hasty employment in the king's affairs.
> (II.i.122-128)

To the Hostess's complaint that she "must be fain to pawn both my plate
and the tapestry of my dining chambers" (II.i.141-142), Falstaff suggests
that she spend "ten pound, if thou canst" (II.i.147) to replace her "fly-
bitten tapestries" with - - among other suggestions - - "the story of the
Prodigal" (II.i.144-147), a story that captures both Falstaff and Prince
Hal within its configuration. While Falstaff's line seems to promise ten
pounds, it shows more clearly that Falstaff has assumed a role that
permits him to offer suggestions for the improvement of the Hostess's
establishment. He poses as a connoisseur of hostelry. The Hostess
presses her plea: "let it be but twenty nobles" (II.i.153-154), which would
be a 10 per cent downpayment on the one hundred marks the Hostess
claims Falstaff owes her. The alternative would be that the Hostess
would have the "pawn [her] plate." Falstaff promises merely to "make
another shift" (II.i.156). The generous Hostess accepts the promise at
full face-value: "Well, you shall have it, though I pawn my gown. I hope
you'll come to supper. You'll pay me all together?" (II.i.158-160).6/ Hal
has chosen to associate with this world, where poverty of pocket is
concealed by empty promises. Against such a "foil" his "reformation"
will "glitter." But more basically, this is the world King Henry V must
control, translating poverty of purse and of spirit into positive national
purpose.

Hal's last effort at controlling Falstaff — as Prince Hal — occurs when Hal and Poins disguise as drawers. The prince, restless in his role as reveller (as II.ii.9-27 suggest), resists the debasement: "From a prince to a prentice? A low transformation!" (II.ii.173-174). But Hal accepts again the strategy he has pursued from the first: "That shall be mine, for in everything the purpose must weigh with the folly" (II.ii.174-175). Here, seeming "lightness" conceals actual "gravity": Hal reverses Falstaff's situation, where "weight," however Falstaff construes it, rests on no basis, other than the "incurable disease" of the purse for which wit offers only temporary antidote. "Substance," as the Hostess says, has disappeared into "that fat belly of" Falstaff's (II.i.74). Doll turns the Hostess's piety into a metaphor that compares Falstaff with a shipload of wine: "Can a weak empty vessel bear such a huge full hogshead? There's a whole merchant's venture of Bordeaux stuff in him. You have not seen a hulk better stuff'd in the hold" (II.iii.63-66).

The final tavern scene turns on the question of rank or hierarchy. Doll rails against the Hostess's "promotion" of Pistol:

> And captains were of my mind, they would
> truncheon you out for taking their names upon you
> before you have earned them. You a captain! You
> slave, for what? For tearing a poor whore's ruff
> in a bawdy house? He a captain!... captains had
> need look to't.
>
> (II.iv.143-153)

The last phrase, of course, is a thrust at Captain Falstaff. Within the tavern world, Pistol, as Doll accurately defines him, represents the threat that Falstaff will embody in the approaching world of King Henry V. Falstaff drives Pistol out, a prefiguration of the play's final scene, in which the ultimate "captain" (Henry V: Act IV. Chorus. 29) of England, King Henry V, will drive Falstaff away.

Yet, while Hal hopes to "drive Falstaff to confess the willful abuse," thereby learning "how to handle" him (II.iv.317-318), Falstaff neatly turns Hal's disguise against him:

Falstaff: Ha! A bastard son of the king's? And art not thou Poins his brother?

Prince.   Why, thou globe of sinful continents, what a life doth thou lead!

Falstaff: A better than thou. I am a gentleman, thou art a drawer.
(II.iv.289-294)

128

Hal must now elevate those Falstaff has defamed: "See now, whether pure fear and entire cowardice doth not make thee wrong this virtuous gentlewoman to close with us. Is she of the wicked?" (II.iv.331-333). Falstaff plays at being a Puritan again, and links possible damnation to the Hostess's position of creditor: "For the boy, there is a good angel about him, but the devil blinds him too... For one of them, she's in hell already, and burns poor souls. For th' other, I owe her money, and whether she be damned for that, I know not" (II.iv.340-346). Venereal disease becomes a "modern" form of damnation. The Hostess's objection about possibly being consigned to Hell because Falstaff owes her money allows Falstaff to be magnanimous: "No, I think thou art not. I think thou art quit for that" (II.iv.348-349). Having again disposed of the question of his debt, however, he tells the Hostess that "there is another indictment upon thee, for suffering flesh to be eaten in thy house, contrary to the law, for the which I think thou wilt howl" (II.iv.349-351). A meal once might have found its analogy in The Lord's Supper. Meat now has its metaphor in prostitution.

While it is too easy to say that the tavern "represents England in microcosm," it is not too much to say that this nadir, where flesh equates to carnality and commercialism, does capture much of what has happened to England since Richard fell from grace in having Gloucester murdered.7/ Falstaff has forced Hal to elevate Doll to "gentlewoman" (again in line 355). "His grace," says Falstaff, "says that which his flesh rebels against" (II.iv.358-359). Hal, as Prince of Wales, can be <u>called</u> "your grace" (II.iv.356), but the word has no intrinsic meaning anymore.8/ Falstaff has maneuvered Hal into a position where even his dubious title as prince, which resides only in a "body natural" ("flesh"), conflicts with the "honesty," "virtue,"and "zeal" Hal has been forced to bestow upon the diseased and besotted denizens of the underworld, whom Falstaff has labelled "wicked." But Falstaff does not recognize that the trap he has improvised for Hal represents only a temporary reversal of hierarchy. Henry IV may believe that whatever order he has been able to maintain in England will revert under his son to the jungle of primitive Britain:

> Now, neighbor confines, purge you of your scum.
> Have you a ruffian that will swear, drink, dance,
> Revel the night, rob, murder, and commit
> The oldest sins the newest kind of ways?. . .
> England shall give him office, honor, might,
> For the fifth Harry from curbed license plucks
> The muzzle of restraint, and the wild dog
> Shall flesh his tooth on every innocent.
> O my poor kingdom, sick with civil blows !
> When that my care could not withhold thy riots,
> What wilt thou do when riot is thy care?

O, thou wilt be a wilderness again,
Peopled with wolves, thy old inhabitants.
(IV.v.123-137)

Hal's plan, however, incorporates a sudden establishment of rank and hierarchy. Falstaff is part of the world he has called "wicked," and, although he maneuvers Hal into a hasty defense of that world, albeit amused and self-aware, Falstaff has defined his own trap, once Hal's "grace" and "flesh" conjoin in the royal personage of King Henry the Fifth. In dispraising Falstaff, placing him among the wicked, indeed in making Falstaff the chief culprit, Henry V will achieve a final revenge for the temporary defeat he suffers in the final tavern scene. As the bruit of battle reaches the doors of The Boarshead, Hal reiterates his restlessness - - and the purpose he holds in abeyance:

By heaven, Poins, I feel me much to blame,
So idly to profane the precious time,
When tempest of commotion, like the south
Borne with black vapor, doth begin to melt
And drop upon our bare unarmed heads.
Give me my sword and cloak. Falstaff, good night.
(II.iv.368-372)

The exit line suggests that Hal will even himself with Falstaff once the prince has been given the scepter and the crown. The foul and ugly mists Hal reiterates here will soon be dispelled. Hal's "good night" is the last phrase Falstaff hears from him. The next words Falstaff hears from someone he mistakes as "King Hal" (V.v.41) will be uttered by King Henry the Fifth.

Falstaff swings away to Gaultree Forest - - an episode that extends his prior equation of honor with nothingness into a national context - - passing through Gloucestershire before and after the "non-battle." John of Gaunt's England - - its grandeur, and the timeless uniformity of its holy purpose - - devolves in Shallow's selective memory to the realm in which "mad Shallow" and "'lusty Shallow'" revelled. His memories of youth coalesce around John of Gaunt and the bona robas Shallow never had. We learn from Falstaff that Gaunt once cracked Shallow across the head "for crowding among the marshall's men" (III.ii.327-328). Falstaff, once Mowbray the elder's page, has survived to become an ironic rejection of Gaunt's vision and a refutation of Mowbray's crusading career, as Carlisle described it (Richard II: IV.i.92-100). Shallow, once summarily rebuked by Gaunt, has risen to become a Justice and owner of land. But it is not Gaunt's "dear, dear land" beyond price, rather an enterprise undertaken with the context of Richard's translation of sacred soil to the debased equations of mere commerce:

Shallow:	How a yoke of bullocks at Stamford Fair? (III.ii.40)
Shallow:	How a score of ewes now?
Silence:	Thereafter as they be. A score of good ewes may be worth ten pounds. (III.ii.51-53)
Davy.	Here is now the smith's note for shoeing and plow-irons.
Shallow.	Let it be cast and paid...
Davy.	Now, sir, a new link to the bucket must needs be had.<u>9</u>/
	And, sir, do you mean to stop any of William's wages, about the sack he lost the other day at Hinckley Fair? (V.i.19-26)

Shallow's world thrives in one sense, yet it is inhabited by the failing or perhaps self-serving memory of the old Justice, who matriculated at Clement's Inn fifty-five years before (III.ii.212-214). Shallow's world is haunted by the approach of death: "Death, as the psalmist saith, is certain to all, all shall die" (III.ii.39-40). This prosperity shadowed by mortality is echoed in the court of King Henry IV:

> And wherefore should these good news make me sick?
> Will Fortune never come with both hands full,
> But write her fair words still in foulest letters?
> She either gives a stomach and no food - -
> Such are the poor, in health - - or else a feast
> And takes away the stomach - - such are the rich
> That have abundance and enjoy it not.
> (IV.iv.103-108)

Falstaff's great appetite suffers from "consumption of the purse" (I.ii.239-240). Shallow can buy "good ewes" and bullocks, but they make him only "This same starved justice" (III.ii.308). The world is at odds with itself. Body natural and body politic are out of sequence, one prospering, the other failing. The only person for whom this is not so is Hal, although no one knows of his purposed transformation but the

131

spectator. In Gaunt's world, essential "substance" was invisible, but lent meaning to the tangible. Now, even real names like "John Doit" (III.ii.20) equate to money (a "doit" being a half-farthing), and false names, or "shadows," line a commander's purse.

Falstaff, of course, employs each visit to Gloucestershire for profit. Again, he abuses his position as king's officer: "We have a number of shadows to fill up the musterbook" (III.ii.137-138), names whose pay goes directly into the commander's pocket.10/ Bardolph negotiates with Moldy and Bullcalf, and tells Falstaff, "I have three pound to free Moldy and Bullcalf" (III.ii.248-249). They are dismissed, much to Shallow's discomfiture: "Sir John, Sir John, do not yourself wrong. They are your likeliest men, and I would have you served with the best" (II.ii.259-261). But Shallow does not recognize that Falstaff's impressment represents profit. Nor does Shallow see that Falstaff is merely using him. Shallow believes that he will benefit from his acquaintanceship with Falstaff: "A friend in the court is better than a penny in purse" (V.i.31-32), but Shallow, like Falstaff, is unaware of the larger stratagem surrounding him. "I have him," says Falstaff, "already temp'ring between my finger and my thumb, and shortly will I seal with him" (IV.iii.130-131). Falstaff's metaphor of solemn compact, ratified in wax, suggests again the reduction of value England has suffered. Even alchemy shrinks to an easy formula, and one that conveys the grossest version of physical coercion; Shallow's "land and beeves" will make him, for Falstaff, "a philosopher's two stones" (III.ii.332-334). Falstaff may believe that he "see[s] the bottom of Justice Shallow" (III.ii.306-307), but his own words might warn him. He arrives too late at Gaultree Forest to hear Lancaster tell Hastings, "You are shallow, Hastings, much too shallow,/ To sound the bottom of the after-times" (IV.ii.50-51). Hastings walks into an immediate trap, the reality of the block suddenly refuting appearances of amity and long life. "Let time shape, and there an end," says Falstaff (III.ii.336-337), having devised a neat trap for some of Shallow's capital, but not recognizing that he himself is subject to another's control of time. Hal becomes Henry V and Falstaff rushes towards a redemption of time itself, the paying of a debt never promised, but one on which Falstaff himself is a final large installment.

Pistol's "tidings" of "golden joys," of "golden times and happy news of price" (V.iii.98-103) encourage in Falstaff a lust for power: "Master Robert Shallow, choose what office thou wilt in the land, 'tis thine. Pistol, I will double charge thee with dignities" (V.iii.127-129):

Master Shallow, my Lord Shallow — be what thou
wilt, I am fortune's steward... Let us take any
man's horses; the laws of England are at my commandment. Blessed are they that have been my friends,
and woe to my Lord Chief Justice!
(V.iii.133-143)

Were Falstaff's megalomania to achieve reality, Henry IV's negative vision of England (IV.v.117-137) would be realized. But Hal has encouraged the "vultures vile" of the commonwealth — Pistol's phrase (V.iii.144) — only to drive them from their anticipated prey. Falstaff's consistent opportunism will not be granted the absolute license he anticipates. Mere anarchy emerges to be dispelled by a few well-chosen and carefully saved words.

The next scene shows us neither the "pleasant days" Pistol predicts (V.ii.146) nor the chaos Falstaff would engender. Instead, we find parish officers dragging Doll Tearsheet off to "a justice" (V.iv.25). As Northumberland had feigned illness to avoid battle, Falstaff deafness to avoid the Chief Justice, and Bullcalf a "whoreson cold" (III.ii.185) to evade the draft, Doll simulates pregnancy to escape incarceration, the pillows she has stuffed under her gown a wry comment on Gaunt's "teeming womb of royal kings." But Doll and the Hostess, for all of their invention and invective, move towards justice, as inexorably as Falstaff rushes towards his final confrontation with the Lord Chief Justice. Falstaff regrets that he hasn't "had time to have made new liveries" with "the thousand pound [he] borrowed" from Shallow (V.v.11-12). We are reminded of the thousand pounds Hal promised Francis, and of the thousand pounds Falstaff claimed Hal owed him. Hal's debt comes due but it is discharged by a sudden new King Henry the Fifth. Falstaff can only turn and say, "Master Shallow, I owe you a thousand pound" (V.v.73-74).

Reno suggests, rightly I believe, that Falstaff's admission of unequivocal truth, unfiltered by any self-interest or irony, shows how shattered he is by Henry V's rejection.11/ Falstaff can attempt to persuade Shallow that "I will be the man yet that shall make you great" (V.v.80-81). yet Shallow - - of all people ! - - can take Falstaff's words and turn them against him: "I cannot perceive how, unless you give me your doublet and stuff me out with straw (V.v.82-83). Shallow defines Falstaff's "substance" as mere straw, and sees himself as merely a player in a scene that is hardly following Falstaff's scenario. The hopes of the survivors of Gaunt's world, hopes predicated on material gain, have turned to straw. Falstaff suggests, half-heartedly, that what Shallow "heard was but a color" (V.v.87). "A color that I fear you will die in, Sir John," Shallow responds, turning the word back on Falstaff (V.v.87-88). Shallow achieves a triple pun - - "collar" (noose), "choler" (disease), and "dye" (the changing of the color of the garment). That Shallow should best Falstaff so completely in the verbal exchange demonstrates the Fat Knight's absolute deflation. The scene is completed as Sir John Falstaff and Robert Shallow, Esquire, one of the king's justices, are led off to incarceration. No words will disintegrate the stones of the prison walls. Falstaff has run headlong into the ultimate trap. An actor in a play he never understood - - of which he did not "sound the bottom" - - he rushes onstage to become virtually a prop within the first scene of a new play in which he can have no part. The new play, of course, is that

directed by and starring King Henry the Fifth of England. The Falstaf
who promised to "deliver" Doll (V.v.39) from gaol is himself imprisoned
"Hal" suddenly becomes a product of Falstaff's imagination. He has beei
that for us since his soliloquy in Part I. Now the humors of idlenes
meet their yoke.

The odd Epilogue to II Henry IV provides yet another dimension o
"the world" of these plays, a world now just over the brink of Henry V'
kingship. It is spoken by "a Dancer" -- strange, when the play has hardl;
featured dancing, as opposed to A Midsummer Night's Dream, Rome
and Juliet, and the heavily choreographed Love's Labour's Lost. Ye
perhaps the Dancer suggests the nimbleness Henry V will need in hi
world, indeed the choreographic skills he will demonstrate is settin₤
England to the "music" John of Lancaster has heard (V.v.110).12/ If th
Epilogue is spoken by the Page, it emerges from a character who, lik
King Henry V, sees through the denizens of Eastcheap, as the Page wil
tell us in Henry V (III.ii.27-54 and IV.iv.68-75). The Dancer suggests th
ad hoc, extemporaneous nature of a world devoid both of the deep rule
of sacramentalism and the contractual laws of feudalism: "what I hav
to say is of mine own making" (4-5). Everything Henry V will say will b
"to the purpose, and so to the venture" (6-7). The Dancer's metaphor i
familiar. It has been the theme of the world of Bolingbroke, and it wil
be that of the world of Henry V:

> I meant indeed to pay you with this, which,
> if like an ill venture, it come unluckily home,
> I break, and you, my gentle creditors lose. Here
> I promised you I would be and here I commit my
> body to your mercies. Bate me some and I will
> pay you some and, as most debtors do, promise
> you infinitely.
>
> (10-16)

An epilogue about payment and debt reminds us of plays about man}
debts, and a variety of payments and promises of payment. In curiou
ways, the Dancer's words reach ahead to the Cambridge plot and to th
many things Henry V says before Agincourt — to Williams, to himself
and to the English troops at large.

The disclaimer that Falstaff is not the historical Oldcastle als￼
applies to the Falstaff of the play: "for Oldcastle died martyr, and thi
is not the man" (27-28). Falstaff can hardly be called a martyr to ₤
ruthless new politics launched without warning by an "instant king."
Falstaff demonstrates in his reaction to Henry V's accession wha
politics would become under a Falstaffian regime. Henry V wil
manipulate a facade across a politics still measured in quantitative an￼
pragmatic terms, a very tangible "measure for measure" that onl}
simulates a return to Gaunt's England, a necessary version of Henry IV'

bitter line: "England shall double gild his treble guilt" (IV.v.128). Henry V will skillfully convert any spiritual issues to commercial terms, unless he happens to conceal a purely commercial "deal" beneath a facade of sanctity and patriotism.

The Dancer's promise to produce Falstaff again in this sequence of plays (26-30) is never fulfilled — unless we believe that Shakespeare is wryly looking ahead to the Hostess's eulogy. Falstaff _may_ "die of a sweat" (30), but we have seen the death wound delivered.

Richard insisted on the substance or reality of sacramentalism after he had rendered it null and void. Falstaff believed in Hal's love, only to discover what we knew all along, that both Hal and his "friendship" with Falstaff were fictive creations of a man who knew he would become king. Richard had failed to observe the truth, and the truth had fled England. Hal/Henry V recognizes that effectiveness lies in successful imitation of "the truth": "Yet herein will I imitate the sun." Hal's soliloquy told us what kind of king he would be — calculating, manipulative, and _alone_ (as the soliloquy convention _per se_ implies). In rejecting Falstaff, Henry V excludes the notion of "fool and jester" (V.v.48) from his kingdom. The king will permit no licensed truth-sayer to puncture his postures. We glimpse in Henry V's rejection speech the inevitable technique of irony Shakespeare must employ with such a character.13/

1. Johnson: Prose and Poetry, ed. Mona Wilson (Cambridge, Mass., 1951), p. 565.

2. Norman Holland, "II Henry IV" (Complete Signet Shakespeare, New York, 1972), p. 678.

3. Bradley wisely suggests that Shakespeare "shows the fact and leaves the judgment to us" (Oxford Lectures, p. 255). Hawkins says, "That Shakespeare intends Prince John's faithlessness to be recognized as Machiavellian is doubtful, but it is clear that he intends our judgment of it to be Ciceronian" (336.n.71) — i.e. we are to censure and detest this horrible violation of faith. What confuses Dr. Johnson is clear to Mr. Hawkins, though a mere assertion of clarity does not make it so. Why should Cicero necessarily obtain, and Machiavelli not apply? — precedents seem valid on some idiosyncratic criteria. I, too, take a "Ciceronian" view of John's act at Gaultree Forest. But I know at least two successful administrators who — though they might condemn John publicly — would hug him inwardly to their corrupted souls. Again, cf. Bradley (although his lecture on "The Rejection of Falstaff" does not always reflect his own wisdom): Shakespeare's "impartiality makes us uncomfortable: we cannot bear to see him, like the sun, lighting up everything and judging nothing" (Oxford Lectures, p. 255). To paraphrase Emily Dickinson, Shakespeare "proceeds unmoved" — his job, after all, not to lay down his judgements, but to force us to make our own.

4. Falstaff plays on the proverb: "Who goes to Westminster for a wife, to Paul's for a man, or to Smithfield for a horse, may meet with a whore, a knave, and a jade." Shakespeare's mention of Paul's, which is Elizabethan times had turned into a marketplace, increases the feeling that the plays occur in Elizabethan London, that is, from the first mention of Prince Hal in Richard II onward. John of Gaunt's "England," indeed John of Gaunt himself, become remote memories inhabiting the minds of the "old men" of the Henry IV plays, who are not Gaunt and York, but Falstaff and Shallow. Both Falstaff and Shallow mention Gaunt in III.ii, although their memories are at variance with each other. Shallow's mention of "bona-robas" (III.i.24.207) indicates that there were whores in Richard II's England. It is as if a different way of looking at the world has made such unsavory elements part of a past wholly alien to John of Gaunt's sacramental vision. The reign of Henry IV, as Shakespeare depicts it, has much in common with an Elizabethan England "confronted," as Robert Eccleshall says, "by numerous rebellions in a period of unprecedented social mobility, rising prices and unemployment." "Richard Hooker's Synthesis," Journal of the History of Ideas XXXVII #1 (January - March, 1976), 116. In a sense, the rebellion led by the Archbiship of York in II Henry IV is similar to rebellions and

conspiracies against Elizabeth — efforts to restore "the old religion." If the plays suggest the similarity, they would seem to be saying that it cannot be done, making Shakespeare a man of the Reformation rather than a recusant.

5.   Falstaff's public relations represent a nice reversal of Prince Hal's, in that Falstaff projects a "positive image" that contradicts "the truth."

6.   One later analogue to this scene is that of Becky Sharp, who operates on great nerve and little capital: "Her aunt was dead. Mrs. Crawley ordered the most intense mourning for herself and little Rawdon.   The Colonel was busy arranging the affairs of the inheritance.   They could take the premier now, instead of the little entresol of the hotel which they occupied.   Mrs. Crawley and the landlord had a consultation about the new hangings, an amicable wrangle about the carpets, and a final adjustment of everything except the bill":   Vanity Fair, pp. 380-381.   For Becky, death is a kind of nineteenth-century credit card: " 'And you had best tell Sparks, your man, that old Sir Pitt is dead, and that you will come in for something considerable when the affairs are arranged.   He'll tell this to Raggles, who has been pressing for money, and it will console pool Raggles' ": Vanity Fair, p. 429.

7.   Cf. Goneril: "this our court. . . Shows like a riotous inn.   Epicurism and lust/ Makes it more like a tavern or a brothel/ Than a graced palace." (King Lear: I.iv.264-267).

8.   No longer is "the word made flesh" — the incarnation Richard aimed for in his coronation.   Flesh is devoid of sacramental significance. Flesh, for Falstaff, equates to damnation, prostitution, and to the "body natural," which is all that even a king has in this world. For Shallow, animal flesh, bullocks and ewes, mean money, and his Gloucestershire estate is little different than the Boarshead in that respect.   Falstaff introduces the equation between man and animal in responding to Hal's "Emboweled" (I Henry IV: V.iv.107) at Shrewsbury. Silence continues it in his song: "When flesh is cheap and females dear" (V.iii.19), perhaps a song he picked up while seeking bona robas long before.

9.   It seems inevitable to link this line with the "bucket" Richard made of the crown (Richard II: IV.i.184.187). Davy repeats the word "bucket" now only in its completely literal sense, and in the context of the homeliest domestic arrangements. If "bucket" in any way still relates to "crown," the line reminds us that by this time in II Henry IV a new king is about to ascend the throne.   A colleague who wishes to remain anonymous says of the Gloustershire scenes, "Shallow and Silence, talking about the price of bullocks at Stamford Fair, bear witness not to the change from mediaeval to modern ways of life, but to the unchanging small-change of conversation in rural England."   Perhaps so,

but that Shakespeare shows us this world and its penny-petty concerns suggests microcosmically what now concerns the world beyond the country fair. Quality and quantity are now equatable; "worth" is signified by monetary price and by monetary price alone.

10. The devalued world of Henry IV is captured, however, in Bullcalf's offer of "four Harry ten shillings in French crowns" (III.ii.236). The ten shilling piece, coined during the reign of Henry VII, was worth only half its face value by 1598.

11. Reno, From Sacrament to Ceremony, p. 247.

12. The ad hoc nature of this world is conveyed if, as has been suggested, the Epilogue is pococurante potpourrie of epilogue scraps.

13. For a corrective to critical stupidity, see Richard Levin, "Refuting Shakespeare's Endings," I and II, Modern Philology 72 and 75 (1975 and 1977), 337-349 and 132-158. I disagree in part with Mr. Levin's generally sound caveats. I am not as secure about the consensus Mr. Levin attributes to Shakespearean critics as Mr. Levin is — what is the "consensus reading" of V.i. of Hamlet for example? Mr. Levin tends to remove from the critic's purview and thus from Shakespeare's creative arsenal a large area of "irony," or manipulation of a spectator's point of view. Mr. Levin warns effectively, however, about elevating minor shadows of irony to the status of "meaning." For a response to Mr. Levin's articles, see my "Shakespeare and the Imposed Vision," Exchange (Autumn, 1979).

138

VI

The England of Harry, Prince of Wales

We watched Bolingbroke setting up the order of his England with promises he did not or could not keep. We watch Hal set up the premises of his kingship by denying any promise, except to "pay the debt [he] never promised" (I Henry IV: I.ii.206). Hal seems to deny even the promise of a prince, except when the emergency of Shrewsbury forces him to be one. His kingship will not be predicated on sacramental premises, nor based on any set of feudal contracts, rather it will depend on the King's personal qualities. Yet, while a pragmatist, Henry V learned, as Prince Hal, how to be a king in the best machiavellian sense.1/

That shrewd realist, Warwick, is correct to suggest that

The prince but studies his companions
Like a strange tongue, wherein, to gain the language,
'Tis needful that the most immodest word
Be looked upon and learned, which once attained,
Your highness knows, comes to no further use
But to be known and hated. So, like gross terms,
The prince will in the perfectness of time
Cast off his followers, and their memory
Shall as a pattern or a measure live,
By which his grace must mete the lives of others,
Turning past evils to advantages.
(IV.iv.68-78)

Warwick's "perfectness of time" picks up Hal's promise to "Redeem... time when men think least I will" (I Henry IV: I.ii.214). If Hal is echoing Ephesians in his soliloquy,2/ the reason for the disguise that Warwick penetrates becomes clear: "Take hede therefore that ye walke circumspectly, not as fooles, but as wise,/ Redeming the time: for the dayes are evil" (V.15-16. Geneva Version). Hal's efforts to learn "how to handle" Falstaff constitute the best possible apprenticeship for a "modern kingship" that must succeed in the midst of "evil days." The Geneva gloss on Paul's exhortation nicely defines the nature of Hal's plan for "instant kingship": "In these perilous dayes & crafte of the adversaries, take hede how to bye againe the occasions of godlines which the worlde hathe taken from you." Hal's "redemption of time" as Henry V occurs precisely in the context of "buying the occasion." The price of kingship has been his long sojourn in Eastcheap.

Bolingbroke had to revert to an older system, largely forced upon him by Richard, who had treated the land as if it were mere land. Henry V cannot restore sacramentalism, and certainly does not line up feudal allegiances before assuming kingship. He can, however, as Reno shows, create a ceremonial sense of kingship. Reno, speaking of the Tudor monarchy he sees Shakespeare reflecting in Henry V, says that "the substance of political power came more and more to be separated from its externals and these latter came more and more to be ceremonial adjuncts of the monarchial office, representative of its importance but not signifying its very origin."3/ Indeed, Henry V will be forced on at least one occasion to obscure the "origin" of his kingship, but he will do so within a ceremony that confirms his throne, no matter where it came from.

As he ascends the throne, of course, he assumes the burden of his father's acquisition of it and becomes the principal member of the court he avoided except when summoned by his father or by the Hotspur emergency, and until, as we notice, his father is dying. Prince Hal enters after an ambiguous fanfare. Henry IV delivers his final public speech about a crusade: "We will our youth lead on to higher fields/ And draw no swords but what are sanctified" (IV.iv.4-5). But sanctity is undermined by lack of "personal strength" (IV.iv.8) and by "rebels, now afoot" (IV.iv.9). Henry's career has come full circle; in his final public scene, we find him merely repeating the pattern of the opening scene of I Henry IV — the concept of the crusade is reitereated only to be interrupted by domestic broils, that have, by now, made the king a tired old man. Henry IV pauses to ask where Hal is. Gloucester thinks him at Windsor hunting (IV.iv.13). The king then delivers a long speech to Clarence, itemizing the qualities of the heir apparent and hoping that Clarence can become "a shelter to thy friends/ A hoop of gold to bind thy brothers in" (IV.iv.42-43). The speech is public and political, sounding a warning to the court. Be careful with him and of him, Henry IV seems to say, and things may work out. But "reality" breaks in. Clarence tells his father that Hal "dines in London... With Poins and other his continual followers" (IV.iv.51-53). The king relapses into predictions of the "unguided days/ And rotten times that you shall look upon/ When I am sleeping with my ancestors" (IV.iv.59-61). Warwick's comfortable words draw only Henry IV's cynical "'Tis seldom when the bee doth leave her comb/ In the dead carrion" (IV.iv.78-79).4/ More comfortable words, news of the victories at Gaultree Forest and Bramham Moor drive the king into "apoplexy" (IV.iv.130).

The prince enters, to be left alone with his father, and the crown. Hal recognizes the crown for what it is, as "hollow" as the eyes of his father (IV.v.6). Hal's apostrophe captures Bolingbroke's career — the higher Bolingbroke reached the greater the price and the more worthless the attainment. Power predicated only on material premises — military strength, for example — becomes finally self-destructive, even when force permits "peace [to put] forth her olive everywhere," as

Westmoreland says (IV.iv.87). Henry IV seems a necessary sacrifice to the peace England has achieved. Henry V will make the same sacrifice a different way. Hal places the proper valuation on the crown. While his words refer to kingship generally, as it had devolved from Richard II, they apply specifically to the "uneasy" (III.i.31) crown of Henry IV:

> O polished perturbation! Golden care!
> ... O majesty!
> When thou dost pinch thy bearer, thou dost sit
> Like a rich armor worn in heat of day,
> That scald'st with safety.
> (IV.v.22-30)

Hal has no illusions — this richness is dangerous, threatening the "body natural" of a king, rather than fusing that body with "body politic." If that fusion is to occur it will do so in spite of the "golden rigol" (IV.V.35: "rigol" means "circle," of course, but suggests "rigor" as well) — not because of it. What Reno says of Tudor monarchs applies to Hal, as he approaches kingship: "Paradoxically, [they] were strong in their own right because they did not claim too much in their own right."5/ Reno is very helpful in describing Hal's confrontation with the crown: "If... the crown is regarded as no more than symbol of power, it is desacramentalized and, in a sense, exorcized of its demonic life. The test requires contact with the dread object. Wearing it, Hal feels no infection of joy, no swelling of ambition, and instead of being victimized by it, he is master of it and thus able to use it as though it were magical — that is, to affect those who 'with awe and terror kneel to it.' "6/

Nor does Hal have any illusions about the sanctity of his inheritance; it is a normal transaction between father and son:

> nature, love, and filial tenderness
> Shall, O dear father, pay thee plenteously.
> My due from thee is this imperial crown,
> Which, as immediate from thy place and blood,
> Derives itself to me.
> (IV.v.38-42)

And, at this moment, he places this strictly "lineal honor" (IV.v.45) upon his head, believing his father to be dead. Hal has conducted his own coronation, knowing well the value of the crown and understanding clearly how it came to him. Coronation per se is now a ceremony for public consumption, not the sacred moment Richard made of it. What matters is the king's knowledge of what power is. As Reno says of the Tudor monarchs "to regard those forms (i.e. coronation, ceremony) as expressing the literal truth about politics was to commit political suicide."7/ The Tudors accepted a machiavellian duplicity as necessity.

Prince Hal, now believing he is king, will not commit suicide. Already a consummate play-actor, Hal retains the literal mind he has inherited from Bolingbroke.

But Henry IV is not dead, merely moribund. He awakens to chastize his son bitterly — and, appropriately, within the profit and loss ethic he himself has encouraged in England: "How quickly nature falls into revolt/ When gold becomes her object" (IV.v.65-66).8/ The indictment contains several levels of irony, not the least of which is that Hal has understood the premises of "this new world" completely from the first, but has expressed them with an objectivity which Henry IV has never enjoyed. Hal has had time to consider kingship, indeed time in which to train for it. As we have just seen, Hal has been exploring the conflict between gold and nature, and recognizing that the man must devise ways of turning a disadvantage — the conflict between the king's "two bodies" — into advantage. Hal has been struggling with the "revolt" of crown against man, realising that the man must control the crown, and not, as with his father, the crown the man. Hal has been clear-sighted about the lineal nature of his kingship, and has expressed the "tenderness" he owes his father for the "due" of inheritance. Bolingbroke expresses the same theme, but in a vehicle of bitter cynicism:

> For this the foolish overcareful fathers
> Have broke their sleep with thoughts,
> Their brains with care, their bones with industry.
> For this they have engrossed and piled up
> The cank'red heaps of strange-achieved gold;
> For this they have been thoughtful to invest
> Their sons with arts and martial exercises.
> When, like the bee, culling from every flower
> The virtuous sweets, our thighs packed with wax,
> Our mouths with honey, we bring it to the hive,
> And, like the bees, are murdered for our pains.9/
> This bitter taste yields his engrossments
> To the ending father.
> (IV.v.67-79)

> Dost thou so hunger for mine empty chair
> That thou wilt needs invest thee with my honors
> Before thy hour be ripe? O foolish youth!
> Thou seek'st the greatness that will overwhelm thee.
> (IV.v.94-97)

Hal's response — as Goddard has shown10/ — does not reflect precisely has actual apostrophe to the crown.11/ Hal's rebuttal is conditioned by his audience — he makes a human-enough adjustment — and also by the politics of the situation — his audience is not merely father, but king. Hal's lines now dwell on his "most true and duteous spirit" (IV.v.147), and his necessary hopes that his father will continue to be king: "And He that wears the crown immortally/ Long guard it yours" (IV.v.143-144). Hal's response contains that piety typical of his father's public utterances (cf. I Henry IV: I.i.1 ff., II Henry IV: IV.iv.1 ff., and IV.iv.253 ff.), and of Henry V's public words (in private, he will address a pagan or Old Testament "God of battles": Henry V: IV.i.289). But Hal does reiterate his assessment of the crown: "'thou best of gold art worst of gold, '" Hal claims he has said to the crown (IV.v.160). He calls himself a "true inheritor" (IV.v.168), but has no illusions about his father's means of gaining it:

> You won it, wore it, kept it, gave it me.
> The plain and right must my possession be,
> Which I with more than with a common pain
> 'Gainst all the world will rightfully maintain.
>   (IV.v.221-224)

Hal correctly anticipated challenges to his crown, similar to those launched against that of Henry IV.

Again — as so often in these plays — the surface of what we have seen must now be reinterpreted. In Henry IV's recapitulation of his career we do not have a wholly biased point-of-view, because Henry IV's words have the legal — and dramatic — weight of a "death-bed confession." The king informs upon himself, a prelude to Claudius's awareness that he must, someday, "Even to the teeth and forehead of [his] faults/ ...give in evidence" (Hamlet: III.iii.63-64).12/

> God knows,
> By what by-paths and indirect crooked ways
> I met this crown, and I myself know well
> How troublesome it sat upon my head...
> It seemed in me
> But as an honor snatched with boisterous hand.
>   (IV.v.183-191)

Bolingbroke's theft encouraged an England of thieves and would-be robbers.13/ Kingship — positive or negative — ramifies into every corner of the land, as the Richard II - Henry IV plays have demonstrated, and as King Lear and Macbeth (in Duncan, Macbeth, and Edward) will.

Bolingbroke may have announced his crusade at the end of Richard II as a means of personal and political expiation, a way of placing himself and England again within the sacramental value system. But the dynamic he, with Richard's prompting, encourages will not be vectored into Gaunt's glorious memory of things past. England comes inexorably to resemble its king, particularly to reenact or attempt to recreate the manner in which Bolingbroke became king. The "substance" of kingship Richard had inherited goes with Richard, indeed had largely been spent by the opening scene of <u>Richard II</u>. Any effort to "draw sanctified swords" (cf. IV.iv.4) is doomed by the sequence of events that began with the unhallowed sword that felled Gloucester. Not only does Bolingbroke not lead his crusade, but the concept of the crusade itself comes inevitably to be translated into political terms:

> I... had a purpose now
> To lead out many to the Holy Land,
> Lest rest and lying still might make them look
> Too near unto my state.
> (IV.iv.209-212)

Dr. Johnson offers this brilliant commentary on the lines: "This journey to the Holy Land, of which the king very frequently revives the mention, had two motives, religion and policy. He durst not wear the ill-gotten crown without expiation, but in the act of expiation he contrives to make his wickedness successful."14/ Like the Crusade become a charade, the prophecy that Henry $\overline{IV}$ "should not die but in Jerusalem" (IV.v.236) shrinks — from the dimensions of "the Holy Land" (IV.v.238) to the narrower space of a "chamber" (IV.v.238) in Westminster.15/

Henry IV recognized that his kingship has been a "counterfeit." The many men marching in the king's coats at Shrewsbury represent the player - king Henry IV has been:

> all my reign hath been but as a scene
> Acting that argument [i.e. deposition, regicide, and civil war],
> And now my death
> Changes the mode, for what in me was purchased
> Falls upon thee in a more fairer sort...
> (IV.v.197-200)

Kingship remains something "purchased." Indeed, the ambiguity of the lines (Henry IV could say "what by me...") suggest that kingship "buys its owner" — property, as Marx would have it, becoming a burden, perhaps more the owner than the person purchasing it. The genre set — a kingship "won," but to be retained only by the means whereby it was won — all that can be changed is "the mode," or sub-genre, the "style" with which a king conducts his monarchy. Basic premises are irrelevant — except perhaps "the good of the kingdom" as the king perceives that good. A corollary to a king's perception must be his own maintenance of power.16/

As Henry V approaches his coronation, the realm's only "valid coinage" seems to be the apprehension in the face of the Chief Justice. "I dare swear," says Gloucester to the Chief Justice," you borrow not that face/ Of seeming sorrow — it is sure your own" (V.ii.28-29). The assembled lords and officers anticipate with Clarence that the Chief

Justice must "now speak Sir John Falstaff fair,/ Which swims against your stream of quality' (V.ii.33-34). They do not realize, of course, that, while Hal as prince was maneuvered by Falstaff into saying "that which his flesh rebels against" (II.iv.357-358), Henry V has planned an "overturning" (cf. Chief Justice: V.ii.19) based on a face he has borrowed for his long sojourn in Eastcheap. When he does appear "all look strangely" on him (V.ii.62). He accepts the Chief Justice as representing "the image of the king" (V.ii. 79), Henry IV and Henry V, but Henry V admits as much only after participating in a long debate with the Chief Justice. The Chief Justice soberly recreates a scene reminiscent of the "play extempore" of Part I:

> Be now the father and propose a son:
> Hear your own dignity so much profaned,
> See your most dreadful laws so loosely slighted,
> Behold yourself so by a son disdained,
> And then imagine me taking your part
> And in your power soft silencing your son.
>   (V.ii.92-97)

Hal has predicted his banishing of Falstaff in that earlier scene ("I do, I will": I Henry IV: II.iv.486). He is now king, therefore no longer must sustain a role seemingly in conflict with his calling. He will no longer, as the Chief Justice suggests "spurn at your most royal image/ And mock your workings in a second body" (V.ii.89-90). As far as possible, the new king will present a "royal image," not a fusion of body politic and body natural, but a conscious subordination of man to crown that allows kingship whatever efficacy it can attain. Bolingbroke's subordination was by the crown. Henry V's is of the crown, and the distinction is vital. Bolingbroke inherits a shattered conception of kingship he cannot reintegrate. Henry V knows the importance of both the imagery and the material basis of a convincing kingly facade. He responds to the Chief Justice with Warwick's weighing metaphor, this time reflecting the scales of justice, of course, but also the quantitative premises of justice as Henry V will administer it: "You are right, justice, and you weigh this well" (V.ii.102). Henry V has recognized the correctness of the Chief Justice's position already, of course, but he allows himself to seem to be convinced by the Chief Justice's speech. It is the pose of a reasonable man accepting a valid argument. And such a stance is characteristic of Henry V. When it suits his purposes he can assume a position — here, affected anger at the Chief Justice, later, seeming trust of the traitors — that in no way reflects the decision he has already made. We can often view the king in the precise light of Hal's initial "I know you all." The career of Prince Hal seemingly refutes a decision only we know has been made — until the precise moment comes for that decision to be revealed to the world.

Falstaff provides such a moment. His interruption of the coronation procession gives the new king the opportunity to establish the hierarchy of "law and order" and to translate potential disruption into the mode of Henry V — ceremonial. Henry V cómmands that the proper subordinate quell the disturbance: "My Lord Chief Justice, speak to that vain man" (V.v.45). But Falstaff insists on speaking to his "heart" (V.v.46), and receives the impact of the heavy monosyllables of a king who claims not to know Falstaff — though the rest of his speech refutes its opening — and whom Falstaff does not know:

> I know thee not, old man, fall to thy prayers.
> How ill white hairs become a fool and jester!
> I have long dreamt of such a kind of man,
> So surfeit-swelled, so old, and so profane,
> But, being awaked, I do despise my dream.
> Make less thy body hence, and more thy grace.
> Leave gormandizing. Know the grave doth gape
> For thee thrice wider than for other men.
> Reply not to me with a fool-born jest.
> Presume not that I am the thing I was,
> For God doth know, so shall the world perceive,
> That I have turned away my former self.
>   (V.v.47-58)

If the king's opening line echoes St. Matthew's Parable of the Wise and Foolish Virgins, then Henry V is creating a quite conscious "resurrection":

> But he answered, and said, Verely I say unto you, I knowe you not.
>
> Watche therefore: for ye knowe nether the day, nor the houre, when the Sonne of man wil come.
>   (25:12-13: Geneva Version)

The Parable of the Talents, with its exile of the unprofitable servant follows, of course, in the same chapter. Henry V, it would seem, is imitating the Son.

The king's speech is a public utterance, delivered not just to Falstaff, but to all in England whom Falstaff represents. Henry V reads a policy statement, conveniently accusing Falstaff of being "the tutor and the feeder of [Hal's] riots" (V.v.63), but not indicating that the ability to spring such an extemporaneous trap so articulately emerges from his constant contest with Falstaff.17/ Henry V knows "how to handle" Falstaff. He denies him a response: "Reply not to me with a fool-born jest." Without language, Falstaff is trapped. What would seem

146

to be an obscene interruption to a solemn occasion becomes an instant ceremony, as Henry V translates discord into a sober lecture on order. While Hal had predicted nothing else, either in soliloquy or to Falstaff directly, we must remember that this is not Hal, but King Henry the Fifth of England, showing Falstaff how to turn diseases to commodity, a bad reputation to a triumphant advantage. At the end of his speech, the king gives a prescription to all within his realm, and redelegates to the Chief Justice the authority he had attempted to give him before Falstaff "forced" the king's direct response:

> And, as we hear you do reform yourselves,
> We will, according to your strengths and qualities,
> Give you advancement. Be it your charge, my lord,
> To see performed the tenor of our word.
> Set on.
>   (V.v.68-72)

From "I know you all," to "I know thee not," to the royal command "Not to come near our person by ten mile" (V.v.65) — the transition is complete. The past lies as in a despised dream. The word is "Set on!"

Falstaff's incarceration is conveniently omitted by the king in his public speech. He has been harsh, yet encouraging. As so often with Henry V, intentions become clear only after public words. Henry V has learned that trick of leadership from his chief "misleader" (V.v.65), Falstaff. And Falstaff learns it — too late — from Henry V. "So a prince," says Machiavelli, "should be so prudent that he knows how to escape the evil reputation attached to those vices which could lose him his state." Richard II attached himself to those vices and lost his state — and the attributes of kingship that went with it, indeed which were his "state." Hal seemed attached to evil reputation — as Bolingbroke charged repeatedly — but in divorcing himself Henry V salvages the "ceremony" that is all a modern king can achieve in a desacralized world. Having defeated the dangerous military energy represented by Hotspur at the end of Part I, as Hal, Henry V contains the equally destructive civil chaos embodied by Falstaff at the end of Part II.18/ In each case, Henry provides the precise dimensions of his rivals' graves: "two paces of the vilest earth" will be "room enough" for Hotspur (I: V.iv.91-92), while "the grave doth gape/ For [Falstaff] thrice wider than for other men" (II: V.v.57-58)). Hal/Henry V knows the measurements of his world and can reduce those who would exceed them to the empirical standard he sets. Henry V proves to be the most able leader in the quantified world this side of Gaunt's "other Eden, demi-paradise." In this world, leadership is self-produced. It has no origins other than those residing in the skills of the body natural. As Reno says of Hal/Henry V, "To counterfeit is to be the very image of the times, and to play a role the only tactic available."19/

1.   I agree with Manheim's description of Henry V as machiavellian: _The Weak King Dilemma in the Shakespearean History Play_ (Syracuse University Press, 1973), pp. 161-182, but I would qualify Manheim's conclusions heavily. I believe that Henry V perceives the nature of the world he inherits and derives from his perception the pragmatic "principle" of leadership it demands. A leader like Henry V recognizes that ceremony is a valuable adjunct to leadership among a people still clinging to sacramental expectations. I cannot agree with Manheim that Shakespeare is prescribing the formula for effective leadership in Henry V. Henry V controls "inevitability" more surely than did his father, indeed Henry V contrives to make himself seem simultaneously to be both the genius and the agent of history. He becomes, however, a victim of his own self-dictated history. Or, to put it another way, England is as much a victim of his "success" as it was on the collusion between Richard II and Bolingbroke. Although the Wars of the Roses have their causes in the deposition and murder of Richard, their specific format is dictated unknowingly by Henry V.

2.   See J. A. Bryant, _Hippolyta's View_ (Lexington, Kentucky, 1961), Chapter 4: "Prince Hal and the Ephesians," and D. J. Palmer, "Casting Off the Old Man: History and St. Paul, "_Critical Quarterly_ 12 (1970), 267-283.

3.   Reno, _From Sacrament to Ceremony_, p. 152.

4.   The lines cast an ironic tone — as if one were needed — over Canterbury's "honeybee" analogy in _Henry V_ (I.ii.187-206), suggesting that all the activity Canterbury happily describes is somehow taking place amid a pervasive rot and corruption.

5.   Reno, _From Sacrament to Ceremony_, p. 182.

6.   Reno, _From Sacrament to Ceremony_, p. 277.

7.   Reno, _From Sacrament to Ceremony_, p. 183.

8.   In his illuminating discussion of the scene, Frank Manley suggests that "when the king wakes, we are once again plunged into the old Lancastrian world, in which the crown is up for grabs." Manley goes on to show that Hal is accused of the archetypal Lancastrian crime, the stealing of a crown, and that "it is within that world that Hal justifies himself." Hal is shrewd enough, Manley argues, to recognize that his father's accusation launches itself from the premises of the Lancastrian world-view, that, having stolen a crown, Henry IV can comprehend only similar motives in others. Henry IV as king provides the motivation for England, where, after his example, there seem to be as many would-be

kings as roam around Prospero's island. "The Unity of Betrayal in II Henry IV," Studies in the Literary Imagination V #1 (April, 1972). Before agreeing totally that the stealing of a crown is an exclusively Lancastrian shortcoming, we must remember that it was Richard's stealing of a great estate that elicited the imperative of deposition.

9.   Bees again, used to contrast points of view (that is, if Shakespeare remembers Bolingbroke's lines here when he gets to Canterbury's lines in Henry V). Although the activity of the bees is similar in each passage, the position of the father differs. In contrast to Bolingbroke's busy parent is Canterbury's satisfied overseer: "Others like soldiers armed in their stings/ Make boot upon the summer's velvet buds,/ Which pillage they with merry march bring home /To the tent-royal of their emperor —/ Who, busied in his majesty, surveys/ The singing masons building roofs of gold..."(I.ii.193-198). As opposed to the father who is killed for his efforts by an ingrate son, Canterbury's king predicts Henry V's career in describing "The sad-eyed justice, with his surly hum,/ Delivering o'er to executors pale/ The lazy yawning drone" (I.ii.202-204).

10.   Harold C. Goddard, The Meaning of Shakespeare (Chicago, 1951), pp. 193-196.

11.   Cf. Manley, "Unity of Betrayal in II Henry IV," 104: "the second speech is rhetorical and rings false... it is concerned only with his father and not with the inheritance, whereas in the first speech the opposite is true."

12.   Johnson's commentary on Bolingbroke's "How I came by the crown, O God forgive,/ And grant it may with thee in true peace live!" (IV.v.218-219) applies, mutatis mutandis, to Claudius: "This is a true picture of a mind divided between heaven and earth. He prays for the prosperity of guilt while he deprecates its punishment": Johnson: Prose and Poetry, ed. Mona Wilson (Cambridge, Massachusetts, 1951), p. 566. Bolingbroke, and perhaps to a lesser extent Claudius and Macbeth, share the characteristics of the "active - negative" political leader described by James Barber: "The activity has a compulsive quality, as if the man were trying to make up for something or to escape from anxiety into hard work. He seems ambitious, striving upward, power-seeking. His stance towards his environment is aggressive and he has a persistent problem in managing his aggressive feelings. His self-image is vague and discontinuous. Life is a struggle to achieve and hold power, hampered by the condemnations of a perfectionistic conscience. Active - negative types pour energy into the political system, but it is an energy distorted from within." The Presidential Character (Englewood Cliffs, N.J., 1972), p. 292.

13.   Cf. Hawkins, 325: "Himself a usurper, a 'cutpurse of the empire,' [Henry IV] gives the sanction of royal example to both the rebel and the highwayman." True, but as I have argued, Richard's crimes predicate Bolingbroke's reign.

14.   Johnson: Prose and Poetry, p. 566.

15.   Although unlike Macbeth, another usurper - regicide troubled by fits, Bolingbroke does not curse the prophecy. His acceptance, as James Black has suggested to me, represents a transcendence of a troubled royal life: "Laud be to God! Even there my life must end" (IV.v.234). It is ironic that Henry IV represents an authentic piety in a world he has helped render very secular.

16.   A further corollary would seem to be that Henry IV is "married" to the crown. We see Richard II's wife and witness Henry V's wooing of Katherine, but we never see Joan of Brittany. The crown is, as Hal says, his father's "troublesome...bedfellow" (II Henry IV: IV.v.21).

17.   And, of course, from the cold Lancastrian blood. Prince John, who can also spring a trap or two, has not had the benefit of Falstaff's tutoring. Manley suggests that Henry V, in his lines about his father's going "wild into his grave" (V.ii.123 ff.), tells us that Henry V has buried "his passion, emotion — whatever it is that makes a person most vital and most individual" (107). Certainly Henry V has buried Prince Hal. Manley goes on to suggest that Henry V's "rejection of Falstaff... carries with it an acceptance of John — a betrayal of the emotions for the calculating political expediency of the Lancastrians. But it is also a betrayal of himself" (109). Perhaps — a betrayal of that Hal that built up a personality within a pose? Certainly a betrayal of "body natural," an abandonment that Henry V believes necessary to his kingship. He expressed that necessity, that "hard condition" (IV.i.219), explicitly before Agincourt, and seems to perceive it in his attempt to pull off a practical joke with Williams and Fluellen after the battle. While the king's political skills are the product of a "body natural" conditioned to look like an old-fashioned "body politic" (as ceremony is meant to resemble ritual), a deeper "nature," a product of unexamined psychic content, seems to want to emerge in Henry V. But his own program has denied him any such release.

18.   Hawkins is excellent in equating Hotspur and Falstaff: "Hotspur's steed is as much a symbol of excess as Falstaff's bottle" (327).

19.   Reno, From Sacrament to Ceremony, p. 272.0

VII

The England of King Henry V

The "apology" of the opening Chorus of Henry V is ironic. Shakespeare could depict a battle. He has imitated many battles — Rouen, Bordeaux, Angiers, St. Albans, Wakefield, Towton, Tewkesbury, Bosworth Field, and Shrewsbury — already. Why does he begin a play by saying, in effect, "my power is suddenly lost"?: perhaps to call attention to the king who stages it all, the king who controls the sequence of events leading to Agincourt. Shakespeare's disclaimer of his mimetic abilities focusses our attention on those of Henry V.1/ Outnumbered at Agincourt, the king must accomplish with his soldiers something similar to what the Chorus asks of us:

> Piece out our imperfections with your thoughts:
> Into a thousand parts divide one man
> And make imaginary puissance.
>
> (23-25)

If Richard's world became "hollow" and Henry IV's was therefore "shallow," Henry V, inheritor of an intrinisically meaningless crown, provides an artistic simulation of true kingship.

The canny Chichele wonders "how his grace should glean" his rhetorical ability, "Since his addiction was to courses vain,/ His companies unlettered, rude, and shallow" (I.i. 53-55). Falstaff's evaluation of Hal may have been "shallow," but we witnessed Falstaff's ability to parody any style — "King Cambyses' vein," for example (I Henry IV: I.iv. 390) — and know that Hal's chief companion was hardly unlettered. We know as well that Hal's addiction was to verbal combat with Falstaff, a tutorial culminating in the one-way communication of rejection. Ely reiterates the Warwick position: "The prince obscured his contemplation/ Under the veil of wildness" (I.i.62-63). And Canterbury admits as much:

> It must be so, for miracles are ceased;
> And therefore we must needs admit the means
> How things are perfected.
>
> (I.i.66-68)

"Miracles" ended, according to Protestant belief, after the revelation of Christ. Only natural causes, then, can explain any semblance of miracle. Shakespeare is guilty of anachronism, of course, in imputing Protestant doctrine to an Archbishop of Canterbury in 1414, but the implication is that spiritual or sacramental premises no longer apply to this world. The world is merely "natural" — raw material for the opportunist, who can, if skillful enough, create the illusion of "miracle."

The scene shifts suddenly from the "wildness, mortified" (I.i.25) of the king back to the practical matters at hand. Even if drama per se permitted characters to indulge long discussions, the brisk pace of Henry V's England will not tolerate digressions.2/ Beneath the surface of whatever seems to be happening lies the reality of quantity. The state of England has devolved to a point where a bill ruinous to the Church is finally being considered: "that self bill is urged," says Canterbury,

> Which in the eleventh year of the last king's reign
> Was like, and had indeed against us passed
> But that the scambling and unquiet time
> Did push it out of farther question.
>
> (I.i.1-5)

The bill reflects back upon Richard's leasing out of lands that were his sacred trust. Its delay in passage recalls Falstaff's escape from justice only because of the "unquiet time" (II Henry IV: I.ii.152). In the present case, Canterbury complains,

> We lose the better half of our possession;
> For all the temporal lands which men devout
> By testament have given to the Church
> Would they strip from us.
>
> (I.i.7-11)

The "they" refers, of course, to Parliament, but it links neatly with the antecedent, "men devout," of whom the principal would be Henry V. Henry is seen, then, as both a protector and a threatener of the Church. Land returned to sacred trust is seen again only as commodity, "valued," as Canterbury continues,

> As much as would maintain, to the king's honor,
> Full fifteen earls and fifteen hundred knights,
> Six thousand two hundred good esquires,
> And to the relief of lazars, and weak age
> Of indigent faint souls, past corporal toil,
> A hundred alms houses right well supplied;
> And to the coffers of the king beside,
> A thousand pound by the year.
>
> (I.i.11-19)

152

One wonders why, if Henry needs an army for his French war, he does not convert Church lands into earls, knights, and esquires. It would seem that, in addition to monetary support from the Church, Henry wants "divine sanction" — at least the lip-service of divines. Whoever has appraised the Church's "temporal lands" has done so with remarkable precision, translating each acre into an equivalent value for the king. We learn, on the other side of the equation, how great that acreage must be.

Ely can only exclaim, "This would drink deep" (I.i.20). Canterbury responds, "'Twould drink the cup and all" (I.i. 20). The Archbishop is interested, obviously, not in the sacramental values of the "cup"; he uses a convenient metaphor for the loss of precisely estimated tangible value. But he has a plan. While the king may be "a true lover of the holy Church," as Ely says (I.i. 23),3/ Canterbury, unwilling to trust the king's love per se, has sought a cancellation of the ruinous bill, a solution based on the king's immediate needs, Who knows how long it would take to convert the church's lands into new "nobles" for the king — that is, to erect a very profitable feudal system for Henry V? His father's advice has been to "busy giddy minds/ With foreign quarrels" (II Henry IV: IV.v.213-214), and Prince John has already surmised that English power will quickly point towards France:

> I will lay odds that, ere this year expire,
> We bear our civil swords and native fire
> As far as France. I heard a bird so sing,
> Whose music, to my thinking, pleased the king.
> (II Henry IV: V.v.107-110)

While we do not learn what Byzantine bird John overheard, we know enough about John to know that he bets on nothing but "sure things." Henry V will mount his war rapidly — a response to his father's advice, and a rebuke to his father's inability to launch a crusade. But Henry IV has also cleared England of almost all vestiges of rebellion. Lest he be dismissed too easily as a failure, we must recall the temporary respite from civil war he bequeaths to his son. His death removes one of the chief sources of unrest and clears the way for Henry V's rapid progress. It would seem that, rather than erect the political structure possible if the anti-Church bill is made law, Henry V wishes to draw power and money into his own hands, so that he can make an immediate move on France.

Canterbury has responded to the danger of the bill with an

> offer to his majesty —
> Upon our spiritual convocation,
> And in regard of causes now in hand,
> Which I have opened to his grace at large,

As touching France — to give a greater sum
Than ever at one time the clergy yet
Did to his predecessors part withal.
(I.i.75-81)

Chichele will not only provide justification for the adventure, he will help finance it as well. The Church has the money to back the king's politics. No "collusion" is necessary. Nor is it dramatized for us. We can with a perfect guess predict the outcome of the scene to follow. In fact, the Archbishop's exposition of Henry's claim to France has been conveniently interrupted by the arrival of the French ambassador, who is about to be given "audience" (I.i. 91). Canterbury knows what the ambassador will say:

Then go we in to know his embassy:
Which I could with a ready guess declare,
Before the Frenchman speak a word of it.
(I.i.96-97)

We do not know yet to what the ambassador is responding, but we do know that Henry V received Canterbury's offer "with good acceptance" (I.i.83). We know, then, that if Henry wants the Church's support for a war on France, and that if Canterbury wishes to stave off the bill that would bankrupt the Church, "special interests" can mesh neatly in public, without seeming to be motivated by the money basic to each interest.

Again typically in these plays, we learn something that forces us to reinterpret what we have already heard when we discover that Henry V has already claimed "several dukedoms in the right/ of [his] great predecessor, King Edward the Third" (I.ii.247-248). This is the claim Canterbury knows will be rejected by the French ambassador. The claim has been made, as Canterbury tells Ely (I.i.84-89) before the king has heard a full exposition of its validity. The final decision to invade, then, waits only on a formal rejection of Henry's claim.

I find it impossible to agree with Kittredge's summary of Act One of Henry V:

> The effect of the first act is to relieve King
> Henry, in the minds of the audience, of any responsi-
> bility for the war that is to ensue. The clergy
> take it all upon their consciences. We also have the
> most favorable exposition of the cause. And at the
> end of the act the Dauphin's wanton insult adds the
> touch of personal injury which makes the conflict
> interesting as the king's own war rather than as a
> mere matter of personal aggrandizement.4/

154

If the "effect" is as Kittredge describes it, then the audience is being fooled, because the effect is only indirectly Shakespeare's. More directly, it is of Henry V's making. Shakespeare has dramatized the anger of John of Gaunt at Richard's betrayal of England's sacred quality. Shakespeare had exposed the fatal posturings of Richard II, had focussed on the dilemma of the Duke of York, has shown the ironic efficiency of Bolingbroke, the opportunism of Northumberland — all of this in Richard II. We have observed the unquiet career of Henry IV and Hal's education as king-to-be, yet we are told that Shakespeare suddenly ceases his examination of politics to indulge in unqualified admiration of "the mirror of all Christian kings" (Chorus: II.6). The mirror reflects what the king chooses it to reflect and, as I will reiterate, the words of the Chorus cannot be accepted "at face value" in Henry V any more than can the public utterances of King Henry V.5/ But, as Palmer says, "Henry of Monmouth has been accepted by most Englishmen, including some of Shakespeare's most famous critics, as the portrait of a stainless Christian warrior and as an heroic example of what every happy man would wish to be."6/

Harold Goddard, however, had filled in Hazlitt's outline and reads the play as a condemnation of Henry V. 7/ One might suggest that Shakespeare has already delivered his judgement on Henry V through Henry VI:

> But, Clifford, tell me, didst thou never hear
> That things ill-got had ever bad success?
> And happy always was it for that son
> Whose father for his hoarding went to hell?
> I'll leave my son my virtuous deeds behind,
> And would my father had left me no more.
> (III Henry VI: II.ii.45-50)

These words, however, are as much a product of the son's pious helplessness as of the father's actions, just as Goddard's harsh view of Henry V is conditioned by Goddard's pacificism, and Hazlitt's by his republicanism. Yet, while Goddard commits the "intentional fallacy" — as he does consistently in his often brilliant analyses of "the meaning of Shakespeare" — he suggests that Shakespeare's habit of qualification works on in this ostensibly heroic play. Shakespeare neither extols nor denigrates Henry V. The play achieves the kind of balance that is the effect of irony, a balance that may expose strength and weakness, but does not deliver moral judgements. As Smith says, "Holinshed praised [Henry V]... and Shakespeare has accepted that surface reputation without relinquishing the sordid details that brought the heroic action into being. Henry V may be the mirror of all Christian kings, but how good or bad that may be depends upon one's idea of Christian kings — that of Erasmus, for example, or of Machiavelli, or of the Tudor myth."8/

Shakespeare does not dramatize Henry's conference with Canterbury, nor does he give us the scene between John of Lancaster and the bird. The audience, moreover, is not taken into Henry V's confidence as we were by Hal when he revealed the rationale behind his sojourn in Eastcheap. No doubt exists about the intentions of either Henry or Canterbury prior to the "justification scene," but the king does not say, "I'll have this bishop here support my claim/ To France," We have instead a brilliant tour de force, a public scene that allows decisions already made to emerge as if the decision is being made within the scene. We are not invited, as we are so often in Shakespeare's plays, to associate ourselves with the manipulator through the revelation of his purpose. Why not? The answer would seem to lie in the fact that Henry is king and in the kind of king he chooses to be. That we view Henry's contrivance of justification at a distance allows us to experience the difference between Hal and Henry V. The king operates from a more remote position, from the lofty place where decisions are not those of an individual, but of a nation. If Hal was "immersed," over-exposed, as Bolingbroke charged, Henry V is isolated, a stance chosen again by design. Thus, while the spectator is armed, as usual, with knowledge superior to that of most of the characters on the stage, our experience of the king is similar to that of the other characters. The king is alone. His is the unique position of personifying a nation, and we gain no "inside view" of that position until the eve of Agincourt. If Henry V is to create "ceremony" — the effect of ritual without sacramental "innerness" — he cannot be revealed as an impotent Wizard of Oz, pulling strings and punching buttons. While we experience this king primarily from the "outside," that view is perhaps the only one available. Henry V deals almost exclusively in externals, the use of rhetoric, the staging of scenes that support his position, in the gestures of war and the postures of monarchy. He must be ready — and Falstaff has made him so — to turn any situation to his advantage, to make it seem consistently that he does represent the England Gaunt celebrated. Since little in Henry V is not subordinate to his role as king — nothing has been subordinate to his role, we know, from Hal's first soliloquy onward — for Henry V suddenly to take us into his confidence would be dramatically jarring. Since he has little or no "inner self," the revelation of an "inner man" would confuse rather than clarify his character. We seldom see Henry outside his role as king because he and the role become gradually inseparable. The apparent exceptions, his disguise and his soliloquies before Agincourt, only confirm that he is king.

The long scene preceding the entrance of the French ambassador ratifies a decision already made, a decision based solidly on a financial transaction. The source of funding for the French war and the cancellation of the bill of confiscation are not brought to the surface of the scene — the deal has been worked out privately, and once consummated, is a "given." But we should not, as spectators, allow ourselves to ignore the basic premises of the scene, which are commercial. As I will suggest, the French war, as Henry sees it, is itself a commercial venture. We cannot believe that Henry's decision follows Canterbury's exposition and the exhortations of the assembled nobility. That belief would be exploded anyway once the France ambassador reveals that Henry has already issued his ultimatum. The point is that it seems that Henry makes his decision during the scene, or, as he would prefer it, it seems that the decision is made for him during the scene. It seems more and more as the scene develops that he has no choice, but is swept along before the irresistible rush of historical necessity. And so he is by the end of the scene. To his followers, Henry V appears helpless before the validity of his claim. He stands at the point of the vector of precisely that momentum he has encouraged.

Tillyard complains of the discrepancy between Hal and Henry V:

> In the debate in I-2 on the French war Henry
> is a different person [than he was as Hal]. He
> hardly interposes much less argues. As a thinker
> he is quite passive, leaving the business to
> others. When these have pronounced their verdict,
> he accepts without a word of comment.9/

Henry's role here is passivity, not revelry. If we deny that Henry is playing a role, then Tillyard is right, but we must also deny what seems indisputable, that the decision to invade France is Henry's alone, and that, once certain of backing, he has made that decision before the scene has begun. He has already done the thinking. In I.ii, he lets people do the talking for him — and for themselves. But the roles of others — Canterbury's, for example — have either been assigned in advance or are easily predicted. Like his father's Council of War in the first scene of I Henry IV, Henry V's scene is neatly veiled behind sanctimonious seemings.

Henry pretends to be a king growing gradually helpless before overwhelming forces; in reality, he nurtures the release of those forces. He delays the entrance of the French ambassador until Canterbury arrives with what Henry knows are words "concerning us and France" (I.ii.6), that is, the kingdom and France. Before Canterbury speaks, however, the king admonishes him:

> For God doth know how many, now in health,
> Shall drop their blood in approbation
> Of what your reverence shall incite us to.
> Therefore take heed how you impawn our person,
> How you awake our sleeping sword of war.
> (I.ii.18-22)

The speech operates on at least three levels. An innocent ear would hear a pious disclaimer of even the slightest of shabby intentions. Yet the words cue Canterbury — awake our sword, but do it convincingly. And, the speech adroitly shifts responsibility to the Archbishop. The dodging of responsibility for which critics have scored Henry is consistent with the passive role he has assumed for this scene. That Canterbury takes the sin on his head, that Ely, Exeter, and Westmoreland exhort him to arms, that France rejects his demand, and that the Dauphin insults him with tennis balls, all add to Henry's role of helplessness before uncontrollable forces. The more he conceals his involvement in the decision, the more he obscures the monetary and political considerations that have dictated the scene, and the more he burnishes his patriotic image. The more Henry can shift responsibility, the more compelling is his pose as a king coerced. Henry bases subsequent actions on the premise that his cause is just; therefore anyone who would deny it (whether the Dauphin in I.iii, the French King in II.iv., or the Governor of Harfleur in III.iii) brings upon himself and the political entity he represents only what he deserves for blocking the highway of destiny. Henry is the instrument of larger forces, controllable, as he explains to the Governor of Harfleur, only if potential opponents submit to them:

> If I begin the batt'ry once again,
> I will not leave the half-achieved Harfleur
> Till in her ashes she lie buried.
> The gates of mercy shall be all shut up.
> And the fleshed soldier, rough and hard of heart,
> In liberty of bloody hand shall range
> With conscience wide as hell, mowing like grass
> Your fresh fair virgins and your flow'ring infants.
> What is it then to me if impious war,
> Arrayed in flames like to the prince of fiends,
> Do with his smirched complexion all fell feats
> Enlinked to waste and desolation?
> What is't to me, when you yourselves are cause
> If your pure maidens fall into the hand
> Of hot and forcing violation?
>
> (III.iii.7-21)

Here, he claims to be in control — tenuously — of the legions of hell itself. 10/ A conscience "wide as hell" is the reverse of conscience, a remorselessness as vast in its appetite as hell is in area. The speech reflects the dynamics of his prodding England into war. At a certain moment, forces are within control. After that moment, mere anarchy or worse is loosed. The speech suggests as well that Henry V has avoided the jungle-law Henry IV had predicted for England by exporting it to France:

For the fifth Harry from curbed license plucks
The muzzle of restraint, and the wild dog,
Shall flesh his tooth on every innocent.
(II Henry IV: IV.v.130-132)

Henry V does not tell us whether Henry V believes in his cause. Belief is irrelevant. The play shows that actions based on the unassailability of the cause make for a marvelously uncomplicated and effective politics. The responsibility for what may happen is, by definition, someone else's. But war, as Henry knows, releases the latent malevolence of "the prince of fiends." Henry may be pointing at himself, a royal plurality which can, if enraged, command that all his army's prisoners be killed, which can, if moved by political considerations, coerce a princess as if she were just another town to be taken.

Henry desires of Canterbury a formal justification of his cause that will convince the king's followers.11/ That Henry is satisfied by its essential justice is neither proved nor refuted. We are no longer in a world partaking of those essential characteristics Gaunt described. The pose of waiting to be convinced, in fact, is curiously similar to that of the character many critics take to be the spiritual antithesis of Henry V — Richard of Gloucester, seemingly so reluctant to be king, yet carefully manipulating the machinery by which he ascends the throne. On the only occasion that the question of Henry's right to France is directly questioned, on the eve of Agincourt, the issue does not come to debate, and he is allowed to argue a subordinate issue. Henry exhibits little evidence of a "conscience." He is troubled before Agincourt by his father's guilt, crimes which may interfere with the morrow's battle, but his own guilt in perpetrating a version of his father's crime — seizing a throne not rightfully his — an issue raised vividly by the soldiers, is simply not an issue for him. It suffices for him that the war is justified as a political expedient best for his own throne and hence best for England. And, if the argument is confined within these limits, that is, if we allow Henry to be our moral interpreter, the war is justified. It may be, as Palmer suggests, that Henry V "is at once the glorification of a patriot king and an exposure of the wicked futility of his enterprise."12/ The play may well yoke such radical levels of irony. "Over [the play]," says Smith, "breathes the spirit of heroic patriotism that can be justified only by such enormities as the Spanish Armada, but that is so often invoked for less worthy occasions. Under it breathe the stubborn and irreducible details of ulterior purpose that characterize most wars."13/ Such a combination of bold exterior image and subversive undertones seems very much at work in Henry V, as in the contrast between what the Chorus says and what we experience in the opening sequences of Act IV, for example. My own feeling, however, is the play, however ironic, avoids the extremes of glory and wickedness, but moderates its irony through the point-of-view of an eminently practical king for whom the war is neither wicked nor futile, but dictated by the strictly literal world he has inherited.

The play is partly, then, an exploration of the limits of Henry's vision. He sees only what is "good for England," and he can make his determination only within the most limited of time-frames, as the pragmatist must, as his father did in responding to the vacuum of rule Richard continued to open. But Henry V controls his steps as his father could not. The borders of England form the limits of Henry V's "morality." Since he is king, this is as it must be. The "justice" of his claim in France is hardly his basic consideration. He deems it necessary. As in Lancaster's trapping of the rebels, morality — whatever that may be in the non-sacramental world of Henry V — subserves policy. Words have efficacy only as they are backed by material power, an "ethic" Richard accepted for England at Flint Castle. What might be considered an international crime if viewed "objectively," becomes "moral" within the narrower viewpoint of a single nation — as a royal plurality interprets the national necessities. The spectator may well bring sanctions against Henry's war, sanctions not merely produced by the conscience of modern liberalism, which sees America's colonialist adventure in Vietnam as a "wicked futility" ungraced with even a phrasable rationalization, but sanctions suggested by the play itself. While the spectator may be invited to question Henry (but not, I think, condemn him), the spectator is also invited to understand that when viewed from Henry's necessarily subjective stance as King of England, his war is justified. A critic's absolute defense of Henry V must become casuistry. Henry's defense would certainly involve omissions and rationalizations — which is perhaps why Shakespeare shows the king avoiding such a direct defense until forced into it on the night before Agincourt. Although the soldiers on stage will not know that a king addresses them, they will be receiving the king's own defense, and a very subjective rationale it will be. But Henry's strength as national leader derives precisely from his subjectivity. Shakespeare shows us the limits of a politician's vision and the power he gains from those very limitations. Rabkin suggests that "the blows he has rained on his country are much more than those of an enemy of the people, and all he had to offer his bleeding subjects for the few years that remain is the ceremonial posture which he himself has earlier had the insight to condemn."14/ Indeed, as Henry V returns from France all he can do is assume the pose the Chorus to Act V accepts at face value. But what can Henry do? He is trapped in a time he did not invent, in a history he can dictate only within limits. That he understands the limits of his control is his strength in one sense — in knowing what he cannot control, he knows what he can. But he has not that control of the future of the office of kingship that Richard inherited and destroyed.

Henry cannot state baldly that he considers war with France best for England. He must work towards war through the medium of a claim he may recognize as dubious. But the claim must seem valid. The

Archbishop's exposition is prolix, even contradictory, but while it makes Henry's claim far from clear, it has the virtue of being confusing — it obscures Henry's lack of a claim. The king at last asks, "May I with right and conscience make this claim?" (I.ii.96). Indeed, the king is pious on this point:15/

> Under this conjuration, speak, my lord:
> For we will hear, note, and believe in heart
> That what you speak is in your conscience washed
> As pure as sin with baptism.
>
> (I.ii.29-32)

"The ceremonial," Reno says, "has its greatest usefulness in a society that is sacramental in its outlook."16/ We have witnessed Hal's "valuation" of the crown, and we have seen an English churchman as worldly as a Medici Pope, but the public overlay of sacramental imagery still has its political effect. An American president, for example, need not be a "born-again Christian," or even a strangely bellicose Quaker, but he must attend church on Sunday and be televised shaking hands with the rector after the services.

Canterbury assumes whatever guilt there be, echoing Northumberland, and Henry stands quietly by while his followers deliver rousing calls to arms. The present enterprise is compared with the chivalric past in material metaphors, predictably by Canterbury, talking of the capture of King David II of Scotland, while Edward III, in France watched the exploits of the Black Prince:

> When all her chivalry hath been in France,
> And she a mourning widow of her nobles,
> She hath herself not only well defended
> But taken and impounded as a stray
> The King of Scots; whom she did send to France
> To fill King Edward's fame with prisoner kings,
> And make her chronicle as rich with praise
> As in the ooze and bottom of the sea
> With sunken wrack and sumless treasuries.
>
> (I.ii.157-165)

England here is a warden for the most aristocratic of dogs. Devoid of the word "chivalry" and the historical content, these words of an Archbishop of Canterbury could emerge from the opulent pagan context of Antony and Cleopatra.

Henry is already convinced, but by allowing others the opportunity to convince him, he permits them to convince themselves. The impassioned rhetoric moves the speakers and the scene further and further away from the question of the validity of Henry's claim in France, until it is simply no longer an issue.

Suddenly, the king interrupts the chauvinistic outpourings with a practical consideration. Suppose the Scots invade while English power is in France? A Scottish invasion of England would be analogous to a British expedition to France. By this time, however, Henry has promoted his own convenient subjectivity in his subjects. The Archbishop's long "bee" metaphor suggests, however, that Henry V's reasonable preference for foreign rather than civil war represents an importation of English "value" far different than that described by Gaunt. While merchants and soldiers are differentiated by Canterbury, their activities amount to the same thing:

> Others like merchants venture trade abroad,
> Others like soldiers armed in their stings
> Make boot upon the summer's velvet buds,
> Which pillage they with merry march bring home
> To the tent-royal of their emperor...
> (I.ii.192-196)17/

The French war and the Scottish threat it invites, as Canterbury has also suggested (I.ii.157-165), offer greater opportunities for monetary gain than mere peaceful commerce.

The invasion of France represents "exploits and mighty enterprises" (I.ii. 121), a perpetuation of England's chivalric past, Ely argues. The Scottish incursion would resemble the visitation of cowardly predator, as Ely also suggests:

> For once the eagle (England) being in prey,
> To her unguarded nest the weasel (Scot)
> Comes sneaking, and so sucks her princely eggs...
> (I.ii.169-171)

The king worries not about the "pilfering borderers" (I.ii.142) and "coursing snatchers" (I.ii.143) only, but about the "main intendment of the Scot" (I.ii.144). That he is keeping the giddy minds of Englishmen busy does not solve the problem of Scotland, "Who hath been still a giddy neighbor to us" (I.ii.145).18/ Some giddiness can be exported, but not all the island holds:

> But that the Scot on his unfurnished kingdom
> Comes pouring like the tide into a breach,
> With ample and brim fullness of his force,
> Galling the gleaned land with hot assays,
> Girdling with grievous siege castles and towns;

That England being empty of defense,
Hath shook and trembled at the ill neighborhood.
(I.ii.148-154)

The threatened England he describes becomes the France he will invade:

He'll make your Paris Louvre shake for it...
(II.iii.132)
Once more into the breach, dear friends, once more...
(III .i.1)

Burgundy will describe France not as gleaned, but as overgrown with wildness, an unprofitable jungle like that Henry IV had imaged, anticipating his son's reign:

her hedges even-pleached,
Like prisoners wildly overgrown with hair,
Put forth disordered twigs...
And all our vineyards, fallows, meads, and hedges,
Defective in their natures, grow to wildness,
Even so our houses, and ourselves, and children,
Have lost, or do not learn, for want of time,
The sciences that should become our country;
But grow like savages — as soldiers will,
That nothing do but meditate on blood.
(V.ii.42-59)

Most subject is the fattest soil to weeds,
And he, the noble image of my youth,
Is overspread with them.
(II Henry IV: IV.iv.54-56)

O... [England] wilt be a wilderness again
Peopled with wolves, thy old inhabitants.
(II Henry IV: IV.iv.136-137)

To avoid the "disordered spring" (Richard II: III.iv.48) and "fall of leaf" (Richard II: III.iv.49), the ruined garden described so often in Richard II, Henry V would despoil "this best garden of the world" (Henry V: V.ii.36), "this world's best garden" (Epilogue: 7), which is no longer England, Gaunt's "demi-paradise," "other Eden," but France.19/ One of the ironies Henry V inflicts on history is that, while he may temporarily spare England the relapse into wilderness, he can do so only by making one of France. The mimesis he calls for, as Burgundy's speech suggests, is "the action of the tiger" (III.i.6). But England, ultimately, will "bleed' (Epilogue: 12), a lingering act that Shakespeare has already "oft... shown" (Epilogue: 13), and that Carlisle predicted in Richard II (IV.i.136-

149). An agent of "historical necessity" becomes, finally, a releaser of larger negative forces over which his own control ceases with his death. Shakespeare does not allow us to forget the larger ironies shadowing the brief career of a king whose power exists only as he is present to direct it.20/

A nation goes to war, however, not with reason that might perceive damning parallels or the transitory nature of personal monarchy, but with the rhetoric that contrasts the puissance of "lions" (I.ii.126) with the annoyance of "petty thieves" (I.ii.177). The parallel between the Scottish and English invasions is suggested by Pistol, who, for better or for worse, is one of the "culled and choice-drawn cavaliers" (Chorus: III:24) whom Henry leads to France:

> To her unguarded nest the weasel (Scot)
> Comes sneaking, and so sucks her princely eggs...
> (I.ii.170-171)

> Let us to France; like horse-leeches, my boys,
> To suck, to suck, the very blood to suck.
> (II.iii.57-58)

Nym. I shall have my eight shillings I won of you at betting?

Pistol. A noble shalt thou have, and present pay;
And liquor likewise will I give to thee,
And friendship shall combine, and brotherhood...
For I shall sutler be
Unto the camp, and profits will accrue.
(II.i.106-113)

As the Boy says, "They will steal anything and call it a purchase" (III.ii.44). However Henry V may overlay his venture with piety and patriotism, he takes with him the "Falstaff ethic," which turns war into commodity. Such undercutting of Henry's rationale is appropriate, since the war does represent, as Hazleton Spencer suggests a "piece of commercial militarism."21/ Smith suggests that "the major issues that animate the war-making classes are muted because they are as self-serving and publicly inacceptable as going to war to preserve foreign investments or to escape economic depression."22/ While Henry V can point at domestic tranquility as his reason for the French war ("What watch the king keeps to maintain the peace,/ Whose hours the peasant best advantages": IV.i.283-284), he takes with him gross reminders of the baser reasons for his war, reasons he has demurely veiled with patriotism. Pistol, as Gower knows, "is an arrant counterfeit rascal... a bawd, a cutpurse" (III.vi.61-62). Bardolph and Nym, of course, are hanged in France for petty theft. Bardolph, who had cried that he "would not take a knighthood for [his] fortune" (II Henry IV: V.iii.131) is hanged for stealing a "pax of little price" (III.vi.45), an anti-sacramental action for which hanging is an appropriate punishment in a Dantean sense, since the pax depicted the crucifixion. Pistol, talking of the theft and approaching punishment, talks of the pax only as being worth little monetarily. Henry V does not punish the sacrilege per se, but measures the crime in political terms, making a dynastic point, as he had upon Falstaff's interruption of the Coronation Procession, but this time employing an emphatic royal plurality:

> We would have all such offenders so cut off;
> and we give express charge that in our marches
> through the country there be nothing compelled from
> the villages, nothing taken but paid for; none of
> the French upbraided or abused in disdainful lan-
> guage; for when lenity and cruelty play for a king-
> dom, the gentler gamester is the soonest winner.
> (III.vi.107-113)

That Henry is hardly a "gentle gamester" is obvious, but he will not allow the rough game of war to keep him from a political pronouncement about "the hearts and minds of the people." All transactions, including war, as he will suggest to Williams, emerge from a commercial base that may encourage petty thievery, in emulation of the great men. But the great men will not tolerate petty theft when exposed. The effort to take a crown is one thing. That effort has been carefully dressed in convincingly counterfeit clothing (and Henry will place false garments on the Cambridge conspiracy to take his crown). Shop-lifting, however, is a capital offense.

It is a tribute to the king's skill that he not only maneuvers his country into such a tainted war, but can do so while remaining so seemingly free of its taint. He does more than this, of course; he contrives to make himself an instrument of destiny, a patriot Tamburlaine. That the Dauphin's "tun of treasure" (I.ii.255) turns out to be tennis balls operates with a neat irony. Henry's premises are still material, as they must be, but his expenditures have been translated from tavern reckonings to outfitting soldiers. Tennis balls become cannon balls. Henry V tells us — in case we have missed the point — what he was doing with Falstaff:

> And we understand [the Dauphin] well,
> How he comes o'er us with our wilder days,
> Not measuring what use we made of them.
> (I.ii.266-268)

He goes on to claim that "We never valued this poor seat of England" (I.ii. 269), a public disclaimer refuted by the precise valuation he placed on the throne from the first. The very skill he employs in turning the Dauphin's treasure into commodity reflects the use he makes of those seemingly "wilder days," where he learned, as Exeter says, how to weigh "time/ Even to the utmost grain" (II.iv.137-138). Here almost as in an "abracadabra," he transforms sporting equipment into weightier missiles, sending the jest back to France with interest:

> And tell the pleasant prince this mock of his
> Hath turned his balls to gunstones, and his soul
> Shall stand sore charged for the wasteful vengence
> That shall fly with them.
>
> (I.ii.281-284)

Henry takes the personality of Hal, as that personality appeared to the world, and neatly applies it to the French Heir. And Henry translates the Dauphin's insult, as he had Falstaff's interruption, into ceremonial:

> But this lies all within the will of God,
> To whom I do appeal, and in whose name,
> Tell you the dauphin, I am coming on
> To venge me as I may, and to put forth
> My rightful hand in a well-hallowed cause.
>
> (I.ii.288-293)

> For , God before,
> We'll chide this dauphin at his father's door.
>
> (I.ii.307-308)

Henry is to the Dauphin as Hotspur would have been to Hal. But Henry is king, Hotspur dead, and the Dauphin, obviously, doomed to defeat. The Dauphin's charge that Henry V is "vain, giddy, shallow" (II.iv.28) will draw from the Constable a correction similar to that administered by Vernon to Hotspur (I Henry IV: IV.i.96-109). Those exposed to Henry V express, more and more, the world's awareness of what he was actually doing in Eastcheap. "You shall find his vanities forespent," says the Constable to the Dauphin, "Were but the outside of the Roman Brutus,/ Covering discretion with a coat of folly" (II.iii.36-37).

The French war is predicated solidly on a mutually beneficial financial deal between Church and Monarchy, but the agreement is kept from the public eye. The conspiracy of Cambridge, Scroop, and Grey is publicly attributed to the profit motive, but its basis is also hidden neatly from public view. The Chorus tells us that the three, "Have for the gilt of France (O guilt indeed!),/ Confirmed conspiracy with fearful France" (II: 26-27), lines which should, for myriad reasons, discredit the

Chorus as "reliable narrator." France has found in England "A nest of hollow bosoms" to be filled "with treacherous crowns" (II: 21-22). The issue is a crown, but the word is allowed to escape to the surface only as it represents a coin. Scroop, says Exeter, will "for a foreign purse... sell/ His sovereign's life to death and treachery !" (II.ii.10-11). And Henry, at the assembly at the Red Lion, will claim that Cambridge,

> Hath, for a few light crowns, lightly conspired
> And sworn unto the practices of France,
> To kill us here at Hampton.
> (II.ii.89-91)

The sell-out of Henry by Scroop is "so strange" (II.ii.102) that Henry compares it to "Another fall of man" (II.ii.142). Scroop "(almost) might have coined [Henry] into gold" (II.ii.98) — it seems no wonder that Henry is amazed at the inexplicable betrayal by his friend. Henry would almost "weep" for him (II.ii.140), like the compassionate punisher of "man's first disobedience." As Wentersdorf says, "If the rebellious Scroop is Adam, then Henry V is God; and this is no mere hyperbole. Henry is subtly reminding all present that... he is their anointed monarch and thus (as the Bishop of Carlisle said of Richard II) 'the figure of God's majesty'."23/ Henry implies that his England is an "other Eden," contaminated by incomprehensible, gratuitous, and original sin. It is a daring case to make, and it is made with effect, in spite of the reduplicated crime of Cain that the previous plays have shown us — Bolingbroke's charges against Mowbray and Exton, for example. We are forced to admire the skill of a judge who can attribute transgressions to mere monetary motives and yet equate the "revolt" (II.ii.141) to pre-lapsarian pre-history. All of this is superbly done and amply fulfills Warwick's prediction that the "memory" of Falstaff and Hal's other "followers"

> will in the perfectness of time...
> ... as a pattern or a measure live
> By which his grace must mete the lives of others,
> Turning past evils to advantages.
> (II Henry IV: IV.iv.74-78)

Henry V has already demonstrated his skill, in rejecting Falstaff and in employing Canterbury as an agent of the king's decision to invade France. We might notice further that the scene with the traitors is a neat reversal of Henry V's confrontation with the Chief Justice at the end of II Henry IV. It that scene, anticipated punishment turned into approbation and reward — a seeming spontaneity that was really an effect calculated to contribute to the "noble change [Hal/Henry] has purposed" (II Henry IV: IV.v.154). In the scene with the traitors, trust and cordiality turn to condemnation and punishment. Each scene treats "justice," and each is designed by Henry to reflect to all on-lookers the proper administration of justice by the king. In each, Henry neatly translates unpromising possibilities into ceremonials in which he has the chief role and most of the lines.24/

The scene with the traitors is analogous to the several scenes in which Hal attempted to trap Falstaff. Here, the king asserts control over agents of disorder, and here there is no humor. Henry is alone in his cold political world, faced with three traitors he must expose and punish. Here, as in his scene with Canterbury — as in his whole career as Hal — resides a central fact that Henry must obscure. The motive for the seemingly inexplicable treason of Cambridge, Scroop, and Grey would be clear to anyone who had followed Bolingbroke's career; it is to supplant Henry V with the heir Richard named, Edmund Mortimer, whose lineal title is better than Bolingbroke's, therefore stronger than Henry V's. The Cambridge conspiracy has already been described in detail in Shakespeare, by the dying Mortimer in I Henry VI (II.v.). One could ask whether the plot does represent treason. To a de facto king it is treason if he says it is and can insist that it is by force. But the plotters are emerging from the principle York enunciated in admonishing Richard. Henry V is not king "by fair sequence and succession" (Richard II: II.i.199). The crown is an "honor snatched with boisterous hand" (II Henry IV: IV.v.191) by Henry IV, which his son has sworn to keep by sheer force:

> And put the world's whole strength
> Into one giant arm, it shall not force
> This lineal honor from me.
> (II Henry IV: IV.v.42-44)

Saccio tells us that "Holinshed adds that Cambridge's formal indictment certainly included the charge of conspiring to crown March."25/ Saccio suggests that the dynastic motive is suppressed by Shakespeare, for "Had he made the dynastic implications of this one episode clear, he might have upset his depiction of the general state of affairs in Henry's reign. England at large was loyal to her hero king. Exceptions to that generalization could be treated as insignificant, and saddled on the French."26/ Dover Wilson says that "it seems odd that Shakespeare did not make [the dynastic motive of the Cambridge Plot] more explicit, until we remember that he must avoid anything that casts doubts out the legitimacy of Henry V."27/ Wentersdorf, however, challenges this position: "is it Shakespeare who must avoid [the question of legitimacy] or Henry himself?... As for the silence of Henry V himself regarding the real motives of the conspirators, how could he mention the plotters' intention to make Mortimer king without drawing attention gratuitously to the weak legality of his own claim to the crown? His problem is to distract attention from the potentially explosive political situation, and he approaches the problem with a rhetorical skill that is little short of masterly."28/

Henry must engineer a trap that exposes the fact of treason, not its underlying motive. To keep the source of this conspiracy hidden, Henry must manage every phase of the manipulation far more overtly than he did in the scene with Canterbury. Knowing already of the plot, he draws from each traitor an expression of loyalty. Grey speaks of "those that were your father's enemies" (Grey is a cousin of Hotspur) who "Have steeped their galls in honey" (II.ii.29-30). On the surface the words suggest devotion to Henry, but they also imply the discrepancy between appearance and reality represented by the conspirators. Their surface is fair, "As if allegiance in their bosoms sat/ Crowned with faith and constant loyalty" (II.ii.4-5), but the galling memory of Bolingbroke's usurpation works within. Seemingly carried away by the optimistic mood of the plotters, Henry decides to free "the man committed yesterday/ That railed against our person" (II.ii.40-41). From the conspirators, of course, Henry can expect the strongest expressions concerning the king's person. Such mercy, Scroop argues, is dangerous; the example of sufferance may "breed more of such a kind" (II.ii.46). Such objections not only undercut in advance any later pleas for mercy in the case of the traitors, but allow Henry to make a prime distinction. The soldier, "set on by excess of wine" (II.ii.42) delivered an extemporaneous insult to the king's person — I assume to his "body natural."29/ If he is severely punished, Henry asks, what recourse have I when faced with conspiracy against king as nation?:

> If little faults proceeding on distemper
> Shall not be winked at, how shall we stretch our eye
> When capital crimes, chewed, swallowed, and digested,
> Appear before us?
>
> > (II.ii.54-57)

Henry has moved the plotters to advocate severity for a minor offense. Now he introduces the theme of capital crime. As in his rejection of Falstaff, the king focusses the issue not on the narrow area of man and insult, but on the wider plane of king and civil disobedience. In his indictment of the three traitors, Henry reiterates the distinction he has made about the soldier:

> Touching our person, seek we no revenge,
> But we our kingdom's safety must so tender,
> Whose ruin you have sought, that to her laws
> We do deliver you.
> > (II.ii.174-177)

The "laws" become effectively impersonal, inalterable, and a priori. Henry's mastery is suggested by his assumption, rhetorically, at least, of the attributes of absolute kingship within a situation where his own legitimacy has been questioned. To achieve this position, Henry has attributed to the conspirators an incomprehensible nihilism:

> you would have sold your king to slaughter,
> His princes and his peers to servitude,
> His subjects to oppression and contempt,
> And his whole kingdom into desolation.
> (II.ii.170-173)

The king's quite proper paternalism, emphasized by the repeated "his," is nicely contrasted with the attitude of the traitors, who become, in Henry's version of the crime they contemplated, something similar to what Henry IV conceived for Hal's reign (II Henry IV: IV.v.117-137). Henry IV, of course, does not know that Henry V, and not Hal, will become king. Henry V, of course, does not know that the England he so piously protects here will be plunged into desolation when Mortimer's heirs overthrow the Lancastrian Henry VI in favor of the Yorkist claim.30/

For all of Henry's talk of "her laws," he knows that he must maneuver around a conflict with the law. He is a king de facto. Regardless of this inheritance from his father and of the skillfully calculated impact of his ascension, Henry must face the legal fact of Mortimer's still outstanding claim. Henry transmits his knowledge of the specific facts and motives of "treason" by handing each plotter written documentation of his complicity. The device of the documents allows Henry to show the conspirators the case against them without revealing the specifics to the assembled nobility and commons. As his expedition leaves for France, Henry can hardly raise the issue of his right to the English throne. Wentersdorf points at "the inescapable fact that Cambridge and Scroop are challenging Henry V's right to the English throne on grounds at least as convincing as those justifying Henry's challenge to the French king."31/ After Canterbury's exposition of Henry's claim, one would suggest that "at least as convincing" is understating the case. Mortimer's claim goes back directly to the generation of Gaunt and his brother, Lionel of Antwerp, a generation Shakespeare has presented dramatically through Gaunt and York in Richard II (and the Duchess of Gloucester, of course). Henry's presentation of written accusations allows him publicly to ignore the motive for the conspiracy, and to emphasize the "strange" (II.ii.103), "gross" (II.ii.104), and "preposterous" (II.ii.112) fact of treason. And so it must seem, as Henry manages the scene.

As in the Justification Scene, Henry adroitly moves away from a troublesome issue — in each case, his claim to a throne. His silence in the former scene was filled with words urging him to launch the claim in France on the vector of military power. His long speech here is so effective that it awakens in the conspirators a belated loyalty to England's king — no matter what the premises of his kingship. Cambridge, however, suggests that the crime is not quite as the king represents it, as a despicable sell-out to France:

> For me, the gold of France did not seduce,
> Although I did admit it as a motive
> The sooner to effect what I intended.
>
> (II.ii.155-157)

This is the closest the scene comes to revealing "the truth." When he wishes to obscure monetary and pragmatic considerations beneath the facade of pious patriotism, Henry does so. When he wishes to emphasize a greed that defies piety and loyalty, Henry also does so:

> You have conspired against our royal person,
> Joined with an enemy proclaimed, and from his coffers,
> Received the golden earnest of our death.
>
> (II.ii.167-169)

The master manipulator can bring to the surface what serves his purpose, knowing in one scene that patriotic and sacramental rhetoric still works in certain ears, and, in another, that the world is more conditioned to accept a purely monetary motivation than it had been before Richard leased out royal lands and seized a great estate to finance an earlier invasion. And Henry V knows that the conspirators dare not defend themselves with their basic motivation. "The conspirators remain silent on this point," says Wentersdorf, "because they do not want to jeopardize the survival of their families: they hope that the king will acknowledge their restraint by mitigating the almost inevitable suffering of their innocent wives and children."32/ Holinshed supports this contention: "what should come to [Cambridge's] owne children he much doubted. Therefore, destitute of comfort and in despaire of life to save his children, he feined that tale [of being corrupted by money], desiring rather to save his succession than himselfe." While some of this historical material becomes too heavy a sub-text for the scene to suggest, one has to take issue with Sherman Hawkins, for example, that Shakespeare's audience couldn't have been expected to remember the reason underlying the Cambridge plot.33/ The scene itself, through Cambridge, alludes to the motive. The primary emphasis, however, is on Henry V's manipulative genius. He can translate a dubious claim in France into a national solidarity that seems absolute until he encounters the Cambridge conspiracy. But he can wrest a situation that raises the troublesome issue of his right into a consolidation of his throne and an auspicious augury for his expeditio against the French throne:

> We doubt not of a fair and lucky war,
> Since God so graciously hath brought to light
> This dangerous treason lurking in our way
> To hinder our beginnings.
> (II.ii.184-187)

Again, Henry translates a scene into a ceremony — Falstaff's interruption, the justification scene, the conspiracy. Henry V seems supremely capable of making any "beginning hindrance" serve "the purpose" that underlies everything Hal - Henry V does (II Henry IV II.ii.175). The purpose is effective leadership. However predicated on sheer personal skill, Henry's successes seem like those of the "body politic" of England, and, in a sense, they are. We have seen, however that Henry preferred the immediate funding of the Church for his war to the more gradual establishment of the hierarchy that confiscation of Church lands would have built. Henry's successes reside solely on this superbly adroit monarch, and will continue only as long as he reigns — unless, of course, equally skillful monarchs succeed him. As Shakespeare has already shown, virtuosity dies with Henry V. God, we must infer, has had no more to do with Henry's success at Southampton than with his manipulation of England into war with France.34/ Once political goals are achieved, they are easily attributable to "the grace of God." We can predict with a ready guess what King Henry will do should he win in France. His victories will absorb the moral Henry ascribes to them Piety, like everything else in the vast arsenal Canterbury attributes to Henry V (Henry V: I.i.24-52), is the adjunct of Realpolitick. Henry V understands, with Machiavelli, that the only intrinsic quality useful in the "real world" is political skill, however veiled by the projection of other, seemingly more platonic or sacramental qualities. The effective ruler, says Machiavelli, must "make himself both loved and feared by his subjects, followed and respected by his soldiers" [my ital. — but the emphasis on political mimesis is valid, I believe]. A critic's love, hatred or ambivalence towards Henry V should not be mistaken for "Shakespeare's attitude," which is that of demonstration, not moral judgement, of dramatic action, not moral preachment or political prescription.

1. Cf. the unidentified critic quoted disapprovingly in Levin, "Refuting Shakespeare's Endings," II, 152: "the real point of the prologue to Henry V. . . is not the inadequacy of the theater. . . but rather the likeness of Henry's campaign to a staged play." The theatricality Bolingbroke stresses in his final words to Hal continues as metaphor in Henry V, as the past is reinterpreted by Canterbury, who translates Crecy into a "tragedy. . . play'd" by the Black Prince before the "smiling" Edward III (I.ii.106-110). Henry V embraces Bolingbroke's metaphor as mode.

2. Unless, as in Canterbury's exposition of the Salique Law, lengthy discourse fulfills a political purpose not necessarily inherent in the speech per se.

3. The historical Henry V seems to have been a devout Catholic, as evidenced by his having his friend Oldcastle executed for Lollardism. Shakespeare avoids this episode in Henry V's career, for a number of reasons, no doubt, one of which would seem to be suggested by his changing Oldcastle to Falstaff in the Henry IV play. Lollardism is hardly an issue in Henry V, but the king does execute two "friends," Lord Scroop and Bardolph. For a discussion of the historical Oldcastle, see Peter Saccio, Shakespeare's English Kings (Oxford Galaxy, 1977), pp. 70-72.

4. G. L. Kittredge, ed., Henry V (Boston, 1940), p. 110.

5. As Gordon Ross Smith says, "a Renaissance mirror is not necessarily an ideal, but may be merely a bad reflector, as is the mirror Richard II looks into and smashes for its dishonesty, or Hamlet's mirror held up to nature, or the title. A Myrrour for Magistrates, which describes more objectionable kings and princes than it does commendable. In Elizabethan English the mirror of something was not necessarily an image of its perfected ideal": "Shakespeare's Henry V: Critical Forest," Journal of the History of Ideas XXXVII (#1: January - March 1976), 9 - 10. George's "Mirror of Knighthood" applied to Ralph in The Knight of the Burning Pestle (II.ii.51) can only be ironic, for example. Richard's mirror "lies," of course, because it tells the truth, reflecting the split between the king's two bodies. What was a fusion is now a concept as fragile as the image in the mirror. For Plato, the reflected image would hardly be "the ideal" — rather a further distortion of the truth (cf. the images reflected to the inhabitants of the cave). The great majority of the uses of "mirror" and its variations in Shakespeare (there are 14) employ a strictly neutral meaning of "reflect." If the meaning is, finally, "neutral" as it relates to Henry V (regardless of the Chorus's often breathless adoration of the king), the

word may reflect Shakespeare's "attitude," which, as artist, is not to impose his meanings but to elicit our response. An exploration of Henry V's "critical forest" suggests that "our response" creates a variety worthy of a jungle.

6.   John Palmer, Political and Comic Characters of Shakespeare (London, 1961), p. 181.

7.   Goddard, The Meaning of Shakespeare, pp. 215-268.

8.   Gordon Ross Smith, "Shakespeare's Henry V: Critical Forest," p. 26.

9.   E. M. W. Tillyard, Shakespeare's History Plays (New York, 1962), p. 351.

10.   That this speech is calculated contrivance is suggested by the Archbishop's previous description of Henry V's "discourse of war" as "A fearful battle rend'red you in music" (I.i. 43-44). One might also suggest that Henry V enjoys his own rhetoric. Alan Howard projected a self-aware delight through speeches like that at the gates of Harfleur. Henry had fun with his own language — perhaps more like Cassius Clay before the first Liston fight than like Tamburlaine. Howard's performance was so convincing that one has to credit his interpretation. Howard's Henry V shared with his audience a personality he could not share with the characters on stage. After his seemingly angry response to the Dauphin, for example, Howard's Henry nodded to himself as if to say, "Hey, not bad!"

11.   James Black offers the interesting — and dramatic — thesis that Canterbury challenges Henry V: "Reminded of both usurpation and glorious conquest, Henry is being offered, as it were, a choice of heritages: if he wishes to clear his title of the dubiety associated with his father's accession, then he had better show himself clearly and by deed in the line of his more respectable forebears," "Shakespeare's Henry V and the Dreams of History," English Studies in Canada I #1 (Spring, 1975), 15. Cf. "No King of England, if not King of France" (II.ii. 193).

12.   Palmer, Political and Comic Characters of Shakespeare, p. 228.

13.   Smith, "Shakespeare's Henry V," 25. A recent brilliant article that defines the "total effect" of Henry V is Norman Rabkin's "Rabbits, Ducks and Henry V," SQ 28 #3 (Summer, 1977), 279-296.

14.   Rabkin, "Rabbits, Ducks, and Henry V," 294.

15. Another interesting reading of the scene is Dorothy Cook's: "When Henry stresses the need for positive moral justification, he slyly appears as the better defender of the faith, whereas the head of the Church takes the position of the scheming politician," "Henry V: Maturing of Man and Majesty," Studies in the Literary Imagination V #1 (April, 1972), 118.

16. Reno, From Sacrament to Ceremony, p. 277.

17. Cf. Henry later to Williams: "Some, making the wars their bulwark, that have before gored the gentle bosom of peace with pillage and robbery" (IV.ii.171-173). Henry's lines capture the politician's clichés, of course (cf. Richard at Coventry: I.iii.124 ff.), reflect back upon his own career as prince, and illuminate his present enterprise.

18. France, of course, is England's "neighbor" (III.vi.159), but becomes, in the subjective view of Henry V as he rises for battle, a "bad neighbor" (IV.i.6). Anyone opposing England, of course, is guilty of the "ill neighborhood" Henry attributes to Scotland (I.ii.154).

19. Is Falstaff's final vision of "green fields" (II.iii.17) ironic? If the image represents a last fleeting glimpse of childhood, it also represents that "other Eden" Gaunt remembers, of which the latter-day Falstaff would have been despoiler. The irony, if there, may be Theobald's, of course.

20. Alan Howard's brilliant Henry V emphasized "community," and thus touched many levels of meaning (or "intention") within and beyond the script — that moment of national unity Henry V creates between civil wars, the uneasy years just before the end of Elizabeth's reign, the sundering of Britain's community in modern times, and even the internal difficulties of the R.S.C. mentioned by Terry Hands in Sally Beauman's The Royal Shakespeare Company's Production of 'Henry V' (Oxford, Pergamon Press, 1976), p. 14. Howard's "band of brothers" speech was not a set-piece delivered from a cart a la Olivier, but an impromptu pep talk given as Henry moved among his troops. The suiting of word to action gave the old words a new vibrancy, fulfilling Michael Goldman's insight that "It is a moment when [Henry V] must respond to the unspoken needs of his men, and we respond to his success as we do when a political leader we admire makes a great campaign speech: we love him for his effectiveness," Shakespeare and the Energies of Drama (Princeton, 1972), p. 70. The Elizabethan topicality of Henry V is treated by Frank Manley, discussing the end of II Henry IV: "the Epilogue. . . obviously links the restoration of order under Henry V with the reign of Elizabeth. . . After Henry, the country was plunged once again into chaos. And in 1598, for all England knew, chaos would come again on the death of Elizabeth," "The Unity of Betrayal in II Henry IV," 110.

21.   Hazleton Spencer, The Art and Life of William Shakespeare (New York, 1940), p. 197.

22.   Smith, "Shakespeare's Henry V," 26.

23.   Karl P. Wentersdorf, "The Conspiracy of Silence in Henry V," Shakespeare Quarterly, XXVII (Summer, 1976), 282.

24.   The Stratford, England, production raised the question of loyalty and treason by employing a bit of doubling Shakespeare himself might have used. The actor playing Scroop doubled as Williams. Grey doubled as Bates. The effect, of course, was to create a relationship between the scenes that raised in the spectator a sense of their thematic similarities. The "Traitor's Scene," as depicted by BBC-TV, and David Gwillam, as Henry V, was, quite simply, one of the most powerful moments of drama I have ever witnessed. It transcended the medium of television — and, even for a debased medium, such a moment is not easy to achieve, simply because we, that passive audience, have such diminished expectations.

25.   Peter Saccio, Shakespeare's English Kings, p. 74.

26.   Saccio, Shakespeare's English Kings, p. 75.

27.   J. Dover Wilson, ed., King Henry V (Cambridge, England, 1947), p. 140.

28.   Wentersdorf, "The Conspiracy of Silence in Henry V," 281.

29.   Though, if this is the case, should not Henry say "my person" — both here and in II.ii.174? Perhaps the king, when speaking of himself as pluralistic personality, even when isolating the singular and mortal aspect of his dual nature, could still employ the royal plural. The question of plurality is consistently worth exploring in Shakespeare simply because, as I suggested earlier, Shakespeare is so sensitive to it. The R.S.C. production realized a brilliant moment when the soldier Henry has freed arrested Scroop. The soldier is loyal, "excess of wine" having worn off and left him in his better senses. The explicitly sober Scroop is a traitor.

30.   Cf. Wentersdorf: "The biblical elements in Henry's rhetoric are obviously intended to suggest that the exposure of the conspiracy is proof of God's adverse verdict on the justice of Scroop's decision to support the Mortimer family. The irony is inescapable: Shakespeare's audience knows that the verdict will be reversed": "Conspiracy of Silence in Henry V," 285. Wentersdorf points also at one of the outer circles of irony in this incredibly interconnected historical sequence by mentioning that the successful Richmond was also backed by France, as was the Cambridge conspiracy: 280, n. 26.

31. Wentersdorf, "The Conspiracy of Silence in Henry V," 283.

32. Wentersdorf, "The Conspiracy of Silence in Henry V," 280.

33. Response to a question from the floor, Shakespeare Association of America Annual Meeting, 1973.

34. The scene with the traitors echoes back to the "expectation mocked" of the Gaultree Forest episode, in which Prince John accepts a written list of grievances, promises redress, springs a trap, and ascribes an unequivocally political success to an approving "God" (II Henry IV: Iv.ii.122). Norman Holland suggests that "expectation mocked," is the running theme of II Henry IV: "Introduction," Henry IV, Part Two (New York: Signet, 1965), p. xxiv. Cf. Hugh M. Richmond: "while Henry has cast off the person and outward vices of Falstaff, he has preserved that virtuosity of mind that Falstaff had devoted to the amusement of his friends, but which the king now devotes with terrifying efficiency to coldly political ends, in which it verges on equivocation — if not downright deceit and hypocrisy." Shakespeare's Political Plays (New York, Random House, 1967), p. 179. Again, while Richmond is correct to point at Hal's tutorial with Falstaff, Henry's "hypocrisy" must be measured against the context of his sense of what is good for England.

CHAPTER VIII

Henry V's France

The French response to Henry's invasion reflects the reverse of Henry's careful calculation. And when Henry's forces and momentum dwindle, the French present yet another reversal of Henry's realistic estimate of the situation at Agincourt — a swelling over-confidence. Henry has succeeded in his "sudden transformation" — through the skills gained in his contesting with Falstaff, but his adventure in France forces him to reach more deeply into his capacity for leadership than has been necessary during the facile early days of his kingship. Henry is consistently aided by an equal if opposite reaction from his French adversaries.

The French react at first with an offer of Katherine, the king's daughter, "and with her to dowry/ Some petty and unprofitable dukedoms" (Chorus: III.30-31).1/ Henry's son will settle for far less, but not Henry V. His further incursion finds the French berating themselves for lack of preparedness. The Constable, one of the few about Charles VI's court worthy of an audience's respect, objects to the loss of France by default:

> if he be not fought withal, my lord,
> Let us not live in France; let us quit all
> And give our vineyards to a barbarous people.
> (III.v.2-3)

While the Constable reflects the typical French attitude towards what the Dauphin calls the "wild and savage stock" (III.v.7) of the English, he knows that abject surrender will devalue the French land and its nobility:

> whiles a more frosty people
> Sweat drops of gallant youth in our rich fields —
> "Poor" we call them in their native lords!
> (III.v.24-26)

Bretagne is even more vehement in his contrast between the "worth" of the contending kingdoms:

> if they march along
> Unfought withal... I will sell my dukedom
> To buy a slobb'ry and a dirty farm
> In that nook-shotten isle of Albion.
> (III.v.11-14)

The question is not value per se — that question is anachronistic, hence irrelevant — but politics, and in the latter area the French are as inept as Henry has been masterful. Once the French king decides to fight, commanding his nobles to bring Henry "in a captive chariot into Rouen" (III.v.54), the Constable indulges in the calculation that will prove so disastrous to the French:

> Sorry am I his numbers are so few,
> His soldiers sick, and famished in their march;
> For I am sure, when he shall see our army,
> He'll drop his heart into the sink of fear,
> And, for achievement, offer us his ransom.
> (III.v.56-60)

Such over-estimation of one's own capacity reflects ironically back on Hotspur, whose confidence expanded even as his own forces dwindled. The cocky wagering of the French nobles — "Who will go hazard with me for twenty prisoners?" (III.vii.87-88) and "by ten/ We shall each have a hundred Englishmen" (III.vii.159-160) — reflects the rebels' division of the kingdom in I Henry IV (III.i) before they have won the necessary battle. As the Constable says to Rambures: "You must first go yourself to hazard, ere you have them" (III.vii.89-90). The French impatience for dawn ("The dauphin longs for morning": III.vii.92) recalls Hotspur's impatience at Shrewsbury: "We'll fight with him tonight" (I Henry IV: IV.iii.1). The Dauphin, of course, is a parody Hotspur, full of words, capable of a Petrachan sonnet on his horse,2/ but revealing, as the Constable suggests, only "a hooded valor, and when it appears, it will bate" (III.vii.114-115). Prince Hal could parody Hotspur good-humoredly (I Henry IV: II.iv.103-110), showing that he knows his man — an important precondition for his victory over "the Hotspur of the North" (I Henry IV: II.iv.104). Henry V scorns the Dauphin, showing again that he knows his "man." Both Hotspur and the Dauphin, of course, under-estimate their man: Hotspur deceived by the reports he receives about Hal — or unwilling to accept Vernon's revaluation — the Dauphin equating Hal with Henry V, a tribute to Hal's "negative public relations" but a fallacy that Falstaff, among others, has been forced to acknowledge. Princess Katherine reveals greater political acumen than her male counterparts by taking a crash course in English (III.iv). The French court at large represents the reverse of the precise calculations with which Henry V has led England into war.

One of the issues explored by Henry V is the French miscalculation of English fighting quality. French estimates are based on a strictly material measurement that ignores completely the "spirit" that can emerge, for example, from "Foolish curs" — as Orleans calls the English (III.vii.145). Foolish curs cornered, warns the Constable, can "fight like devils" (III.vii.153). But the French tendency is to ignore the precedent cited by their king — "our too much memorable shame [at]

Crecy" (II.iv.53). Indeed, the Constable sees the situation as the reverse of Crecy, where the Black Prince and a third of the English crushed the main force of the French, while Edward III and the rest of the English looked on:

> There is not work enough for all our hands,
> Scarce blood enough in all their sickly veins
> To give each naked curtle ax a stain,
> That our French gallants shall today draw out
> And sheathe for lack of sport...
> (IV.ii.20-24)

That Shakespeare intends the equation to be precise is suggested by the Constable's echoing of the stance Charles VI attributes to Edward III:

> Whiles that his mountain sire [Edward III] — on mountain standing,
> Up in the air, crowned with the golden sun —
> Saw The Black Prince, his heroical seed...
> (II.iv.57-59)

> 'Tis positive against all exceptions, lords,
> That our superfluous lackeys and our peasants,
> Who in unnecessary action swarm
> About our squares of battle, were enow
> To purge this field of such a hilding foe,
> Though we upon this mountain's basis by
> Took stand for idle speculation.
> (IV.ii.26-32)

The Constable, of course, does not consciously draw the parallel, hence does not heed Charles's previous warning. Were he to do so he might wonder whether the odds are as favorable as they seem. Grandpre looks upon the English as if they were Falstaff's crew staggering towards Shrewsbury:

> Yond island carrions, desperate of their bones,
> Ill-favoredly become the morning field.
> Their ragged curtains poorly are let loose,
> And our air shakes them passing scornfully.
> Big Mars seems bankrout in their beggared host.
> (IV.ii.40-44)3/

But the French bankrupt themselves in their assumptions of a victory yet to be won, complaining about the paucity of the prize before it is achieved. The Dauphin utters a final scornful jest — shall we even the odds a little?:

Shall we go send them dinners, and fresh suits,4/
And give their fasting horses próvender,
And after fight with them?

(IV.ii.58-60)

While Shakespeare has never attributed a Christian or a chivalric past to the French, except by implication, in that they have been English opponents, and although Shakespeare renders the English "garden" equivocal by transferring it to France, we find the French trapped into the same scheme of calculation and miscalculation which became the English "standard" once Bolingbroke became king. Ironically, the French valuation of English forces fails to account for that strain of English spirit which survives the collapse of Gaunt's world, the "quality" which Henry has released through a variety of calculated moves, a quality that is not totally doused by the likes of Nym and Pistol, and that Henry V, for all his machiavellian traits, also shares.

Perhaps Henry V's ultimate achievement is his encouraging of "spirit" — fighting spirit as opposed to spirituality — from the almost wholly calculating and materialistic attitude of the England he inherits from Bolingbroke. We learn that England is composed of a Williams as well as of a Pistol, and the former is as ready to respond to effective leadership as he is to reject false claims, whether they come from a soldier in the night or from a king in the daylight. Pistol may reflect the dominant ethic and he may be a parody of Henry V. But the king is skillful enough to reverse for a moment the world's remorseless rule of and by mere weight and measurement — as he must if his vastly outnumbered army is to win at Agincourt.

Henry V has carefully maneuvered his nation into war. The French response to invasion is to attempt to accomplish by kingly fiat what Henry V has achieved by expert leadership. Montjoy delivers Charles VI's ultimatum:

> For our losses [Henry V's] exchequer is too
> poor; for the effusion of our blood, the muster
> of his kingdom too faint a number; and for our
> disgraces, his own person kneeling at our feet
> but a poor and worthless satisfaction. To this
> add defiance; and tell him for a conclusion, he
> hath betrayed his followers, whose condemnation
> is pronounced.

(III.vi.130-137)

The lines sound almost like those Bolingbroke heard so often, as his own example kept rising to face him in rebellion. One might expect Henry V to hurl defiance back at Charles VI, or perhaps to allow the French king's rhetoric to drive itself and its speaker into a trap of Henry's construction. While the French do run headlong into disaster, Henry's response seems to lack his characteristic calculation, unless we read into it a level of irony I personally do no perceive there. Henry seems to realize that "honesty" is the only policy, and he expresses a character distinctly different than, perhaps deeper than, we expect of a mere machiavel. It is the response of a brave and over-mastered military commander:

> Turn thee back,
> And tell thy king, I do not seek him now,
> But could be willing to march on to Calais
> Without impeachment; for, to say the sooth,
> Though 'tis no wisdom to confess so much
> Unto an enemy of craft and vantage,
> My people are with sickness much enfeebled,
> My numbers lessened...
> The sum of all our answer is but this:
> We would not seek a battle as we are,
> Nor, as we are, we say we will not shun it.
> So tell your master.
>
> (III.vi.141-168)

Henry gives nothing away here — he merely reiterates military intelligence to which the French are already privy. But Henry's words here seem to emerge from no "hidden agenda." He reveals his own strain and weakness, the weariness of his army, and his resolve to complete his campaign. But the choice, he recognizes, is, for the first time, not his. Those who make the case for Henry's "greatness" might well employ Henry's honest and public appraisal of his insecure military position as "best evidence." He seems to recognize that no matter how perfectly he has planned every sequence of his foreign (and domestic) policy, he must now face pressures beyond his manipulative skills. The point is that he does face them, and comes closest here to revealing a true piety:

Gloucester.   I hope they will not come upon us now.

King.   We are in God's hands, brother, not in theirs.
               (III.vi.170-171)

On the one hand, the Henry of the day before Agincourt reminds us of Falstaff: "honor comes unlooked for, and there's an end" (I Henry IV: V.iii.62-63), and on the other Hamlet: "there's a divinity that shapes our ends,/ Rough-hew them how we will" (V.ii.10-11). The king seems willing to relax into a fatalistic pose, or to place himself within a frame of intention that is not his to shape — much of the ambiguity of the Grave-yard Scene pertains here. The world of the play, as far as we are able to define it, would seem to suggest that "God" has little to do with anything that happens in England or in France, but that the career of Henry V has driven past his ability to control it. All the forces he claimed to hold on leash seem now to face him from the enemy ranks. Such a reversal may be appropriate, creating a sudden image of his father's long and troubled reign, but Henry's response seems admirable, whether we read it as a shoulder-shrug in the face of the invisible event or as a belief in the validity of God's judgement. My own response — and any response to Shakespearean characterization is necessarily subjective — is of admiration for this complete king who, his completeness suddenly frail and endangered, has the grace to admit as much as man.5/ Bolingbroke was characterized as a literalist posing initially as "justicer" for England. He could be a king, finally, only in the most literal sense of the office. Henry V, also a literalist beneath his disguise as Hal, manages to endow monarchy with a facade of ceremony that suggests sanctity. But in France, during the moment when Henry is confronted by Montjoy and by his own assessment of the odds against him, all pretense is stripped away — and Henry can acknowledge as much.

The Chorus to Act IV misleads us into believing that Henry V walked among his troops on the eve of Agincourt "with cheerful semblance, and sweet majesty" (40), and that the soldiers received "A little touch of Harry in the night" (47). Anne Barton takes the Chorus at face value: "Henry V pays two quite different visits to his despondent troops. Although the first of them, made in his own person as king, is not enacted, the Chorus testifies eloquently to its success."6/ We are invited, I believe, to contrast what the Chorus tells us to anticipate with what we actually witness. Again, the mock apology of the "dramatist" the Chorus represents tells us that his effort will be paltry: "mean and gentle all/ Behold, as may unworthiness define,/ A little touch of Harry in the night" (45-47). In other words, not "the king made two separate tours of his camp," but "I am scarcely able to render the touching quality of Harry's visit," a disclaimer that sets us up neatly for the discrepancy between what the idolatrous Chorus says and what the penetrating dramatist does. Only one visit occurs.7/ What we see is Henry wandering incognito into the glow of the campfire of Williams, Bates, and Court.

In disguise, Henry V reveals many things — his conception of himself as body natural, his conception of the war he has encouraged towards this emergent occasion, and the trap he has set for himself in becoming the king he has chosen to be.

Henry is not characterized as having much of an "inner life." Any "personality" independent of the role of king would clash with that role, as it had in the case of Richard II, Henry VI, as Shakespeare has already depicted his career, as it will in the case of Claudius, the machiavellian who really does love Gertrude, and Marc Antony, the triumvir ensnared by Cleopatra. Henry V has allowed the "personality" he exhibited as

184

Prince Hal to emerge only through the political techniques he mastered as prince. But it would seem, as he faces the ominous morning, that he is also characterized as wishing he had "interiority":

> I think the king is but a man, as I am; the
> violet smells to him as it doth to me; the ele-
> ment shows to him, as it doth to me; all his senses
> have but human conditions. His ceremonies laid by,
> in his nakedness he appears but a man...
> (IV.i.101-105)

One irony, of course, is that this is Henry speaking, although the "on-stage audience," as so often in Shakespeare, does not know the truth. But Henry has had relentlessly to avoid "being human" in his public scenes 8/ — although his straightforward speech to Montjoy could be called a moment of "nakedness," a prelude to the scene with his own soldiers. Henry has had to rely on a "ceremony" that he knows has no merit other than to evoke a predictable response from those assembled around the king. Ceremony creates no links with "truth," indeed becomes a necessary falsehood that the man producing it comes to hate:

> And what have kings that privates have not too,
> Save ceremony, save general ceremony?
> And what are thou, thou idol Ceremony?
> What kind of god are thou, that suffer'st more
> Of mortal griefs than do thy worshippers?
> What are thy rents? What are thy comings-in?
> O Ceremony, show me but thy worth!
> What is thy soul of adoration?
> (IV.i.238-245)

Ceremony is barren, producing no value even within a strictly "commercial ethic"; the king's divorce from meaning can be traced back to the divorce between land and sacredness that Richard unwittingly perpetrated. Henry seems very much the alienated capitalist Marx describes — and Henry seems aware of his position. Ceremony is the means of retaining power, of suggesting to willing worshippers that power rests on something more than its own premises. Henry gazes, in a sense, at The Lord of the Flies, glimpsing the utter emptiness residing at the heart of his modern politics. Ceremony is the false god, the pagan idol Henry V has been forced to erect in the place of the symbols of sanctity Richard erased with his self-destructiveness, his self-pity, and his tears. Ceremony lacks even the medicinal potency Hal had ascribed to "gold" (II Henry IV: IV.v.161-162). Now, Henry V asks,

> What drink'st thou oft, instead of homage sweet,
> But poisoned flattery? O, be sick, great greatness,

And bid thy ceremony give thee cure !
Thinks thou the fiery fever will go out 9/
With titles blown from adulation?
(IV.i.250-254)

The healing power that Richard II admitted he could not contact — the divine curing that only Edward the Confessor among Shakespeare's kings is capable of soliciting — cannot pertain to a kingship that Henry V has had to puff up to seeming substance with the air of adulation. The organic and sacramental principle the Duchess of Gloucester stressed in her appeal to Gaunt, the deep natural and sacred roots of the Jesse Tree she imaged have been erased totally, and replaced only with painted scenery and inflated figures hollow at the heart. Henry can control the poisoned flattery — those who "steep... their galls in honey" (II.ii.30) — only through artfully contrived ceremony. He can ascribe such staging to God, but he knows who the manager is. Henry has no choice but to continue to develop the role that creates the vacuum. Ceremony cannot lead into "substance," cannot release sacramental latency. Ceremony leads only in the direction of the haunting emptiness Henry must explore as king. It is little wonder, then, that he would like to breathe for a moment or two as a "private," indulging the family insomnia (cf. II Henry IV: III.i.4-31 and Henry V: IV.i.281-284) under a borrowed cloak, hiding from the dawn that will reveal him as king again.

Falstaff has already parodied the dilemma of the sleepless king:

You see, my good wenches, how men of merit are
sought after. The undeserver may sleep, while the
man of action is call'd on.
(II Henry IV: II.iv.381-384)

Falstaff is at once playing the part of a great man rushing to war and mocking that pose. Henry IV and Henry V are so committed to the political world that they can neither develop nor afford the ironic vision of Falstaff — one reason why "political realities" clench in so painfully on Bolingbroke and his son. But satire might make politicians look like fools: "Peace, chewet, peace !" Hal had commanded Falstaff during a sober parley (I Henry IV: V.i.28). Falstaff's words on sleep show us, as do the words of Henry IV and Henry V, the private limitations accruing to wholly public figures like Henry V. For Falstaff, when he is at his most effective, "true value" lies in the exploration and exposure of "apparent value." He has his own hard lesson to absorb in this context — as has Henry V.

For Henry, ceremony is a "proud dream" (IV.i.257) that denies him the "Elysium' (IV.i.274) he envies but cannot enjoy. Shakespeare reveals in very human terms the plight of the total politician, the literalist and materialist who employs ceremony to mask meaninglessness, but who finally must see beneath the mask. Granted the premises of his inheritance, Henry has had no choice but to perpetuate a role that denies him whatever humanity he might have grown to realize. That he should awaken to his condition long after surrendering the seeming personality he had displayed during his long acquaintanceship with Falstaff is not the least of the scene's ironies. Perhaps Henry's successes have led him to believe what he knew was untrue when he assumed the throne. Perhaps when faced with the probably disastrous culmination of his policies, he must learn again that kingship brings with it only a "farced title" (IV.i.263).

A further irony is that the scene will demonstrate in multiple ways that "the king is but a man, as I am" (IV.i.101). Henry's role may be a relief from his constant public posture. He may achieve a further catharsis in discussing the king as mere man. As king he can show no public fear — nor should any soldier as he says (IV.i.110-112), almost schizophrenicly, talking as a part of himself that might communicate with "the king" in or around the self.10/ Here, Henry can indulge the luxury of describing a private man who might feel fear beneath his crown. He may begin the scene as "mere soldier," but quickly he is forced into his role as King Henry, developing a corollary to one of his consistent public premises — if war lies within God's will (cf. II.ii.289, for example), so does the fate of each soul within the army. The scene suggests, as did his speech to Montjoy, that while Henry might have once controlled his role as king, the role now controls him. His opportunity to discern the human and internal coordinates underlying his consistent projection as king surrenders to the necessity of keeping the role inflated.

The cynicism and doubts of the soldiers force Henry to "speak [his] conscience of the king" (IV.i.123), and to state that the king "would not wish himself anywhere but where he is" (IV.i.124). He claims that he "could not die anywhere so contented as in the king's company, his cause being just and his quarrel honorable" (IV.i.126-128). As for the justice of his cause, Williams replies, "That's more than we know" (IV.i.135). Critics who dislike Henry claim that he dodges the issue of the rightness of his quarrel: "the question," says Goddard, "is in the justice of the cause not in the morals of his soldiers."11/ But Goddard is inaccurate. Henry himself has introduced the king's cause, not as question but as conclusion. Since little in the play suggests that Henry questions the validity of his cause — regardless of the specious rhetoric he, and others, use to "sell the war" — we cannot expect that he considers it debatable. The soldiers themselves dismiss it as irrelevant to them: "If his cause be wrong," says Bates, "our obedience to the king wipes the crime of it out of us" (IV.i.132-133). "But," says Williams, "if the cause be not good, the king himself hath a heavy reckoning to make, when all those legs and arms and heads, chopped off in a battle, shall join together at the latter day and cry all, 'We died at such a place' ..." (IV.i.134-138). "I am afeard there are few die well that die in a battle,"

Williams continues, "for how can they charitably dispose of anything, when blood is their argument? Now, if these men do not die well, it will be a black matter for the king that led them to it: whom to disobey were against all proportion of subjection" (IV.i.141-146). Williams argues that, regardless of the justice of the king's cause, men cannot die well in battle and that the king who leads them is responsible for their souls. Williams provides at once a "medieval world picture" in a post-sacramental world and a version of pacifism in an Elizabethan England that was not notably pacific.12/ It is to Williams's argument about the king's accountability and not to the question of his cause that Henry responds. The latter question, even if debatable in Henry's mind, has been dropped.

Henry's reply is not quite as "poor, muddled, and irrelevant," as Palmer suggests.13/ Henry attempts to meet Williams's contentions, but only through Henry's conception of the war: "So, if a son that is by his father sent about merchandise do sinfully miscarry upon the sea, the imputation of this wickedness, by your rule, should be imposed upon his father that sent him" (IV.i.147-150). We are reminded that Henry is about _his_ father's business. Williams's argument, Henry maintains, would blame a master who sends a servant on a mission only to have the servant "die in many unreconciled iniquities" (IV.i.160); "the business of the master [becomes] the author of the servant's damnation" (IV.i.161). While analogy is never proof, in the context of this debate the equation of war with commerce is wholly invalid. The "cause" that generates commerce is obvious, seldom requiring the defense of an Archbishop of Canterbury. Williams has contended that men cannot die well "when blood is their argument" (IV.i.150), and blood is not ostensibly the argument of commerce, as that word is normally understood. Henry ignores Williams's assertion that battle per se causes men to sin. Not only does Henry make war the same as commerce, but he shifts his emphasis to the sins a man may have committed before he embarks on what has now become an innocent enough economic venture. Henry can now respond to a contention Williams has not made — indeed that no one would make. "No king," Henry says, reiterating the "given" of the justice of his claim, "be his cause never so spotless, if it come to the arbitrament of swords, can try it out with all unspotted soldiers" (IV.i.159-160). Henry can now assume — for the sake of argument — that this hypothetical king's cause might be tainted, though Henry's, clearly, is not. He dwells on the various vices his army may represent, and suggests that "if these men have defeated the law and outrun native punishment, though they can outstrip men, they have no wings to fly from God. War is his beadle, war is his vengeance" (IV.i.166-169). We might almost accept such an Old Testament vision, were we to forget that this war is not God's, but Henry's. Predictably, he has placed the war under God's aegis, neatly swinging his weltanschauung into conformity with Williams's fundamentalism, but doing so on Henry's terms. War is a moral institution, and the argument follows logically enough from Henry's previous assignment of politics to the will of God.

Henry does not willfully neglect William's contention that to participate in battle is to sin; the king simply cannot grasp a conception so alien to his own. Williams has uttered "the thing that is not." Henry can respond only with his view of the war. If the war is necessary for England, it is ipso facto "moral". If necessary for England, war becomes, rhetorically at first and then more than rhetorically, the instrumentality of God. One might argue with Henry on the basis of the aristotelian theory of causes, claiming that final cause must be God and not England, but as king, Henry can determine what final cause is, and as king, he must, unlike his son, determine final cause to be England. History may say that Henry V is wrong, possibly short-sighted. But how far he can be blamed for the ambiguous situation he inherits or for the inept son he leaves behind are questions that must be raised if his politics be condemned.

Since the "world" of Henry V emerges from no absolute premises, is not encompassed by a specifically purposive cosmos — as opposed to that of Macbeth, for example — the play throws varying and sometimes conflicting fragments of morality to its surface. Morality tends to be what power says it is. God does not object in the guise of a storm to the use of raw power against a saintly king. The rules of sainthood do not obtain in the world of The Second Henriad. Henry's war is predicated on the only "ethic" available — the good of England measured in material terms. Foreign war is vastly preferable to civil war, hence is equatable, in Henry's view, to any venture that profits England. The equation between war and commerce, a false analogy blatantly irrelevant to William's suggestions about blood as argument, is absolutely consistent not merely with Henry's policy, but with his view of things. "The business of America," Calvin Coolidge once said, "is business." American history since 1940 has demonstrated to some that "war is good for business."

The dislocation of an economy into what President Eisenhower called a "military - industrial complex" results in an inevitable effort to maintain that complex for commercial reasons, even after, perhaps particularly after, a misadventure like Vietnam. The effort and its extensively promulgated rationale may seem irrational to some, but, like Everest, they are "there," and cannot be dismissed as merely specious argumentation. They must be met as fact, as those trapped into combatant roles in real wars - no matter what politics and the English language may call them - or those thrown out of work by the shut-down of steel plants can attest. Although Henry rests on the comfortable ground that war is a version of commercial venture, the scene is set on the eve of a battle, one we know will come, unless the Chorus has been describing Gaultree Forest to us, and in which Henry will have to make do as the Chorus's dramatist must make do: "With four or five most vile and ragged foils" (IV: 50). In Henry's defense, it must be noted that unlike a staff officer, he is personally there to supervise his venture.

Having swung the debate to his ground, he interestingly imputes "many irreconciled iniquities" to the servant "assailed by robbers" (IV.i.152-153). Be war what it may be, this is the world as it is, a world where the iniquitous are themselves robbed. While he cannot glimpse the full thrust of his metaphor, Henry, in the heat of debate, reveals not merely the basis of his kingship, but a basic negative pattern imposed on England by Richard's crimes and Bolingbroke's response to them. Once a crown is stolen in response to a robbery (of the Lancastrian estates), England becomes immediate prey to robbery. Robbery proliferates. Henry IV complains of his son's support of the "dissolute crew" that "beat our watch and rob our passengers" (Richard II: V.iii.1-12). Gad's Hill parallels the dynastic seizure Hotspur, Glendower, and Mortimer would perpetrate, however buttressed they are with a de jure legality. The "crusade - rebellion" of the Archbishop, aimed at a usurper who happens to be king de facto, makes the late Richard "a traitor with the rest," as he predicts (Richard II: IV.i.247). The possible robberies of the Scots are anticipated as response to an actual campaign against France, that Goddard, perhaps overstating the case, calls "the royal version of Gad's Hill."14/ Henry's campaign is conducted, as he admits in theory, and as the play shows, partly by profiteers and petty thieves, by the commons necessarily engendered in a world that reflects what is happening at the top. Henry's argument illuminates much of the historical wilderness between Richard's seizure of Bolingbroke's inheritance and the showdown at Agincourt. Henry accepts the world as he has found it, and his translation of war to commerce is a product of that world, not just of some bizarre personal idiosyncrasy. The larger dramatic pattern may raise sanctions against Henry's war, but Machiavelli would raise none: "A prince should... have no other object or thought, nor acquire skill in any thing except war, its organization and discipline." Regardless of Shakespeare's "intention," the career of Henry V develops ironies that undercut his machiavellian successes. The basic irony, perhaps, is what is lost in succeeding.15/ We must grant, at least, that Henry himself sees through "ceremony." But there is nothing behind or within ceremony, and Henry can only produce more of the magnificent same, meaningful only as it can inspire his followers to victory. Victory, once achieved, can be translated only into further ceremony. As Rabkin suggests, "The play contrasts our hope that society can solve our problems with our knowledge that society has never done so. The inscrutability of Henry V is the inscrutability of history."16/ The play generates ironies too large to be contained within or controlled by the title character.

After Agincourt, Henry reduces God to the status of English functionary: "God fought for us" (IV.viii.119). The aftermath of victory is framed in religious ritual:

> Do we all holy rites:
> Let there be sung "Non nobis" and "Te Deum,"17/
> The dead with charity enclosed in clay.18/
> (IV.viii.121-123)

And Henry stages a return to London, reflecting his rejection of vanity more subtly than did his rebuff of Falstaff on the same streets:

> his lords desire him to have borne
> His bruised helmet and his bended sword
> Before him through the city. He forbids it,
> Being free from vainness and self-glorious pride;
> Giving full trophy, signal, and ostent
> Quite from himself, to God.
>
> (Chorus: V.17-22)

The Chorus, like England, seems conditioned to take all this at face value. Henry knows that his efficacy lies in his acting "as if" sacramental values still obtain in this world, however ruthlessly aware he may be that they do not. Henry V prudently assigns the achievement of his political goals to "the will of God."

With the soldiers before Agincourt, Henry translates battle into ultimate religious significance. Battle is a Judgement Day, encompassing salvation and damnation:

> Therefore should every soldier in the wars
> do as every sick man in his bed — wash every mote
> out of his conscience; and, dying so, death is to
> him advantage; or not dying, the time was blessedly
> lost wherein such preparation was gained; and
> in him that escapes, it were not sin to think
> that, making God so free an offer, He let him
> outlive that day, to see His greatness, and to
> teach others how they should prepare.
>
> (IV.i.177-183)

Henry has translated war into a context where "virtuous men pass mildly away." He himself has assigned to Canterbury, the Dauphin, and (through Exeter) the French king precisely the responsibility Williams has ascribed to the English king. The "guiltless drops," Henry says to Canterbury, "Are every one a woe, a sore complaint/ 'Gainst him whose wrong gives edge unto the swords/ That makes such waste in brief mortality" (I.ii.25-28). Through Exeter, Henry makes the French king responsible "For husbands, fathers, and betrothed lovers,/ That shall be swallowed in this controversy" (II.iv.106-109). The Governor of Harfleur is himself the "cause" (III.iii.19) of the havoc Henry holds on the outer reins of control. It would seem, then, that in denying the very responsibility he so readily assigns to others, Henry is guilty of grossest hypocrisy. The charge is valid, however, only if we deny the premise from which all Henry's words and actions emanate - he is destiny's lieutenant and his war "lies within the will of God" (II.ii.289). The single exception — the honest resignation of his response to Montjoy (III.vi.141-148) — remains predicated on his publicly stated stance that "We are in God's hand... not in theirs" (III.vi.171). Henry's position as "the voice out of the whirlwind" is philosophically untenable, of course, but his reply to Williams is consistent with Henry's program, a program whose shortcomings he has to face before Agincourt, but a program whose basic tenet — the welfare of England — he never questions.19/ War may be "evil" in and of itself, as Williams asserts, but if war is an adjunct of national policy it loses moral colorations. War, subordinated to a "larger purpose" — the civil peace of England — does not become "holy." It merely becomes necessary:

> The slave, a member of the country's peace,
> Enjoys it, but in gross brain little wots
> What watch the king keeps to maintain the peace.
>   (IV.i.281-283)

Henry is, clearly, making war to keep the peace, conducting a version of "preventive war." Such policies may well lead to greater difficulties than they are designed to prevent, and the precarious position of the English before Agincourt suggests that they have, but what would seem like shocking hypocrisy is consistency in this king, the result of a clearly formulated set of priorities. To apply the Marxist or "Vietnam" sanctions against the French war is probably to be too stringent as well as unhistorical (whether in the context of the Sixteenth or the Fifteenth Century). One could point at Henry's easy use of "slave," as well as his earlier bizarre and self-refuting simile:

> We are no tyrant, but a Christian king,
> Unto whose grace our passion is as subject
> As is our wretches fett'red in our prisons.
>   (I.ii.241-243)

Some of the attitudes Henry releases seem to deny him a modern "social conscience," but he does not come before us as an example of the best in Victorian England. Certainly Henry's war partakes of the shabby management Smith ascribes to it: "Mottoes and slogans of patriotic affirmation are all insults to intelligence, the work of intelligent and predatory elites manipulating dullard populations against their own proper self-interest."20/ To argue Henry's "sincerity" is probably irrelevant, since the same praise could have been rendered Hitler, had he died in, say, 1938. Posthumous public relations would probably have obscured the firm foundations of "The Jewish Policy" and would have diminished the racism of the 1936 Olympic Games. The blonde beast had yet to be released, and the world had yet to glimpse the blackness of the Hitlerian nightmare. But Henry V is no Hitler, obviously, nor does he demonstrate the "foolish consistency" of the well-meaning men of measured merriment who stumbled deeper and deeper into the jungles of South East Asia (by proxy, of course) in increasing contravention of hobgoblin facts from which they ultimately had to barricade themselves. Historical parallels looked to more closely consistently break down, as did, for example, Secretary Rusk's application of the situation of industrialized central Europe in the late 30's to the rice-producing South East Asia of the early 1960's.20/

Henry V shows that for King Henry, the issue is the domestic tranquility of England, and he maintains himself within that narrow national framework, regardless of the ironies into which his policy presses him, regardless of the international or historical qualifications Shakespeare may suggest. Henry is not lying — consciously, at least — to his soldiers. He is revealing the limits of his vision, the very limits which make him such a superb political leader. He believes in the "justice" of his cause because he believes in its efficacy for England. He may know, as Richard II must at the lists at Coventry, that no intrinsic justice can emerge from the battle — although it will be convenient for him to view the result as that of a judicium dei. Since intrinsicity is available neither to him nor to his world, as Henry knows very well, he must also know that the battle, or any battle, cannot be a model of platonic form, even though he makes a case for battle as virtual sacrament. Henry employs, without necessarily believing in it, the Christian teleology in which at least part of the world — as Williams proves (IV.i.127-138) — does believe. While Henry's program may be narrow, it is based on that value a king must recognize — the good of his country, and Henry does not deviate from that value. The play invites us to glimpse the limitations of Henry's moral vision, but the play asks us as well to recognize that Henry cannot admit those limitations, lest the insight undermine the political effectiveness that is a leader's sole reason for being. Henry must accept the ambiguous world Richard and Bolingbroke have left him. To do otherwise would be to perpetuate some version of Richard's error — to misconstrue the nature of the world — albeit a very different world than Richard inherited. History will make its subsequent judgement, partly through the instrumentality of Henry VI, but we witness Henry V allowing his island kingdom to dictate his program and fitting that program to the precise dimensions of that kingdom. He pays a price, of course — he cannot allow either an objective moral vision or a private personality to develop within him.22/ Instead, the man and his morality must serve his program, must be his program, since kingship rests only on the strength of the man who wears the empty crown. As morality becomes subservient to politics — a condition Richard II engendered, not Henry IV or Henry V — the man becomes dominated by the role dictated by Richard and by the nature of Bolingbroke's response to Richard. Henry V is hardly a glorification of patriotism, but it has much to do with the price of patriotism. In spite of the falseness of the rhetoric with which England rushes to France, it could be argued that Henry really is a patriot, however masked by an ironically patriotic face, and that patriotism is not merely a scoundrel's refuge, but the necessary premise of a king.

The mood of the scene in which Henry confronts the soldiers may be "lightened" by the quarrel between Henry and Williams, but the exchange of favors recalls the vicious charges and counter-charges in Richard II that are never brought to legal combat or conclusion (cf. IV.i.1-106), largely because the death of Richard II renders them irrelevant and insignificant. We should observe also that, while Henry seems to be a mere soldier accepting the challenge of another soldier, Henry is acting in defense of the very king he is. It would seem that he cannot be merely "a man," but must, even in disguise, be what he is, a king — indeed a king who has denied a jester to himself, but who finds himself in the uncomfortable position of knowing that William's scorn is valid:

> You pay him then ! That's a perilous shot out
> of an elder-gun, that a poor and a private dis-
> pleasure can do against a monarch ! You may as well
> go about to turn the sun to ice with fanning in his
> face with a peacock's feather. You'll never trust
> his word after ! Come, 'tis a foolish saying.
>   (IV.i.196-201)

While Henry finds that the faults of all men are laid to the king — a position into which his own debating skill maneuvered him — and that he is denied the felicity of being a mere man, his position is the inevitable consequence of the forces he himself has released. He has been so successful in developing a program, that now he himself is subject to it. Like his father, Henry has become the controlled, rather than the controller.

Henry's soliloquy invites us to place ourselves against the "real" Henry. While we see that there is virtually no "real" Henry, that any man within the king has been almost thoroughly subdued by the king, the pain of the soliloquy is real. In search of himself, Henry discovers that he has already surrendered the self he seeks. The play has educated us to the shortcomings of Henry's program, and the soliloquy brings us vividly against those limitations. Yet here, when we see the character's limits most strongly, we sympathize most strongly with him — partly, of course, because he himself is speaking. While multiple ironies still apply, as they did in the scene with the soldiers, the dramatic effect is very different. Here we find Henry trying to grapple with irony of his own making, yet an irony already strong in the world into which he was born. We discover what prior conditions and his own version of kingship have done to the man. Henry has publicly expressed his vulnerable military position, and here he explores the meaninglessness of kingship itself, the nothingness he has consistently manipulated into a semblance of substance. But he must lead his men in the morning. He must recognize that kingship is only "negatively sacramental" at best; obedience to the king absolves the subjects of the blame of battle, but the cosmic coordinate intersects and indicts the king's decision to go to battle.23/ It is a "hard condition" (IV.i.233), but one that became inevitable once Henry V made it seem as if that dimension, that sacramental centrality, had returned. Henry can complain of his success, now that it is suddenly confronted by a massive adversary, but he clenches whatever fears he may feel to the dimension of the "fault [his] father made in compassing the crown" (IV.i.293-294).

Henry's only recourse has been a quantitative effort at contrition:

> I Richard's body have interred new,
> And on it have bestowed more contrite tears
> Than from it issued forced drops of blood.
> Five hundred poor I have in yearly pay,
> Who twice a day their withered hands hold up
> Toward heaven, to pardon blood;
> And I have built two chantries,
> Where the sad and solemn priests sing still
> For Richard's soul. More will I do:
> Though all that I can do is nothing worth;
> Since that my penitence comes after all,
> Imploring pardon.
>
> (IV.i.295-306)

Henry's "sincerity" here cannot be doubted. He is, although he doesn't quite express it, in a position similar to Claudius's, retaining the crown while repenting the method whereby he gained it. While Henry is hardly as guilty as Claudius, Henry doubts the efficacy of God's grace. Claudius does not; he admits his human incapacity to attain it. Perhaps Henry might recognize that the grace of God is not to be "bought." In a play that seems to reflect a Protestant point of view, Henry does not recognize that God's grace, according to Luther, is not a quantity, but an attitude, shared by God and by the individual who can intercept God's constant. But perhaps such an attitude — a belief in "all things visible and invisible" — is simply not available in the world of these plays, a world predicated so ruthlessly on tangibility. The most contrite of spirits must, it would seem, attempt to reflect contrition quantitatively, and must, then, fail. Henry's effort reflects merely more vain ceremony, no matter how much he may wish it were otherwise. Trapped in irony as is Claudius, Henry falls short of the attitude that would permit sacramental potency to develop from contrition. Like Alonso in The Tempest, Henry V comes dangerously close to despair here. Typically for Shakespeare, the questions are explored without arrival at an "answer." Significantly, however, Henry begins by praying to the

"God of battles" (IV.i.289), more a pagan Mars than the Christian deity towards which the prayer seems to turn.24/ The end of the prayer forgets its beginning. In a world in which, as he has just said, ceremony is a "proud dream" that keeps a king awake (IV.i.257-258), Henry seems almost to use his precisely measured repentance as a bargaining position from which to request God's aid in the coming battle. Sincere though he may be, his sincerity is shadowed by the irony of the situation into which his prayer is placed. Perhaps the most that can be said about the lines is that they raise profoundly the issue of ceremony vs. sacrament.

Henry's speech to his troops before Agincourt, however, betrays none of the ambivalence of his soliloquy. Again, he translates a seemingly unpropitious moment into a superb ceremonial. Westmoreland looks wistfully over his shoulder at England:

> O that we now had here
> But one ten thousand of those men in England
> That do no work today!
>   (IV.iii.16-18)

Henry pretends to overhear his "cousin" (IV.iii.19) and with a splendid show of spontaneity retorts with Hotspur's argument before Shrewsbury, disinterring the obsolete concept of "honor," dusting it off, and holding it aloft for admiration:

> No, my fair cousin.
> If we are marked to die, we are enow
> To do our country loss; and if to live,
> The fewer men, the greater share of honor.
> God's will! I pray thee wish not one man more.
> By Jove, I am not covetous for gold,
> Nor care I who doth feed upon my cost;
> It earns me not if men my garments wear;
> Such outward things dwell not in my desires:
> But if it be a sin to covet honor,
> I am the most offending soul alive
>   (IV.iii.19-29)

While Henry can claim that "outward things dwell not in [his] desire," they are all he has, as his speech proves. While he can summon up a spirit for the occasion — from himself and from his men — he can make no basic case for the "honorableness" of his cause. While Henry attributes humility and honor to himself, the thrust of his rhetoric is that his soldiers accept such values as their own. Thus is his speech more effective than that of a Hotspur, who spoke as the embodiment of honor but who could not extend that quality, who was jealous of its possession even to his last breath. Henry V is hardly the most covetous soul alive — but his stance invites others to emulate his lust for honor. Henry V knows the difference between belief and rhetoric, and knows how to use the latter — no matter what he may believe. When he tells his troops that he is not "covetous for gold" we, too, can believe him, for, regardless of the commercial premises of his war, we have heard him expose "Ceremony" as worthless to him. But it is useful to a king, particularly when the king can imply sacramental values as Henry does in contrasting outward show and inner spirit.25/ Henry V is not hampered at Agincourt by the rebutting premises of rebellion, nor is he a victim of duplicity as Hotspur was at Shrewsbury. Henry V has already eliminated those who would betray him, as Worcester betrays Hotspur. While Henry leaves the question of his own guilt in the matter of Richard II unresolved — as he must if he chooses to raise the issue — his confrontation with the deep guilt that haunts about his reign seems to clear his mind for the next production — the transformation of the night's ominous predictions into the bright promise of daylight. He is indeed capable of projecting a French feast day — "the Feast of Crispian" (IV.iii.40) — into the future as an English celebration, which it will become after 25 October 1415:

> And gentlemen in England, now abed,
> Shall think themselves accursed they were not here;
> And hold their manhoods cheap whiles any speaks
> That fought with us upon Saint Crispin's day.
> (IV.iii.64-67)

"Rare words! Brave world!" Falstaff would say (I Henry IV: III.iii.213), having learned the difference between anticipation and reality. After the battle, "To boast of" the victory becomes a capital offense (IV.viii.113-114). But Falstaff is not present to project the shadow of sudden irony behind this glorious morning. No matter what profiteers and petty thieves are present, Henry parades names in an almost Miltonic array,26/ incorporating them within future celebrations, festivals that will have sacramental overtones:

> Then shall our names
> Familiar in his mouth, as household words —
> Harry the King, Bedford and Exeter,
> Warwick and Talbot, Salisbury and Gloucester —
> Be in their flowing cups freshly rememb'red.
> (IV.iii.51-55)

The shedding of blood will bring "advantages" (IV.iii.50):

> For he today that sheds his blood with me
> Shall be my brother; be he ne'er so vile...
> (IV.iii.61-62)

While sacrament per se have no efficacy, Henry can suggest that the coming battle carries with it a sacramental value — that of flowing cups, and blood shed to advantage.28/ The ceremony can contact "holy mystery" only indirectly — and, in view of Williams's argument, ironically — but the appeal is to an archetype that, however outmoded in practice, is real enough in theory, or is at least present as heritage within the individual psyches of individual soldiers, as Williams, Bates, and Court have proved by their literal acceptance of Judgement Day. Henry's subliminal suggestion of sacramental possibility has to be powerful — as powerful perhaps as Shakespeare's dramatic mimesis of sacramental action within his plays.29/

Henry's response to the Dauphin's undelivered offer to "send... fresh suits" (IV.ii.58) is clear enough:

Our gayness and our gilt are all besmirched...
But, by the mass, our hearts are in the trim;
And my poor soldiers tell me, yet ere night
They'll be in fresher robes, or they will pluck
The gay new coats o'er the French soldier's heads
And turn them out of service.
                    (IV.iii.110-119)

The poverty of the English army is decked in hope — "by the mass" — either of the "new clothes" of heaven, or in garments seized as prizes of war. Henry employs the concept of immediate afterlife — and blanket salvation, regardless of what he has said about certain elements of his army and of what Williams has said about the argument of blood. Thus he sets up, rhetorically at least, a winning situation for his troops no matter what happens. Though Henry can say that he doesn't care "if men my garments wear" (IV.iii.26), no counterfeit kings emerge from his ranks to the field of Agincourt. Poverty becomes "genuine," the outward garment betokening no "bravery," but fortitude, endurance, the will to continue, the Churchillian virtues Henry so brilliantly encourages from his men. The quantitative question of ransom will be answered by the quality of a response — a response reflected, however, in a tangible activity:

If they do this [i.e. pluck the French coats over the French heads]
(As, if God please, they shall), my ransom then
Will soon be levied.
                    (IV.iii.119-121)

Henry translates the situation before the fact into his receiving, not giving, ransom. By stressing quality he answers the "material" question. It is rhetoric, of course, but the skill with which Henry shifts equations — the odds are "five to one" (IV.iii.4), and "besides they are all fresh" (IV.iii.4) — from a quantitative disadvantage that shows in numbers and in garments to a qualitative reality that poor clothes demonstrate makes his public statements a kind of magic, a version of "mass," as his oath suggests. Perhaps we see the magician's hand and perhaps Henry asks ceremony to show him its worth, but, in public, in his role as leader, Henry makes it work. In spite of the desperate situation, Henry seems almost to have won the battle before it has begun. The doubting Westmoreland, who so gloomily begins the scene wishes, after Henry's verbal alchemy, "you and I alone/ Without more help, could fight this royal battle" (IV.iii.74-75). Westmoreland elevates the value of the battle per se. Henry is allowed to respond in the context of the value the men represent individually, not in their collective numbers: "Why, now thou hast unwished five thousand men !/ Which likes me better than to wish us one" (IV.iii.76-77). With a superb "reverse alchemy," Henry V takes the only value really at large in this world — the sheer materialism exemplified by many of his soldiers — and exposes it to scorn: "he which hath no stomach to this fight,/ Let him depart; his passport shall be made/ And crowns for convoy put into his purse;/ We would not die in that man's company" (IV.iii.35-38). By implication, other values — courage, fellowship, and loyalty — go deeper than mere "crowns." The speech seems almost to become what it imitates.

Whatever we may think of war per se, or of Henry V's contrived quarrel with France, his leadership here is more than merely dazzling. It works. Put to the ultimate test, albeit by the forces he himself has set in motion, he succeeds. Praise Henry V or condemn him as we may, Shakespeare forces us to witness a virtuoso performance. The man who could stage his own resurrection — his own "birth" — can also encourage a situation to the point where he can assume the stance of God in Creation, naming what he has done: "Then call we this the field of Agincourt,/ Fought on the day of Crispin Crispianus" (IV.vii.89-90). But, for the record, he has been careful to deny his own powerful role in victory:

Montjoy.   The day is yours.
King.   Praised be God, and not our strength for it !
                  (IV.vii.85-86)

But "our strength" — which means, partly, the strength of the kings' totality — has not been a negligible factor.

Shakespeare comments on Henry's superb performance in the scene in which Pistol captures a French soldier. We might be inclined to believe that some of Henry's magic has rubbed off on Pistol, but the scene shows only that it has touched the French. They seem willing to capitulate even to the likes of Pistol, whom Monsieur le Fer takes for

199

"the most brave, valorous, and thrice-worthy signieur of England"
(IV.iv.64-65). For Pistol, of course, the scene is merely an opportunity
for bluster and hard bargaining; his actions support Smith's suggestion
that Pistol "is a constant parody of the king."30/ While York and Suffolk
engage in the pathos of their bodiless flight towards heaven — the scene,
as described by Exeter (IV.vi.7-32), itself a mawkish parody of chivalric
and epic dying — Pistol demands "forty moys," insists that his prisoner
deliver more than "brass," and promises "some mercy" once he is
promised "two hundred crowns" (IV.iv.14-65). Cheated of his "ransom"
by Henry V's order to kill the prisoners, Pistol will turn the cudgelling he
receives from his own "comrade-in-arms," Fluellen, into profit. Pistol
will reimport to England the very "quality" Henry V has managed
temporarily to draw out of England:

> Well, bawd I'll turn,
> And something lean to cutpurse of quick hand.
> To England will I steal, and there I'll steal;
> And patches will I get unto these cudgeled scars,
> And swear I got them in the Gallia wars.31/
> (V.i.86-90)

While Monsieur le Fer finds himself in Falstaff's position — achieving a
comforting illusion that quickly becomes deadly — the defeated forces
achieve a small and ironic revenge when "Doll" dies "Of malady of
France" (V.i.83).

Pistol's capture of le Fer is a debased version of Falstaff's
capture of Coleville. Falstaff had been at least willing to "sweat" (II
Henry IV: IV.iii.12) in combat against Coleville. And Falstaff's "victory"
is couched in the self-knowing mockery of the valiant pose he assumes
before Prince John. Falstaff endows his effort with a far richer effect
than Pistol can achieve. Falstaff controls the irony with his "double
vision." Pistol merely reflects a fragment of the irony that gathers a
solid shadow beneath Henry V's "miracle" at Agincourt.

We learn in Henry V that the loss of chivalric value is all-
pervasive. Assuming it once applied in France, it certainly does not
pertain to the French conduct of the battle. Like Williams, the Boy —
Falstaff's former page — asserts an ethic contrary to that which gave
Henry's French war its "endowment" and to that which will provide
Pistol with his "livelihood." The Boy resists the squalid example he is
constrained to serve:

> They would have me as familiar with men's pock-
> ets as their gloves or their handkerchers: which
> makes much against my manhood, if I should take from
> another's pocket to put into mine; for it is plain
> pocketing up of wrongs. I must leave them, and seek

some better service. Their villainy goes against my
weak stomach, and therefore I must cast it up.

(III.ii.47-54)

The Boy's "counter-ethic" emerges from what he considers his "manhood"
— it is isolated and "existential," making no appeal to any premise or
commandment other than what the Boy considers right and wrong. If so,
his decision to leave his masters is more admirable than Hal's resolve to
reject Falstaff. Hal, of course, as prince, cannot choose on the basis of
any objective moral framework. A non-sacramental world, however,
does not preclude the growth of what must be an individual moral
viewpoint. Indeed, such development is encouraged, in spite of the
seemingly inevitable spread of mere materialism, of the pervasive
opportunism displayed at the outset by Bolingbroke, who becomes a king
attempting to repress the very prize-taking anarchy he had been forced
to embody in response to Richard.

But the Boy is not permitted to find better service. His self-
developed creed is extinguished almost immediately. The Boy remains
"with the lackeys and the luggage of the camp," and knows that "the
French might have a good prey of us, if they knew of it, for there is none
to guard it but boys" (IV.iv.75-78). The Boy becomes mere "prey," like
the victims of Gad's Hill, England defenseless before the "weasel Scot,"
or Harfleur, facing the potentiality of "Herod's bloody-hunting
slaughtermen" (III.iii.41). While one cannot accuse Henry V of having
encouraged in the French the "English quality" displayed at Gad's Hill,
we find the Boy dying in the debased battle at the English rear, a
"battle" containing certain reminders of the episode at Gad's Hill:

'Tis certain there's not a boy left alive,
and the cowardly rascals that ran from the battle
have done this slaughter; besides, they have
burned and carried away all that was in the king's
tent; wherefore the king most worthily hath caused
every soldier to cut his prisoner's throat. O,
'tis a gallant king.

(IV.vii.5-10)

Falstaff, who ran from Gad's Hill, would, figuratively, have carried away
all that was within the king's tent: "Rob me the exchequer the first
thing thou doest," he says to Hal, "and do it with unwashed hands too" (I
Henry IV: III.iii.191-192). Falstaff abuses the king's press before both
Shrewsbury and Gaultree Forest, delivers a cowardly thrust to a dead
Hotspur, and demands reward for his "defeat" of Coleville. But the Boy
who rejects the "Falstaff ethic" ends up as much a victim of it as
Falstaff himself. Individual morality seems defenseless before the
forces rampant here, as later and more profoundly in King Lear.

Whether Henry V has recognized the "way of the world" and directed dangerous energies along the vectors of his political intentions, or whether he has loosed mere anarchy which cannot be contained once released — or both — are questions the play keeps raising. That Henry has "gallantly" ordered the execution of the prisoners in response to the incursions of cowardly predators is Gower's inference, but not what the play shows us: "The French have reinforced their scattered men./ Then let every soldier kill his prisoners" (IV.vi.36-37). Henry's command issues from a battlefield emergency, not as a quid pro quo for treachery.32/ The order stands unambiguously, no matter how Gower fits it into a possibly more acceptable sequence.33/ The Boy's death is described in a scene recalling the rejection of Falstaff specifically, not through analogy (IV.vii.31-52).34/ Henry V, it seems, can eliminate some of the symbols of rapacious appetite in "this new world," and perhaps disguise others, but he cannot eliminate the principle, a principle seemingly intent on killing those who, like the Boy, would oppose it, as well as killing those who, like Nym and Bardolph, are hanged for their petty reflection of it — or in the case of Bardolph hanged in the service of a "larger principle," however expedient and commercial. Pistol may be cudgeled, but he will turn diseases to commodity.

The Boy is killed, but Williams survives. The Williams episode after Agincourt illuminates the career of Henry V with multiple ironies. Fluellen praises Henry's valor, echoing Richard ("Not all the water in the rough rude sea/ Can wash the balm off from an anointed king": Richard II: III.ii.54-55): "All the water in Wye cannot wash your Majesty's Welsh plood out of your pody" (IV.vii.105-106). Fluellen goes on to say that he "need not be ashamed of your majesty, praised be God, so long as your majesty is an honest man" (IV.vii.112-113). Henry responds with the piety that seems almost a conditioned reflex: "God keep me so" (IV.vii.114). Yet immediately, Henry indulges in a manipulation reminiscent of the several through which he attempted to ensnare Falstaff, and of the scene in which he made Francis a puppet. He summons Williams and asks why the soldier wears "that glove in [his] cap" (IV.vii.118). Williams responds that the glove belongs to

> a rascal that swaggered with me last night;
> who, if alive, and ever dare to challenge this
> glove, I have sworn to take him a box of the
> ear; or if I can see my glove in his cap, which
> he swore, as he was a soldier, he would wear (if
> alive), I will strike it out soundly.
>   (IV.vii.122-127)

Williams is in the position of Falstaff after Gad's Hill. Williams does not know the identity of his antagonist any more than Falstaff knew who robbed him. Henry asks Fluellen whether it is "fit this soldier keep his oath" (IV.vii.128), and the Welshman responds that "He is a craven and villain else" (IV.vii.130). According to Fluellen, who "knows the rules of the game," even if the other party be "a gentlemen of great sort, quite from the answer of [William's] degree," that gentlemen must "keep his vow and oath" or be "perjured" (IV.vii.132-137). While Henry admits that he "by bargain should/ wear it" himself (IV.vii.170-171), he gives the glove to a delighted Fluellen: "Your grace doo's me as great honors as can be desired in the hearts of his subjects" (IV.vii.156-157). In doing so, however, Henry admits that he cannot play the role he assumed in the night — yet he seems to wish to play the scene out on his terms, enjoying that anonymity into which he escaped temporarily before Agincourt. There, however, his identity was forced back upon him. Henry has explained to Fluellen that he plucked the glove from Alencon, and that therefore, "If any man challenge this, he is a friend to Alencon, and an enemy to our person" (IV.vii.152-154). Having sent Williams to fetch Gower, Henry now dispatches Fluellen on the same mission. Williams, remembering Henry's promise before the battle, is certain that the king intends "to knight" Gower (IV.viii.1). Fluellen, of course, intercepts Williams and Gower, and promises to "give treason his payment" (IV.viii.15). The scene parodies the Southampton conspiracy, and Henry's manipulation of the traitors. Upon apprehending Williams, Fluellen echoes the words of Henry V after uncovering the plot of Cambridge, Scroop, and Grey, also in league with France:

> here is (praised be God for it!) a most contagious treason
> come to light...
>
> (IV.viii.21-22)

> Since God so graciously hath brought to light
> This dangerous treason...
>
> (II.ii.185-186)

The king enters upon the contention and accuses Williams: "'Twas I indeed thou promised'st to strike;/ And thou hast given me most bitter terms" (IV.viii.41-42). Fluellen — forgetting his argument that no matter who the opponent is he must answer the challenge directly, and overlooking his own employment as unknowing deputy in the dispute — demands that William's "neck answer for it, if there is any martial law in the world" (IV.viii.43-44). The king, it seems, is above the law he administers. Henry's power over his subjects is such that even a "strict constructionist" like Fluellen shifts to Henry's whim. Here — unlike the scene with Francis — we have no Poins to ask Hal what the point of the joke is. Poins's absence is another index of the difference between Hal and Henry V, a difference Henry insists on in one way here — by insisting on sovereignty — but ignores more basically in trying to pull a practical joke.

"How can you make me satisfaction?" Henry demands (IV.viii.45). Williams responds with a direct statement of loyalty: "All offenses, my lord, come from the heart: never came any from mine that might offend your majesty" (IV.viii.46-48). But Henry will not allow the matter to rest. He has indicted Williams for "poor and... private displeasure... against a monarch" (IV.i.197-198), and, although he has not led Williams into a trap as overtly as he led Cambridge, Scroop, and Grey, Henry had not, on the eve of Agincourt, discouraged the quarrel that "comes to light" after the battle. He claimed to seek no "revenge" against the conspirators "Touching our person" (II.ii.174-175), yet he shifts the argument against Williams suddenly into the royal plurality: "It was ourself thou didst abuse" (IV.viii.49). Accurate enough in the context of the Southampton conspiracy, the charge is manifestly unfair when lodged against Williams. The soldier meets it head on:

> Your majesty came not like yourself: you ap-
> peared to me but as a common man; witness the
> night, your garments, your lowliness. And what
> your highness suffered under that shape, I be-
> seech you take it for your own fault, and not
> mine; for had you been as I took you for, I made
> no offense. Therefore I beseech your highness
> pardon me.
> (IV.viii.50-56)

Williams turns the tables on the king who descended to the lowliness of mere manhood, much as Falstaff did to the prince who donned the outfit of a drawer.

While the scene has been viewed as an amusing interlude after all the high tension of battle, I find it markedly unfunny. It would seem that Henry V would have indulged his role as Hal, wandering around "in disguise" with base companions. The scene with the soldiers demonstrates that Henry V cannot enjoy such relaxation. He is pushed hard against his role as king, one who knows only the emptiness of the practitioner's side of ceremony, and who must bear guilt for everything, it seems, including the death of Richard. With no trust in God's grace — or perhaps in the face of the absence of God35/ — Henry must bear guilt with no hope for redemption. His placement of his own obligation upon Fluellen's shoulders suggests that he might like to place the deep issues raised before Agincourt into the context of a practical joke.36/ But the joke falls flat. Henry again asserts himself as king ("ourself"), as he had to, however incognito, in debate against his soldiers. He does not, however, meet the evasion of a Falstaff ("By the lord, I knew ye as well as he that made ye": I Henry IV: II.iv.270-271). He has ruled such responses out of order through his rejection of Falstaff ("Reply not to me with a fool-born jest": II Henry IV: V.v.55). He meets, instead, the direct defense of Williams, a plea for "pardon" that indicts the king as one of the guilty parties, that pulls the king down to the human plane Henry V might seem superior to — even as the "joke" suggests he is not. William's defense reiterates the ironies of Henry V's "Imploring pardon"

(IV.i.306) before the battle, and, in implicating Henry further, Williams deepens those ironies. That Henry has set his plot up so that Williams "is a friend to Alencon" (IV.vii.153) reminds us that between the disguise that Hal perpetrated in Eastcheap and the king who stands on the field after Agincourt has intruded the wholly political career of that king. The complete politics demanded by that king has included an explicit exposure and punishment of the very "treason" he imputes to Williams. As Hal "came not like himself," neither did Henry V. Practical jokes, the opportunity to indulge the "I" as opposed to the "ourself," no longer lie within the province of this all-too-complete king. While he can take dangerous political situations — Falstaff's intrusion, conspiracy, the unfavorable odds at Agincourt — and transform them into successful ceremonial, his effort to translate his quarrel with Williams into joke or ceremonial fails.

Apparently accepting William's assertive "apology," Henry orders a monetary reward for Williams, shifting the scene towards the ethic of this world. The king moves through a subordinate, reminding us of his order that the Chief Justice quell Falstaff's disturbance (II Henry IV: "My Lord Chief Justice, speak to that vain man": V.v.44):

> Here, uncle Exeter, fill this glove with crowns,
> And give it to this fellow. Keep it, fellow,
> And wear it for an honor in thy cap,
> Till I do challenge it. Give him the crowns;
> And, captain, you must needs be friends with him.
> (IV.vii.57-61)

Fluellen, willing to see Williams though the king's eyes (as he had reversed his opinion of Pistol after Gower's evaluation: III.vi.61-85), offers Williams "twelve pence... to mend [his] shoes (IV.viii.66-69). Fluellen attempts to repeat the king's largess on a smaller scale, but Williams rejects the offer: "I will none of your money" (IV.viii.67). Williams's response seems directed at Fluellen, who replies that "It is with a good will, I can tell you" (IV.viii.68), hence Williams might be saying, "I will none of your money!" The episode might reflect the spirit "shining through" the tattered English coats, the "trim hearts" Henry has emphasized to Montjoy — and to his own troops — before Agincourt. The scene could be staged to expose Henry's prior rhetoric by having Williams reject both Fluellen's insulting offer and Henry's gratuity: "I will none of your money!" Williams could be suggesting that he, at least, cannot be bought off on a point of honor. Fluellen would then be left misunderstanding William's rejection (IV.viii.68-71), Exeter left holding a glove full of crowns, and Henry relieved by the timely entrance of a Herald. The full glove captures the emptiness of the ceremonial Henry has attempted to engineer. The loyalty of Cambridge, Scroop, and Grey may have had its price — so Henry publicly construes it — but Williams, the common soldier, refuses to yield to the dominant ethic. He turns his back on what amounts to a "pay-off," just as he has obviously refused Henry's earlier offer to give him "which hath no stomach to this fight" a "passport" and "crowns for convoy put into his purse" (IV.iii.35-37).

If Williams accepts the glove full of crowns, while rejecting Fluellen's twelve pence, he suggests that he accepts royal reward but rejects the petty effort Fluellen makes to carry out Henry's command "to be friends" with Williams. Williams cannot select his king, but he can choose his friends. If Williams turns away all reward, his action accords with his direct rebuttal of the king's charge qua king, and he shows that he embraces neither the Falstaff ethic (abuse of power for personal gain) nor the Henry V ethic (use of power for effect). The staging of the scene as William's total rejection of any "reward" drives the irony of Henry's kingship home completely. The king cannot enjoy the life that once he led as prince, nor can he impose his ceremonial vision as completely as perhaps he believes he can. The scene has no major political point, so that the failure of ceremony is inconsequential. But the scene makes a major point about the limitations of Henry's "personality" — or "I" — and the limitations of his kingship — "ourself." The first is gone forever, "wild" into his father's "grave" (II Henry IV: V.ii.123). The second is limited by the inevitably individual qualities Henry has had to impose upon the empty concept of kingship. He has created a structure that must be maintained in its falseness, as he recognizes before Agincourt and as the scene after the battle suggests. The scene focuses finally on the integrity of a single English soldier. Henry may in one sense be "the hero of Agincourt," but in another sense, Williams is. Against the twelve pence Williams rejects, Shakespeare places the "groat" Fluellen gives Pistol (V.i.59-60). The cowardly Pistol attempts to out-face his acceptance of the coin by calling it an "earnest of revenge" (V.i.65), but his fingers on the coin suggest William's integrity. Williams has not allowed "Honor" to be "cudgeled" from him, as Pistol has (V.i.86). Pistol, as Gower says, is "a counterfeit cowardly knave" (V.i.71). Fluellen, at last, places a proper value on something:

> If I owe you anything, I will pay you in cudgels;
> you shall be a woodmonger, and buy nothing of me
> but cudgels.
>
> (V.i.66-68)

Williams's assertion of individual integrity is reiterated immediately, if ironically. Success in battle is measured numerically, by a list. Of the great men mentioned by King Charles before the battle, most are dead: "Charles Delabreth, High Constable of France... Alencon, Brabant, Bar.../ Jaques Chatillon, Rambures, Vandemont,/ Beaumont, Grandpre, Roussi, and Falconbridge,/ Foix, Lestrale" (III.v.40-45). Others are POWs: the "Duke of Orleans, Bourbon [and] Bouciqualt" (III.v.41-45). Of those listed by Charles, only Burgundy, Berri and Charlois remain alive and uncaptured. Exeter adds to the list of French dead "The brother to the Duke of Burgundy" and the Earl of Marle (IV.viii.96-99). The English have lost

> Edward the Duke of York, the Earl of Suffolk,
> Sir Richard Ketly, Davy Gam, esquire;
> None else of name; and of all other men
> But five-and-twenty.
> (IV.viii.102-105)

The staggering quantitative imbalance can be attributed to the "arm" of "God" (IV.viii.105), but we might notice that "This day" — as opposed to Holinshed's account — has gentled no one's "condition," as Henry promised it would (IV.iii.64). Contrary to William's conviction, Gower has not been knighted. And Williams, had he been killed, would have been a number but not a name among the English dead. The promise of ceremony that assisted, perhaps assured, the victory, Henry's projection of "brotherhood" to all his troops (IV.iii.60-63), is reduced to quantity, conveniently enough now that ceremonial has fulfilled its pragmatic purpose. Henry's immediate order for "Non nobis" and "Te Deum" (IV.viii.122) introduces another ceremony, one that praises God, appropriately enough, no doubt, but that, more importantly, "changes the subject," ending the battle phase of Henry's program with an example of piety. While this is the ceremony we may have come to expect after we have witnessed, for example, Henry's attribution to God of the uncovering of the Southhampton conspiracy, we have also been led to anticipate the knighting of Gower, Jamy, MacMorris, Fluellen, et. al., the Captains of the British Isles who have banded together to produce the victory. Henry may be incapable of bringing Williams within the ceremonial context — even if Williams accepts the king's crowns, his rejection of Fluellen's twelve pence jars the "peacemaking" scene Henry would project onto his fiasco of a practical joke. But Henry is capable of framing victory to the dimensions he orders — a temporary "religious" pause before he humbly pursues domestic politics (Chorus: Act V), then returns to France to drive his total demands home without exception, and hardly as the "gentler gamester" he advocated as adjunct to success on the battlefield (III.vi.113).

The "wooing scene" represents Henry's successful pursuit of what he has achieved in battle. Katherine is, as Henry says, "our capital demand, comprised/ Within the fore-rank of our articles" (V.ii.94-95). Whether he is Hazlitt's butcher boy or Van Doren's hearty undergraduate in a letter sweater, he is direct, non-ceremonial, and honest in his "capital demand." He claims "uncoined constancy" (V.ii.156), which means both not yet touched by the market place and unalloyed by base metal. A "capital" becomes, in Katherine, it seems, another town to be taken:

207

> No, it is not possible you should love the
> enemy of France, Kate; but in lóving me you
> should love the friend of France; for I love
> France so well, that I will not part with a vil-
> lage of it — I will have it all mine. And,
> Kate, when France is mine and I am yours, then
> yours is France, and you are mine.
>> (V.ii.173-179)

Henry can make the conquest, as he admits, only as a soldier, by force:

> O Kate, nice customs curtsy to great kings.
> Dear Kate, you and I cannot be confined within
> the weak list of a country's fashion: we are
> the makers of manners, Kate; and the liberty
> that follows our places stops the mouth of all
> find-faults, as I will do yours for upholding
> the nice fashion of your country in denying me a
> kiss. Therefore patiently, and yielding.
>> (V.ii.272-279)

Here he would create a ceremonial that suggests the subsuming of mere custom by high position — a ceremonial ironically reflecting the absence of "ritual." The argument, however, seems more akin to Henry's speech to the Governor of Harfleur than it is to his usually graceful technique of transforming an obstacle to an advantage. Here, Henry claims a mutual privilege for himself and the French Princess, but the claim is at the service of his will. Like the Governor of Harfleur, Katherine is made an accomplice by Henry's overwhelming rhetoric.

Henry claims that he "cannot see many a fair French city for one fair French maid that stands in my way" (V.ii.319-321). But Charles completes the equation between "love" and acquisition — and the dynastic "bargain" to boot:

> Yes, my lord, you shall see them perspectively,
> the cities turned into a maid; for they are all
> girdled with maiden walls that war has never entered.
>> (V.ii.322-324)

The optic glass would create a distorted image of the France Henry will have, a duplication of town after town, maid after maid. Henry as conqueror is Henry as wooer who looms large upon the maidenhead of France, indeed upon the sequence of "fresh fair virgins," "pure maidens," and "shrill-shrieking daughters," he mentioned in passing to the Governor of Harfleur (III.iii.14.20.35). Perhaps Charles suggests that the "perspective" — the projection into the future — is warped and unattractive.37/

The scene reflects both past and future. Henry's bad French, he suggests, would make Katherine think him "such a plain king that... I had sold my farm to buy my crown" (V.ii.127-128). 38/ Bolingbroke was thrust, willingly, unwillingly, or half-willingly, into that position when he returned to England from exile. To buy his "farm" he had to "sell" a crown as he bought it. He then reneged on the feudal basis of his kingship and continued to buy his crown dearly in the face of feudal revolt. In relinquishing possession of church lands, Henry V has purchased France. He has achieved France at the expense of England — as Canterbury's extensive list of all confiscation would purchase shows (I.i.11-19) — and, although he considered that expense justified in light of larger domestic and commercial concerns — he makes war to keep the peace — his conquest of France will become bitter for the next generation of Englishmen. Katherine will not "prove a good soldier-breeder" (V.ii.208). Henry's vision of the future would seem to project a combined French and English crusade, an effort launched on a grander scale than that fruitlessly proposed by Bolingbroke:

> Shall not thou and I, between Saint Denis
> and Saint George, compound a boy, half French,
> half English, that shall go to Constantinople,
> and take the Turk by the beard?
>   (V.ii.208-211)

Wentersdorf suggests cogently that "It is not by chance... that the successful invasion of France is capped by a series of striking dramatic ironies. During the wooing of... Katherine, Henry roguishly boasts that he and his wife-to-be will together breed a warrior son... Can this have sounded anything but laughable to those who recalled that the son born to them would one day sit on a hilltop sighing for a hermitage, while his doughty wife leads his army in battle? When the French king is compelled to disinherit his son the Dauphin and adopt Henry V as his heir, what historically-minded playgoer would not have reacted with the sobering thought that the weakling Henry VI will also have to face a warlike challenger and will likewise be compelled to disinherit his son? Above all, there is the French king's pious hope that the peace treaty between England and France will plant 'Christianlike accord/ In their sweet bosoms': is this a genuinely felt expression of hope, or is it nothing but a platitude, the face-saving rhetoric of a king trying to justify his inglorious surrender? In any case, it is belied only minutes later by the gloomy predictions of the Epilogue".39/ Since those "predictions" have already occurred historically and have already been dramatized, they carry more than merely a predictive weight.

Henry V recognizes that he may not survive to carry out his programs — he deals with aging (V.ii.161-164) in the scene. But he does not seem to recognize that the skills he acquired in constant contest with Falstaff and sharpened during his career as monarch are not inherited characteristics. Such virtuosity is a product of Hal - Henry's calculated gaining and use of his own experience, and that consciously acquired ability will die with him. He can ridicule his father good-naturedly, excusing his own behavior on genetic grounds: "Now beshrew my father's ambition ! He was thinking of civil wars when he got me..." (V.ii.227-228). Hal inherits his father's crown, which, however dubiously acquired, permits Henry V a scope for his skills that Bolingbroke never enjoyed. What may preoccupy Henry V as he gets his son we are not told, but civil wars, leaping a generation, will be the issue. While Henry may create a brief parenthesis in civil turmoil, and while he uses his marriage to Katherine as a means of binding France to him ("Then shall I swear to Kate, and you [the peers of France] to me": V.ii.373) — ignoring Erasmus's warning that the marriage of a monarch for dynastic reasons was likely to lead to strife — his victory in France will rebound disastrously in England. The genetic line from Bolingbroke to Henry VI carries no political skill, but does seem to convey domestic strife. The piety Henry V employs so effectively surfaces ironically in his son, for whom it proves a political liability — along with the yielding tendency he may inherit from Katherine. Simple bad judgement, however, seems to be the primary factor in the negative career of Henry VI.

Whatever victories Henry V achieves are the product of a personality superbly conditioned to the ambiguous modern world that issues out from the cracking of the firm foundations Gaunt described. Bolingbroke's smooth pragmatism returned to confront him in rebellion. Henry V's consummate skill achieves all it can in a world in which materialism has "evolved" to replace the devolutionary principle, the Christian version of platonism, Gaunt celebrated. Predicated on personality — although, for reasons, that personality might be concealed — the career of Henry V is not designed to restore "sacramentalism" to England. Even were that restoration possible — and it is not — Henry V employs sacramental "value" as an adjunct to policy, a facade for machiavellian means that justify the end of "the good of England" — though some, including history per se, might argue that the means defeat the end. However much Henry V succeeds, his success is individual, and no other individual stands in the historical wings, trained to carry on. Quite the contrary. Mortimer's line remains unfulfilled, and anti-Lancastrian energy will emerge from there in abundance. The career of Henry V must be placed against the shadow history casts upon it, against the civil wars mentioned in the play's final, ironic sonnet, "Which oft our stage hath shown" (Epilogue: 13). France was "lost" and England made to "bleed" (Epilogue: 12), and the brief glow of a great leader becomes, finally, only a comet, portending disaster, predicting the black-hung heavens England will know for some seven decades after the "miracle" of Agincourt.

Time measures Henry V, finally, as it measures all men. He is able to avoid war, as he sees it, only be waging war, but the war he avoided during his reign crashes in on England as soon as he rests in peace. Unlike Richard II, Henry V only seemed — as Hal — "to profane the precious time" (II Henry IV: II.iv.369). Finally, however, Henry V is the victim of the marching time Richard released from out of that timeless England of Gaunt's vision. "Let time shape, and there an end," Falstaff had said (II Henry IV: III.ii.336-337), perhaps having the last word.

1.   Even the Chorus, usually given to inaccurate generalizations that provide a "popular view" of Henry V and his activities, embraces the "profit" metaphor inevitable to the world beyond the reign of Richard II.

2.   While Hotspur is probably consciously "anti-literary," except when it comes to imaginative flights on "honor," his "my horse, my love — my horse !" (I Henry IV: II.iii.78) is echoed by the Dauphin's "my horse is my mistress" (III.vii.45). Hotspur's "my love," admittedly, is vocative, but also, I believe, self-amusedly ambiguous.

3.   The fine English actor, Patrick Stewart, has pointed out to me, however, that Grandpre's speech suggests that the character is really looking at the English and that he does not understand what he sees. He perceives something more than natural in the English host because they are so much less than natural. Grandpre, having measured the ground between the armies, has had a closer look at the English than any Frenchman other than Montjoy.

4.   Henry V rejoins to Montjoy that "my poor soldiers tell me, yet ere night/ They'll be in fresher robes, or they will pluck/ The gay new coats o'er the French soldier's heads/   And turn them out of service" (IV.iii.116-119). Henry's reference to the angelic garments of salvation is one of several in Shakespeare in which fresh clothes signal positive spiritual change. Cf. King Lear: "in the heaviness of sleep/   We put fresh garments on him" (IV.vii.21-22), Gonzalo in the The Tempest: "Sir, we were talking that our garments seem now as fresh as when we were at Tunis at the marriage of your daughter..." (II.i.99-101), and the "fresh array" given the reformed Oliver in As You Like It (IV.iii.142).

5.   Henry V's behavior is vivified by the 1977 David Frost interviews of Richard Nixon.   As Roger Rosenblatt suggests, "Who but someone who didn't really believe it would say... 'I know that my political career is over.'"   "To observe this self-deceiving man fall in slow motion," Rosenblatt goes on, "his possibilities of failure seemingly as infinite as his possibilities of success must once have seemed, was very close to watching genuine tragedy...   Of course, Nixon isn't really a tragic figure.   Real tragedy involves more than a fall from power; it requires the intensity of a conspicuous life — a force that threatens (promises) extinction, and a life that fights back, holds fate off for a time, in which the audience comes to admire that life, and eventually to weep for its defeat.   Few can weep for Nixon's defeat because his 'tragic flaw' encompasses his whole character." The New Republic 176 #5 (18 June 1977), 42. While Henry V hardly qualifies as "tragic hero" in either the Renaissance of the de casibus traditions, and while he is the victim of a massive historical self-deception, his ability to face the truth about his position before Agincourt is a refreshing quality in a character who

could be absolutely stultifying. Alan Howard's self-aware Henry V had prepared us for the "human" Henry of the scenes before Agincourt, and thus allowed that humanity to emerge not unexpectedly but with unexpected power. Howard's performance qualifies much that has been written about Henry V, including parts of this chapter.

6. Anne Barton, "The King Disguised: Shakespeare's Henry V and the Comical History," The Triple Bond, ed. Joseph G. Price (Pennsylvania State University Press, 1975), p. 92.

7. In fairness to Mrs. Barton, whose analysis of Henry V is typically brilliant and illuminating, I must point out that, later in her essay, she makes the very point I am making about the relationship of the Chorus to the "play": "Throughout this play, the relation between the Chorus's unequivocal celebration of Henry and his war in France and the complicated, ambiguous, and sometimes flatly contradictory scenes which these speeches are made to introduce is productive of irony and double focus. This duality of attitude is particularly striking in Act IV, where the Chorus's epic account of the king dispensing comfort to his troops in his own person leads directly into that altogether more dubious scene in which Henry visits the army a second time..." "The King Disguised: Shakespeare's Henry V and the Comical History," The Triple Bond, p. 99. I remain puzzled by Mrs. Barton's insistence that the "first visit" has occurred. It seems to me that the Chorus clearly tells us that that visit is what we are about to see. That we do not see the visitation as the Chorus has chracterized it, creates precisely the irony Mrs. Barton nicely describes.

8. An exception to the display of personality qua personality is Henry's long diatribe against Scroop, which, however, confirms the king's supremely isolated status. As Anne Barton says, "Precisely because Scroop is someone Henry has imagined was bound to him as a man by private ties of affection and liking, his treason is far more painful than the more neutral betrayal of Cambridge and Grey ['neutral' as it touches on 'body natural,' I take it]. With the latter he deals in an efficient, almost perfunctory fashion. Only Scroop evokes a long and suddenly emotional remonstrance in which Henry effectively bids farewell to the possibility of personal relationship. Significantly, this scene at Southampton is placed between the two episodes in London dealing with the death of Falstaff. The epic voyage to France is thus preceded by three scenes dealing not merely with the death of former friends but with the final severance of the new king's remaining personal ties." "The King Disguised: Shakespeare's Henry V and the Comical History," p. 103. Henry has now had to reject the entire spectrum of mankind, in a sense, from the "surfeit-swelled" Falstaff (II Henry IV: V.v.50) to men "spare in diet,/ Free from gross passion," as are the Cambridge conspiratators (II.ii.131-132). Peter Saccio offers the brilliant observation that, assuming that Shakespeare knew that it was March himself who betrayed the conspiracy to Henry (a possibly unprovable

assumption, although the facts are stated in the Gesta Henrici Quinti),
"his handling of the episode is a beautiful example of his purposive
ruthlessness in adapting his sources: he takes a story whose most
striking element is the loyalty of the king's cousin and friend [March] and
reverses it into a scene making just the opposite point — the king finds
to his dismay and bitter disappointment that he cannot afford to have a
close friend (Scrope)." A letter to me, 21 June 1977. I believe an
equally strong argument could be made to the effect that Henry
emphasizes Scroop's "friendship" further to exaggerate the gross nature
of the conspiracy and thus to obscure its rational and legally-based
premise.

9. Cf. Bardolph on Falstaff: "Well, the fuel is gone that maintained
that fire: that's all the riches I got in his service" (II.iii.43-44), and
Fluellen on Bardolph: "His face is all bubukles and whelks, and knobs,
and flames o'fire, and his lips blows at his nose, and it is like a coal of
fire, sometimes plue and sometimes red; but his nose is executed, and his
fire's out" (III.vi.102-106). Henry V's control over fire, like Othello's
(V.ii.7-13), is limited.

10. Henry's use of the plural — ostensibly to include the soldiers and
himself vis a vis the king — could be construed as an ironic use of the
royal plural, in which the king qua king speaks of himself: "and though
his affections are higher mounted than ours, yet when they stoop, they
stoop with the like wing; therefore, when he sees reason of fears, as we
do, his fears, out of doubt, be of the same relish as ours are" (IV.i.105-
109). To attribute a conscious use of royal plurality to Henry here is to
give the lines the same wry humor that the true identity of the speaker
gives so many of the other lines. The scene, of course, explores "the
nature of identity," and, characteristically for Shakespeare, leaves us
with the question, however profoundly probed.

11. Goddard, The Meaning of Shakespeare, p. 242.

12. Against Erasmus's attacks on war, Dulce Bellum Inexpertis and the
Querela Pacis, influential and widely reprinted, could be placed
Machiavelli (in the Discorsi, for example), Raleigh (Discourses of War),
La Noue (The Politicke and Militarie Discourses), Digges (Foure
Paradoxes, or Politique Discourses), Essex (The Apologie), et. al. For
some Tudors, war was an avenue towards peace, as Sir Richard Morison
suggested in 1539: "Let us therefore work lustily now, we shall play for
ever after. Let us fight this one field with English hands and English
hearts, perpetual quietness, rest, peace, victory, honour, wealth, all is
ours" (Exhortation to Stir All Englishmen to the Defense of Their
Country). Bolingbroke echoes these sentiments: "Come, lords, away,/
To fight with Glendower and his complices./ A while to work, and after
holiday" (Richard II: III.i.42-44). As one might expect, war, like other
basic human activities, was a debatable topic in Tudor England, and we
would anticipate that the debate, but not a resolution, would carry into

Shakespeare's plays. Bolingbroke, of course, never finds his holiday ("So shaken as we are, so wan with care/ Find we a time for frighted peace to pant": I Henry IV: I.i.1-2). Peace is not necessarily a blessing, of course. King John's negotiated settlement is a "base and vile-concluded peace" compared to "a resolved and honorable war" (King John: II.i.585-586). But that is Philip the Bastard talking, and we must take his character into account, however much he may be "England's spokesman" in the play. Truces, however, are often preludes to greater wars, as is that in Troilus and Cressida and that in Antony and Cleopatra, which evokes the cynicism of Enobarbus (Antony and Cleopatra: II.ii.103-107). Richard II's version of "peace in our time," as he stops the trial by combat (I.iii.124-143), is self-refuting (as Goddard demonstrates), but reveals a latent truth — this kind of peace means ultimate war ("peace... Might... fright fair peace"). Richard has "basely yielded upon compromise/ That which his noble ancestors achieved with blows./ More hath he spent in peace than they in wars" (Richard II: II.i.253-255). Such a peace insists on war, as the Archbishop of York, referring back to Richard, suggests in II Henry IV (IV.i.53-66). Although York claims to be no "enemy to peace," he invokes "fearful war/ To diet rank minds sick of happiness,/ And purge the obstructions which begin to stop/ Our very veins of life." Beyond Henry V, and his forcible marriage of the French and English crowns, lie the black-draped heavens of his son's gloomy reign, and the loss of everything, domestic and foreign, that his war was to win: "With Henry's death the English circle ends;/ Dispersed are the glories it included" (I Henry VI: I.iii.136-137).

13. Palmer, Political and Comic Characters of Shakespeare, p. 238.

14. Goddard, The Meaning of Shakespeare, p. 260.

15. The irony undercutting perhaps Shakespeare's most successful politician, Octavius Caesar, is that his cold and narrow world has no room in it for the expansive warmth of an Antony or of a Cleopatra. Octavius's successes are not shadowed by the dynastic disaster lying beyond the reign of Henry V. Both Henry V and Octavius must eliminate extraordinary energies to achieve political success — as they define it.

16. Rabkin, "Rabbits, Ducks, and Henry V," 296.

17. One might argue a certain irony in the singing of the "Te Deum" after the battle, particularly in light of William's argument about battle per se, since the "Te Deum" incorporates the line, "Vouchsafe, O Lord, to keep us this day without sin."

18. Reno, From Sacrament to Ceremony (p. 302), notes a parallel between Agincourt and Bosworth Field. While Shakespeare uses a portion of Holinshed in Henry V's command ("he caused Te Deum, with certeine anthems to be soong; giving laud and praise to God, without bosting of his owne force or anie humane power"), he seems also to

incorporate Richmond's command at the end of the Battle of Bosworth Field, an incorporation that strengthens the parallel with Agincourt: "willing and commanding... the dead carcasses to be delivered to the sepulture." Richmond promises <u>after</u> the battle what Henry V promised before (IV.iii.60-64): "[Richmond] also gave unto them his hartie thanks, with promise of condigne recompense for their fidelitie and valiant facts." Richmond looked on Bosworth Field as a <u>judicium dei</u>, as Henry V may view Agincourt (cf. "this lies all within the will of God": II.ii.289, and "We are in God's hands... not theirs:" III.vi.171).

19. Dorothy Cook suggests that, until the confrontation with Bates and Williams, "possibly [Henry] himself has not understood the gravity and extent of his own responsibility," "<u>Henry V</u>: Maturing of Man and Majesty," 124. Rabkin says that "the king's answer evades the issue: the suffering he is capable of inflicting, the necessity of being sure that the burden is imposed for a worthy cause," "Rabbits, Ducks, and <u>Henry V</u>," 289. I would reiterate that the "cause" is never an issue in Henry's mind. Even his father's fault is treated only as a possible inhibition of the "cause."

20. Smith, "Shakespeare's <u>Henry V</u>", 26.

21. Cf. historian Warren I. Cohen: "Rusk came to see Stalin's Russia — and later Mao's China — playing the role of Hitler's Germany in the 1930's." Quoted in Karen J. Winkler, " 'Making Sense' of the War in Vietnam," <u>The Chronicle of Higher Education</u> (24 April, 1978), 3.

22. Alan Howard's sharing of such a "private personality" with his audience is a dramatic convention that suggests the "roundness" (Forster's term in <u>Aspects of the Novel</u>) of his character. Henry V cannot, however, share that personality with any of the characters <u>on stage</u> — the results of that inability are dramatized before and after Agincourt.

23. Cf. Kernan: "Identity is now no longer God-given but only a role within which an individual is imprisoned by political necessity... In the process of becoming a ruler his personal self, the essential 'I', is lost forever, as the man disappears into the role his work demands." "The Henriad: Shakespeare's Major History Plays," 274-275.

24. Dorothy Cook overstates the case, I think: "Repudiating his assumed role as God's champion and spokesman for His way, he humbly asks God to be his champion." "<u>Henry V</u>: Maturing of Man and Majesty," 124-125. Henry employs God in public with a convenient duplicity. Henry poses as God's champion <u>and</u> suggests that God is the English champion.

25. The rhetoric of his battlefield oration seems the reverse of his argument with the soldiers about the "naked" king. Yet, in talking of borrowed garments, he seems to recall his discussion with Williams, Bates, and Court, while hiding under Erpingham's cloak. That Henry has talked of his troops as "warriors for the working day," "all besmirched," and "worn... into slovenry" (IV.iii.109-114) finds its point in Fluellen's offer to give Williams money enough to mend his shoes (IV.viii.63-66). Crispin and Crispian, brothers, fled the anti-Christian persecutions of Diocletian in the middle of the Third Century. They supported themselves as shoemakers, so that the day of the battle is appropriate in view of the condition of English clothing and foot-wear. Professor James Black tells me that The Second Battle of Tobruk was fought on St. Crispin's Day, 25 October 1942. Although Montgomery was a Shakespeare buff, he could not, in 1942, have seen Olivier's splendid Henry V. The date apparently coincided with a full moon favorable to British gunnery.

27. Perhaps the most Miltonic sequence in Shakespeare is the exotic list of "The kings of the earth" provided by Octavius (Antony and Cleopatra: III.vi.60-75). James Black, however, suggests the contrast between Henry V's "household words" and the exotic list in Antony and Cleopatra. Black points out that Henry's oration is about "peace, domesticity, posterity," "Shakespeare's Henry V and the Dreams of History," 24. The speech is similar, then, to his translation of war into moral institution at the campfire, a wonderfully effective "doublespeak" in which "war is peace." The calm posterity Henry V images for his troopers contrasts markedly with the world Pistol predicts for himself (V.i.85-94), further described by Norman Rabkin: "the reality of the postwar world the play so powerfully conjures up — soldiers returned home to find their jobs gone, falling to a life of crime in a seamy and impoverished underworld that scarcely remembers the hopes that accompanied the beginning of the adventure," "Rabbits, Ducks, and Henry V," 293.

28. Cf. Charles Harris, D.D.: "Not only are the religious associations of the Chalice of a most moving kind, but the common cup powerfuly suggests human fellowship of an intimate unselfish, generous, and uplifting nature (cf. the institution of 'the loving cup')." "Communion of the Sick, " Liturgy and Worship, ed. W.K. Lowther Clarke, D.D. (London, 1932), pp. 614-615. Cf. also Bolingbroke's "those blessed feet/ Which fourteen hundred years ago were nailed/ For our advantage on the bitter cross" (I Henry IV: I.i.25-27).

29. For this argument see my Christian Ritual and the World of Shakespeare's Tragedies (Bucknell, 1976).

30. Smith, "Shakespeare's Henry V," 24. Parody, of course, tends to diminish the stature of what is parodied; but Pistol is an antidote to the

adulation of the Chorus. Pistol provides, as Rabkin suggests, a "mocking persective on the rhetoric and pretensions of the warrior," "Rabbits, Ducks, and Henry V," 282.

31. An ironic fulfillment of Henry V's line about "show [ing] scars" (IV.ii.46).

32. Yet many critics accept Gower's version. Cf. Dorothy Cook: the "slaying of the young boys... along with new alarms, so angers Henry that he orders the French prisoners killed both as retaliation and as a means of preventing further treachery," "Henry V: Maturing of Man and Majesty," 126. Henry cannot know what causes the "new alarm" when he gives the order for execution (IV.vi.35). He attributes the alarm to the French reinforcement of "their scattered men" (IV.vi.36). In Holinshed, he gives the order in response to the noise made by the French attack on his camp.

33. One of the strange effects of the battle as Shakespeare renders it is that we meet characters like le Fer and the Boy and later learn that these specific characters have died in a general slaughter of "prisoners" or "boys." Agincourt suggests, finally, a "collective fatality," appropriate to an event in which an individual hero can only temporarily hold back — and perhaps even encourages — a negative historical pattern. As James Black points out, the "personal endeavor of Henry at Agincourt [is] played down" by Shakespeare, "Shakespeare's Henry V and the Dreams of History," 26. Even individuals like York and Suffolk die communally, as "brothers" (cousins, at least: IV.vi.15). In the Olivier film, of course, Henry V and the Constable square off in the finale of an epic battle, like Hal and Hotspur, Edgar and Edmund, Macduff and Macbeth. While necessary for cinematic purposes, no doubt, the individuation of Henry during the battle seems contrary to Shakespeare's intention.

34. The thrust of Fluellen's allusion may suggest that Cleitus, like Falstaff, was a "truth-sayer" whom Alexander, like Henry V, could not allow to inhabit, or inhibit, a single-minded rule.

35. "The determinism [of the plays of the second tetralogy following Richard II] is entirely naturalistic," suggests Robert G. Hunter, and I concur. Shakespeare and the Mystery of God's Judgements (University of Georgia, 1976), p. 102.

36. Henry V seems to believe that he can dismiss "fathers" with a snap of his fingers, as if heritage has no basis in the past, but is relevant only in (a) the results of his training with Falstaff, and (b) the crown he receives from Henry IV. But the unexamined psychic content he would exile into oblivion emerges in (a) his concern before Agincourt with his father's crime (which, as is the nature of unexamined psychic content, becomes his own), and (b) his effort to play a game with a "Falstaff

figure" after the battle. Henry V's "two fathers" rise from the "graves" he has assigned them (II Henry IV: V.ii.123 and V.v.53) to haunt him. For an excellent psychological approach to Shakespearean characterization, one that I believe would be effectively applicable to the Second Henriad, see Bernard Paris, "Hamlet and His Problems: A Horneyan Analysis," Centennial Review XXI #1 (Winter, 1977), 36-66.

37. The scene would seem to reflect a version that Bourbon has described:

> Let him go hence, and with his cap in hand
> Like a base pander hold the chamber door:
> Whilst by a slave, no gentler than my dog,
> His fairest daughter is contaminated.
> (IV.v.15-18)

The English have been described previously as "Foolish curs" (III.viii.145). Henry V, of course, is better than a dog, even if the French are forced into the role of "base panders."

38. The linguistic difficulty reminds us of the scene between the disinherited Mortimer and his Welsh bride (I Henry IV: 198-210). Henry V, however, does manage to turn his small French into an amusing "virtue."

39. Wentersdorf, "The Conspiracy of Silence in Henry V," 286.

INDEX

ABOUT THE AUTHOR

H. R. Coursen was born in 1932, and grew up in New Jersey. He graduated from Amherst College, Wesleyan University, and The University of Connecticut. For the past eighteen years, he has taught at Bowdoin College, Brunswick, Maine. His seventh book of poetry was Hope Farm, from Cider Mill Press in 1979. His new collection, Winter Dreams, will appear in early 1982. His novel, After the War, based on the life and death of Manfred, Baron von Richthofen, appeared in 1981, from Heidelberg Graphics, Chico, California. His previous books on Shakespeare include Christian Ritual and the World of Shakespeare's Tragedies (Bucknell, 1976), and Hamlet's Mousetrap (Wisconsin, 1969). His books on writing have been As Up They Grew (Scott, Foresman, 1970), and Shaping the Self (Harper & Row, 1978). His reviews of Shakespeare on stage, in film, and on television have appeared in many journals, most frequently in the annual review issue of Shakespeare Quarterly. He lectured on Shakespeare for several summers at Westfield College, University of London. He is currently completing a manuscript on "Jungian Approaches to Shakespeare."

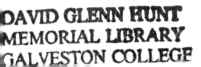